Surya Green's mystical experien . . . *ul,
and she has the power to expres* . . . *ful*
she has written this book. *Whatever can increase faith in the
world is precious, a gift of God. Her book will serve a lot of
people.*
  Irina Tweedie, author of *Chasm of Fire* and *Daughter of Fire*

*. . . very interesting personal logbook of a pilgrim culling any
possible clue to a higher wisdom . . . .*
  Pir Vilayat Inayat Khan, Sufi master

*Surya is, of course, a fine writer and I hope her book will be made
available to the wider public.*
  Ram Dass, spiritual teacher

*Travelling with Surya Green will help you to wake up and see you
are a member of the sun family.*
  Rabbi Zalman M. Schachter-Shalomi, New Age pioneer

*Surya Green's book very much captured me. She takes the reader
along on her fascinating spiritual journey . . . we receive, in many
different ways, a message of inner deepening and oneness with the
source of all life . . . Surya bridges the differences between East
and West, which is what the world really needs . . . an
exceptionally informative and inspiring book.*
  Dr. H. J. Witteveen, former director of the International
Monetary Fund

*I have never met a woman with such an energy and such a creative
inspiration as Surya. Her book gives me a proof that the road of
true spirituality still exists.*
  Bruno Mertens, founder of the Handcraft Welfare Centre for
Maoris

*Surya's book really surprised me. I couldn't put it down until I
reached the very end. Surya gets to the spiritual essence, and at the
same time the book captured me like a novel. I love her deep
human feelings and honesty. It is a very inspiring book which I
recommend to everyone.*
  Diana Vandenberg, meta-realist painter

Surya Green, born in Manhattan, completed her formal education in the United States with a B.A. in American Studies from New York's Barnard College, Columbia University, and an M.A. in Communication from California's Stanford University. When a work assignment drew her to Europe she discovered her writing home in Amsterdam and established herself as a freelance journalist. Later she consciously began her spiritual search. The inner journey and her writing work became one. Both in the West and in Asia, where she lived for many years, she met and interviewed leading spiritual teachers and other exceptional persons. For two decades she published articles on transformational themes internationally. Entering deeply into various disciplines of self-realization encountered on her quest, she has developed a lifestyle based on positive attunement, surrender and acceptance.

The Call of the Sun

A Woman's Journey to the Heart of Wisdom

SURYA GREEN

ELEMENT

Shaftesbury, Dorset • Rockport, Massachusetts

Brisbane, Queensland

© Element Books Limited 1997
Text © Surya Green 1997

First published in Great Britain in 1997 by
Element Books Limited
Shaftesbury, Dorset SP7 8BP

Published in the USA in 1997 by
Element Books, Inc.
PO Box 830, Rockport, MA 01966

Published in Australia in 1997 by
Element Books Limited
for Jacaranda Wiley Limited
33 Park Road, Milton, Brisbane 4064

Cover design by Slatter-Anderson
Page design by Roger Lightfoot
Typeset by Bournemouth Colour Press, Parkstone, Dorset
Printed and bound in Great Britian by
Creative Print and Design Wales, Ebbw Vale, Gwent

British Library Cataloguing in Publication
data available

Library of Congress Cataloging in Publication
data available

ISBN 1–85230–898–2

*Lovingly
dedicated*

*to everyone
and everything
under the sun*

O Beloved Sun,

I salute your Light
        within
        and
        without.

When we look at you,
may we see our Self.

Contents

Part III The Task

Part IV The Continuity

Om Suryaya Namah

Just as the sun has countless rays, so would there be countless names in a full listing of all the persons, places and energies that helped me bring to completion *The Call of the Sun*.

To the Almighty Sun, my source of inspiration;
to the high beings and the spiritual teachers who opened themselves to me;
to the men and the women who are part of the story unfolded in these pages;
to Heinz Frehse whose sensitive editing helped me continually to refine the text;
and to all the others who contributed in whatever way to the life of this book, I offer my deep thanks.

My gratitude to Swami Purna cannot be expressed in words.

Acknowledgments

Grateful acknowledgment is made for the use of copyrighted material from the following publications:
How to Know God: The Yoga Aphorisms of Patanjali, by Swami Prabhavananda and Christopher Isherwood, Mentor Books, copyright© 1953 Vedanta Society of Southern California; *The Sufi Message of Spiritual Liberty: The Mysticism of Sound and Music* by Hazrat Inayat Khan, Volume II, revised edition, published by Element Books, Shaftesbury, England, in association with The International Headquarters of the Sufi Movement, copyright© The Representative General of the International Headquarters of the Sufi Movement; *The Sufi Message* by Hazrat Inayat Khan, Vol. V, published by Servire, copyright© The Representative General of the International Headquarters of the Sufi Movement; *The Sufi Message and the Sufi Movement* by Hazrat Inayat Khan, published by Barrie and Rockliff, copyright© 1964 The Representative General of the International Headquarters of the Sufi Movement; *Women in Training* ('The Beaming Faculty of Women') by Yogi Bhajan, published by 3HO Transcripts, copyright© 3HO Foundation; *Born in Tibet*, by Chögyam Trungpa, the eleventh Trungpa Tulka, as told to Esmé Cramer Roberts, published by Penguin Books, copyright© George Allen & Unwin, now Unwin Hyman of HarperCollins Publishers Limited; *The Path* by Maharaj Charan Singh, published by Radha Soami Satsang Beas, copyright© Radha Soami Satsang Beas; *On the Birth of My Mission* by Martinus, published by The Martinus Institute, copyright© The Martinus Institute; *Martinus* by Erik Gerner Larsson, published by The Martinus Institute, copyright© The Martinus Institute; *Rumi and Sufism* by Eva de Vitray-Meyerovitch published by The Post-Apollo Press, copyright© The Post-Apollo Press; *Sufism, The Transformation of the Heart* by Llewellyn Vaughan-Lee published by The Golden Sufi Center, copyright© The Golden Sufi Center; *Chasm of Fire* by Irina Tweedie published by Element Books, copyright© Element Books; *Life and Teaching of the Masters of the Far East* by Baird T. Spalding published by De Vorss & Co, copyright© De Vorss & Co.

Foreword

At this time when the world is caught in many conflicts and controversies, while at the same moment reaching the heights of technological advancement, people as a whole – both those who have and those who have not – are urgently seeking a genuine fulfillment in their lives.

Starting out as someone quite representative of modern Westerners, Surya Green lived in various parts of the world in search of whatever might lead her to a true contentment. Along the way she had to confront many obstacles, negativities and disappointments, yet did not give up and carried on courageously.

Having discovered that beyond all apparent confusion there is a spiritual energy with which one can attune, she opened herself to bring out the light that is dormant within. Her journey makes clear that before one will receive the true guidance and knowledge, a humble attitude towards spiritual learning is required. The story of Surya's transformation is, in various ways, a mirror for other people.

Concerned with transformation both personal and planetary, *The Call of the Sun* is pioneering in its suggestion that global problems can be solved when there is respect for the Sun-principle.

This unique book will help others immensely.

Swami Purna
London
2 October 1996

Introduction: The Challenge

After 33 years on this planet, I suddenly came face to face with other realities. Voices and visions took me by surprise and, when I looked at the sun, I saw myself. My life turned upside down and inside out. Significant experiences often occur unexpectedly.

A New York City transplant to Amsterdam in the early 1970s, I was freelancing as a writer when journalistic assignment jetted me to India. Maharani-style accommodation in former princely estates, dinners in magical surroundings recalling courtly splendor, a ride to a magnificent Mogul palace on elephant-back – these and more privileges were afforded me as a guest of the Ministry of Tourism.

The simpler travels undertaken on my own, after the Grand Tour ended, led to spiritual places and persons. Astonishingly enough, these had correspondence with places and faces inside me. I discovered that the invisible world, situated beyond our normal perception, is not only real but accessible to anyone.

I had long sensed that life is more than the daily routines of being alive, and that our presence on earth has deep purpose. But it was not until India that clues and answers emerged spontaneously, without apparent cause on my part. An inner knowledge revealed itself. I saw light within.

Once connected with the higher energies, my individual fleeting existence opened to wider dimensions. In addition, I awakened to the fact that the entire human race is one family, and that all life belongs to an inseparable Whole.

To be spiritual, I realized, means not only to participate consciously in my own evolution, but also to help cultivate that mutual garden which is our earthly home. Such thoughts began to motivate my everyday activities.

My writings shifted from outer to inner destinations, and transformational themes were to predominate. My work and my quest became one. As a pilgrim with journalistic shoulder bag, I wended my way around the globe to sacred sites and power spots, to holy celebrations of all kinds, and to diverse groups and communities.

Both in the West and especially in Asia, where I spent six years, I have had the *darshan*, holy audience, of literally hundreds of spiritual figures, representing diverse traditions and attainments. Leading teachers of our time as well as the unknown and the unsung have generously given themselves to my tape recorder, camera and notebook.

The one influenced me more strongly than the other, but each helped me progress. Each passed on ideas and ideals, or imparted experiences, which further opened my eyes. The seeds of understanding enlivened in me by the Indian sunshine rooted more deeply. Until attuned with the supreme guru who resides within us, outer guides can assist our sprouting and blooming.

Over the years I have sowed and harvested much while continually watering and weeding, a task that never seems to end. Season in, season out, the garden of our development needs nurturing.

Looking beyond my little patch of green to the heavily damaged land of our Mother Earth, I see many precious buds of awakening consciousness ready to burst into flower. I feel challenged.

This is the right moment to take up my pen and tell my story, which is our story, because we all share the same journey from darkness to Light.

PART I

The Awakening

Getting Started

Aboard Air-India flight AI-124, heading for New Delhi via Bombay, I had no idea I was on my way towards a destination no airplane could ever reach.

Next to me sat Wim Freni, the publisher of a Dutch travel trade magazine. It was his desire to see India which led the Ministry of Tourism to roll out the official red carpet for a two-week work visit. Contrary to many people in those flower power days of the early 1970s, I had no particular interest in that country. Nevertheless, when Wim asked me to write an English-language supplement on Indian tourism, I gladly accepted the plum assignment.

The moment my feet touched Indian soil, the government's carefully planned itinerary fell apart, giving a first hint that other forces were at work behind the tour expressly created for us. Ordinary occurrences, which normally I would have overlooked, called my attention and made me notice the meaningful messages they contained.

It all began rather prosaically, in Bombay, when Wim and I failed to catch our connection to Delhi. Although we both listened carefully every time distorted sounds came from the loudspeakers in the hot and muggy waiting hall, neither of us heard the boarding call. Finally it was discovered that the aircraft had left, and hotel rooms were hastily improvised. This would cost us the valuable orientation day in Delhi because, to keep up with the tightly scheduled tour arrangements, we had to fly directly to Agra, city of the Taj Mahal. The inconvenience was all the greater as our suitcases were on that missed plane.

Arriving in Agra, still in the same clothes since our departure from Amsterdam 48 hours earlier, we found no one at the airport to receive us. Tired and exasperated, Wim and I decided to phone our local hosts. Just then a bearded Sikh gentleman wearing a bright red turban came rushing over to us.

'Miss Norma Green? Mr. Wim Freni?' he asked. Upon our affirmation, he bowed grandly and introduced himself as A. S. Sawhney of the Government of India Tourist Office. I could not help but think of the charming maharaja in Air-India publicity. Requesting us to excuse his lateness, he emphasized 'Please, do not worry,' before announcing that my luggage was lost. He regretted this from the bottom of his heart, but it could have been worse. At least Mr. Freni had his suitcase.

During the ride to the hotel we drove through a very poor neighborhood of shabby streets and primitive housing, little better than the pathetic shacks of mud, canvas, cardboard and even newspapers I had seen in Bombay. Many of the dwellers were thin and appeared unhealthy; some literally wore rags. The sight of such unbelievable indigence, filth and stench, caused me to weep.

The hotel greeted us with a large sign – 'Strike' – on its door. It could not admit guests, news Mr. Sawhney took much more calmly than Wim and I, and on the spot he arranged accommodation for us elsewhere.

After the missed plane connection, the disappeared luggage and this latest change of plans, I started to feel all this was not happening by accident. Was there some purpose behind these occurrences? It looked as if I was being asked to adapt myself more easily to revised situations, as Mr. Sawhney did, and to leave the past behind. When I realized I had left my appointment book at the airport while trying to phone the Tourist Office, I mentioned these thoughts to Wim. He laughed and said that Indians were nice people but terribly disorganized.

Before our sightseeing tour could begin, an unplanned visit to Agra's main clothing shops had to be squeezed into our program. Urgently, I had to search for an alternative to the wide-legged trousers and matching top I had worn on the plane and which, on my third day in this hot and moist climate, were becoming a kind of second skin.

In all of Agra there were no Western fashions available. A sari with its six meters of cloth I considered too difficult to wear, taking into account the journalistic equipment I had to carry. A *salwar-kameez*, a blouse and pants combination, was rejected because of its tight trousers.

My salvation became a *lungi*, a long skirt, worn with a *kurta*, a collarless, long-sleeved top. The only example in my size came in flaming orange, and having no other choice I bought it. When I emerged from the dressing room Mr. Sawhney smiled and said, 'You're wearing the color of the saints.'

Traditionally used in India by Hindu ascetics, orange is associated with renunciation, sacrifice and courage.

I got my initial taste of India's other-worldly pursuits as Wim and I entered the lobby of the Lauries Hotel after dinner.

'Let me read your palm,' requested a well-dressed man, sporting a bow tie, who approached us. Radiating a great confidence, he greeted me specifically.

'I know many things about you,' he declared, presenting a leaflet which bore his photo and read: 'Gayane – World Renowned Star Gazer and Astro-Palmist-Psychologist'.

'How much?' I inquired.

Even before he examined my palm he described several of my problematic character traits and then said: 'The two years before this one were difficult for you; very bad, very low. You're out of it now.'

Absolutely correct he was, and I showed him my palm.

'Excellent hand,' he informed me, going on to say that my health was good and that two of my important qualities were my fine manners and my talents. Very favorable things were happening for me and I would travel a lot. Something was coming up in November. After asking my birth date, he said I was at the age when everything in the life of a Taurean would improve. I was leaving the negative influence of one planet and entering the positive sphere of another.

Several other revelations followed before he offered to give me a full reading, which would cost more of course. I politely refused. Even if I had wanted a long consultation with 'The Modern Cheiro', as his leaflet termed him, my agenda left no free time.[1]

On our first excursion at the government's planning, Wim and I strolled through the magnificent Taj Mahal, a mausoleum dedicated to love. This splendid example of Indian Muslim architecture fullfils the vow of the 17th-century Mogul Emperor Shah Jahan. When his wife Mumtaz Mahal died at the age of 41, after bearing him 14 children, he promised to build her the most beautiful monument the world had ever seen.

Another packed day of sightseeing included a visit to the Red

Fort, a massive Mogul fortress-palace surrounded by 70-foot-high walls, a stop at the tomb of the 16th-century Emperor Akbar, whose central purpose was to unite Hindus and Muslims, and a trip to the deserted Mogul capital of Fatehpur Sikri, founded by Akbar southwest of Agra. The city with all its glorious marble structures had to be abandoned after 16 years because of water shortage.

Over the following weeks we made further acquaintance with the India the Tourism Ministry wished to promote, starting with the country itself as a varied assortment of highlands, plains and shorelines and continuing with the cultural by-products of a 5,000-year-old civilization. We looked at countless temples, historic sites and ancient ruins, viewed fine examples of old paintings and sculptural art, attended concerts of Indian classical music and dance, watched the production of traditional crafts, and more.

Into this concentrated timetable was added a stop at Delhi airport to claim my reappeared luggage. Curiously enough, my Western clothes hardly interested me any longer. I now felt much more at ease in the Indian styles I had been forced into wearing.

Our last destination on the Grand Tour took us to the southernmost tip of India, to the lush and lovely tropical state of Kerala, 'land of coconuts', where people still lived harmoniously with nature and tourists rarely visited. In this idyllic setting, overlooking the beautiful beach at Kovalem, Wim and I were lodged in the Palace Hotel, formerly an estate of the Maharaja of Travancore.

The undisturbed serenity of this green paradise made it hard for me to quit India. With my manuscript not due just yet and my air ticket having an open return, I decided to stay and travel on my own for a while. As I watched Wim leave for his plane, carrying with him my portable typewriter, I wondered where my next steps would lead.

After weeks of good weather, the clear blue sky suddenly grew dark and water came down in torrents, accompanied by violent winds. My individual travel was inaugurated by continuous rain from morning until evening. It pained me to lose a full day of exploration, but I profited from the opportunity to clean out my suitcase and organize my papers. Because I had to stay in my room – the Maharani Suite of course – I relaxed with a book purchased before my departure at a friend's last-minute suggestion.

Be Here Now is the story of its author, Dr. Richard Alpert. He was a psychology professor at Harvard University when a chance trip through India directed him to the Indian ascetic Neem Karoli Baba, who appeared to be guiding him on subtle levels. After a life-transforming few months, Alpert returned to his native America as 'Baba Ram Dass', arriving at Boston airport in Indian clothes, beads and a full beard. His book fascinated me because in a way I recognized myself in it.

Although I had not met the spiritual teacher to reshape my life, very soon I had given up the notion that my tour was being orchestrated solely by the Indian government. Numerous incidents had made me suspect a larger design. I could not escape the idea that everything had been necessary, even inevitable, and I had been brought to India for more than tourism writing.

The book reinforced my thoughts on this matter. No longer would I work out in advance the details of what tomorrow might bring. What if I simply flowed with each day, trying to heed the signs and other indications that I trusted would be offered? Free of any musts or shoulds, I ate when I was hungry and went to sleep when I was tired. Time did not exist for me.

My main occupation in Kovalem was to listen to the never-ending pulse of the Indian Ocean. I sat all alone on the pale-sanded beach in the shade of the palm trees, or on my balcony which faced the sea, musing on the sources and forces of life. Many reflections passed through my mind, especially about my recent experiences. They led me to think that nothing happened without reason. Not the reason of our intellect, but something beyond the mind.

Every evening my inner explorations came to a temporary halt as I witnessed the southern sun cover the blue canvas of the sky with blazing shades of red, pink, orange and purple before vanishing into black, restful night.

Now I was ready to begin the real journey, the one for which the first two weeks had been but an introduction.

Ahalya, linking Modern with Ancient

An overcrowded rattletrap bus, courageously manoeuvred by a barefoot driver sitting sidesaddle, carried me away from the luxurious official trip. Having been privileged to discover some of the wonders of India's past, I now longed to know the secret of her living present. What was it about *Bharat Mata*, 'Mother India' as her Sanskrit name translated, that caused people to think of her in spiritual terms?

I began by choosing transport and accommodation that would take me closer to the locals. My idea was to stay in hotels frequented by the ordinary Indian budget traveler. If India's spirituality is real, then it has to live in the inhabitants of the country.

In Ernakulam I was directed to the Bharat Tourist Home, a guesthouse catering to Indians. For a nominal price I had a spartan but clean place. The cool stone floors prompted me to walk in the room without shoes.

In the restaurant I stood out, as a Westerner of female gender, on her own. Women in India traditionally travel in the company of others, for protection.

Very shyly I sat at a table in the back, where I watched the guests, mainly men, receive a folded banana leaf which they opened and covered with rice, soupy curry, and condiments. They all ate without cutlery! I was fascinated to see how they could handle the hot, wet food with nothing but the fingers of the right hand. Still lacking the courage to try this manner of eating myself, I ordered only tea. All the while I noted that each banana leaf was washed before use and thrown away after the meal, a very natural and non-polluting procedure.

Eventually I adapted to my new situation, and the slow and easy rhythm of South India gave me an increased sense of well-being. I noticed how I took everything more lightly, trying to tune with each day as it flowed – my Kovalem resolution. Soon I found the uncomplicated approach to life very pleasant. Eating with my hand and walking barefoot in my room were only two of the experiences which brought me closer to myself.

Friendship developed between me and my surroundings. I was even becoming accustomed to the geckos clinging to the walls of my hotel room. These curious lizards with their oversized toepads were the declared enemies of the profuse insect population.

The growing sense of familiarity with India intensified my wish to know her people, and I recalled some of the hospitable persons I had met on the official trip.

In Madras our program had introduced me to Ahalya Narayanan, a Brahmin woman guiding for the local Government of India Tourist Office. Sightseeing with her had been a brief course in the ideas and principles of Hindu thought. She had helped me to understand its essence: in this world, with all its physical diversity, there is a spiritual Oneness.

I had right away valued Ahalya's calm and balance, as I had her loving heart. An instant empathy existed between us, and before I left Madras she invited me to stay with her family.

Upon my return, Ahalya welcomed me like a long-lost relative. From my side I felt I was coming home to an older sister. The immediate ease I had enjoyed in her presence now extended to her husband and to Krishna, Subrahmanya or 'Mani', and Usha, respectively 11, 13 and 15 years old.

Introducing the children, all named after Hindu deities, Ahalya remarked: 'Usha is the goddess of dawn, Subrahmanya the warrior god, and our very popular Krishna you surely know.'

'Only slightly,' I responded.

'He's probably the god people love the most, and there are innumerable charming stories about him,' commented Ahalya, going on to explain that Krishna was an *avatar*, one who comes to earth as a messenger from a higher region. Hindus recognize ten such 'descents' of their god Vishnu, who incarnates whenever the world's balance is severely threatened. He took his eighth incarnation, as Krishna, when Mother Earth pleaded to be rescued from evil forces.

The children obviously knew these basics, but nevertheless listened attentively. Their respect for elders impressed me, and I enjoyed hearing them call me 'Auntie'.

A great surprise awaited me at bedtime. Although the generations-old house contained space enough for a second bedroom, the family slept together in one room, according to Hindu custom. Now I was included. The parents in a high, elaborately carved wooden bed, the children and I on the floor, we talked and giggled in the darkened room until Ahalya gently suggested we be silent.

Lying on my mat, I reviewed the day's happenings. A spacious calm came to me, or was it just the love and closeness of this tightly-knit family? I forgot all about my cherished privacy. Preparing for sleep in such a warm atmosphere brought me to an inner place of absolute safety and security. I remembered my happiness when, in my childhood, we moved to a larger house and my sister Bonnie and I each received a separate room. In the Narayanan home I saw a new set of values that stimulated me to re-examine my own.

Well before dawn, everyone else still asleep, Ahalya arose to answer the milkman's knock. So began my day, in which I followed her while she performed the numerous household chores, observing how she integrated the principles of Hinduism into practical life.

First she swept and washed the front and rear entrances to invoke Lakshmi, goddess of prosperity, who entered to bless a house only through a sparkling clean doorway. 'Cleanliness is next to godliness,' Ahalya explained.

At both entrances she then arranged rice flour in a design of traditional spiritual significance, explaining: 'Small insects and birds eat the flour, enabling me to start the morning with an act of charity. It is also an act of worship, to the oneness of all.'

After waking up her husband and children, she similarly adorned the prayer room. The *puja*, or prayer service, could begin only after we had all bathed and put on fresh clothes. When we gathered, Ahalya's husband lit small oil lamps and incense. Assisted by Mani, he led us in the chanting of Sanskrit hymns. From the walls, pictures of various Hindu deities watched over us during the 20-minute ceremony.

The end could not come soon enough for Krishna. 'Mummy,' he said as soon as we finished, 'the stomach asks for something.' It was time for breakfast.

'Such a daily prayer service is necessary', Ahalya told me while we moved to the kitchen, 'to remind us of God's nearness. It also helps us remember the relativity of earthly existence.

'Our religion is not just a belief or faith,' she went on. 'It is actually a philosophy. There are no compulsions, only suggestions about the way to act positively and harmoniously on every level. All is left up to the individual.'

I noted more and more that she was not blindly following a prescribed code of behavior, but organized her life around a subtle discipline based on deep comprehension.

When I expressed my wish to know more about the philosophic wisdom of India, Ahalya remarked that for most Westerners the study of Indian thought stays an end in itself. 'But for us', she said, 'it must be incorporated into our daily routines and form the basis for a purposeful and happy life.'

With perfect timing the fruit merchant arrived, just after the *puja* finished and before the meal. Ahalya purchased bananas and oranges for our breakfast of steamed rice cakes and fresh coconut chutney. Everything was served in metal trays, directly on the floor.

Later on, my feeling of intimacy with Ahalya allowed me to ask how she and her husband worked out their sex life with the family around.

'The main purpose of sex is procreation,' she said, letting me know she and her husband did not want any more children.

Ahalya explained that to a Hindu, marriage is a fusion of two hearts, minds and souls rather than just of two bodies. It is a duty, a willing sacrifice for the good of the partner and the family. A man or woman is not considered complete without a spouse. Husband and wife together form a spiritual whole. The alliance is a sacred bond preserved by the couple with purity, loyalty and devotion. Hearing all this, I started to question the true worth of the sexual freedom so treasured in the West.

'First comes marriage, then understanding,' Ahalya said. 'Understanding leads to love, the placing of the partner's needs before one's own.'

She had only a brief 15-minute meeting with her future husband before entering with him into a union arranged by their parents. Liberated as she was in her work, occasionally tour-guiding away from Madras for periods as long as one month, she still would not call her husband by his first name, out of respect. I myself called him 'Sri Narayanan', using the formal Indian address.

To my remarks about the unequal position of women in most

Eastern countries, Ahalya replied: 'If a woman is treated as secondary, there is no happiness. Women in India are equal, but our custom is to pay men genuine respect.' From her answer I saw this was not a subject a Westerner could immediately understand.

The matter became more complex when she went on to elaborate that traditionally a woman surrenders to her husband. Together with him, through love and dedication, she can realize fulfillment. Marriage and family give her the possibility to manifest this fulfillment in ordinary life. In this way marriage can become a spiritual path.

During my talks with the children, Usha told me she wanted to be an accountant. Besides her school subjects, of which she especially loved mathematics, she was learning to cook, taking lessons in Indian classical dance and studying the *vina*, the most ancient of India's stringed instruments. She wanted to get married in her mid-twenties, but would do it sooner if her parents wished. The choice was up to them. Family life was her supreme consideration. As she answered my questions, I noted how well-balanced and clear she was, certainly in comparison with teenagers in the West.

That afternoon Ahalya dressed me in a sari. After draping it gracefully around me, she surveyed the effect and smiled. 'You look like an Indian woman. From the North,' she said.

Between my eyebrows she made a dot of *kumkum*, red powder, to symbolize the third eye of wisdom, the energy center which, when open, gives one spiritual insight. Then she tied a string of jasmine flowers around my hair, but my own hands finished the process.

'Oh, you know how to do it,' she observed. 'Do you wear flowers in Europe?'

'No, and this is the first time I've worn my hair braided up like this,' I answered in wonder. So much in India seemed familiar! Ahalya said that of course it was not difficult to wrap flowers around the hair. Nevertheless she thought I must have lived in India before, in a former life, and probably we had even known each other. That was one reason we had met again now. We were like soul sisters.

The soul, Ahalya explained to me, is a core of divinity within us, a link between the Supreme and our mortal frame. Upon the death of the physical shell, the soul eventually comes back to the earth in another body or form, to receive further lessons. The process goes on for innumerable lives until we reach full knowledge of Self, or our true divine identity. Then, 'Self-realized' or 'enlightened' and no longer needing earthly experience, we are freed from the endless compulsion of birth and re-birth.

To a Hindu, liberation through Self-knowledge is the ultimate objective of life on this planet. The more conscious we become, the closer we move to this supreme end. According to the law of karma – the law of action and its consequences – as we sow we shall reap. All that occurs to us, we create ourselves. Whatever we think, speak or do will have its effect, either in the present or in a future life.

In Ahalya's household, which combined centuries-old traditions and customs with a modern outlook, Hindu thought lost its abstractness for me. I discovered an unexpected kinship with Hindu ways. Had I had prior acquaintance with them? Or was my fertile imagination influencing me to see more than existed? I clearly felt I must have been here before, in this strange, exotic India.

At the same time, Ahalya showed me in concrete examples how the family can be more than just a training-ground for our better functioning in society. I observed how Hindu customs from the past, integrating acceptance of the Supreme into all undertakings, can give guidance along the path to Self-knowledge. Of course I wondered if the lifestyle of the Narayanan household was the rule or rather the exception in modernizing India, where traditions are fast being undermined by secular developments, at least in the cities.

Ahalya had a set of finely developed values acknowledging the sacredness of everything. The way she applied them quite naturally in all situations, so that each detail of her daily life made sense, helped me see the incompleteness of my own understanding. I needed to widen my consciousness and increase my awareness.

'It is sad to think you are leaving us,' Ahalya said on the last day, as I packed my bag. 'You fit in so well here.'

With full heart I agreed, but I had to move on.

I left Ahalya's loving family as a different person. A light had been turned on, awakening old memories long dormant within me. Although kumkum powder no longer marked the spot between my eyebrows, I had found out about my inner spiritual eye, and the potential to activate it.

First Revelation of the Sun

Along with the old and traditional, in South India I came into contact with revolutionary modern ways too. One hundred miles below Madras was being constructed Auroville, a city of the future. Its unique charter begins: 'Auroville belongs to nobody in particular. Auroville belongs to humanity as a whole. But to live in Auroville one must be the willing servitor of the divine consciousness.'

The experimental township had first caught my attention the previous year, through an article in the *International Herald Tribune:* 'Utopian Living on Bay of Bengal'.[2] I learned more about Auroville at the United Nations Conference on the Human Environment held that summer in Stockholm, where the Indian delegation circulated an official paper on this model city based on a shared spiritual vision.

Then, shortly before my departure for India, a peculiar series of coincidences led me to the president of the Sri Aurobindo Auroville Society in the Netherlands, Willie Perizonius. I was captivated by his accounts of Auroville's leader, a French woman called simply 'the Mother'. She lived in the nearby seaside town of Pondicherry and guided an *ashram*, a residential centre where people who aspire to higher understanding can study and practice spiritual teachings. One of her visions led to the establishment of Auroville, with UNESCO sponsorship.

The Mother was born of Jewish descent in 1878 in Paris as Mira Alfassa. When only four years old, she spontaneously sat in yoga positions as well as meditated. In her childhood she had revealing dreams, knew she had come to help humanity, and repeatedly received signs.

Once, in the Fontainebleau Forest, she heard a tree speak to her.

'Please listen to me,' it said. 'Save me from being cut down.' She went straight to a forest ranger, who agreed to her urgent request. Back at the tree, it thanked her.[3]

At 15 Mira Alfassa joined a well-known art studio in Paris to learn drawing and painting. For her tendency to focus undistractedly on her work no matter what was going on around her, she became nicknamed 'the Sphinx'. Although the youngest of the students, it was to her that the others went for advice. At 19 she married the painter Henri Morisset, a disciple of Gustave Moreau. The next year their son André was born.

All along her inner powers were unfolding and Self-realization became her main objective. By 1906 she formed a study group to discuss spiritual and occult topics, a circle which later on was joined by the well-known Tibetologist, Alexandra David-Neel.

A significant detail in her development was that she was able, while asleep, to receive occult instructions from several teachers. With one of them, whom she called 'Krishna', a strong psychic and spiritual relation grew. She realized they would eventually see each other on the physical plane.

It was in 1914 that she travelled to India, for the first time, in the company of her second husband, the philosopher Paul Richard. There, in Pondicherry, she met the Indian mystic Sri Aurobindo and immediately recognized him as 'Krishna', the guide of her meditations. Although she was quite certain that her work was in India with Sri Aurobindo, a prolonged stay was not then possible. The years of the First World War she spent in France and Japan, returning to Pondicherry only in 1920, on her own, never again to leave.

Noting my interest in the Mother, Ahalya suggested I visit her. She had her doubts, though, whether it would be possible for me to meet the 94-year-old saint of Pondicherry after all, as people waited months for an appointment. Ashram members saw her privately only once a year, on their birthdays. Four times annually, on certain designated occasions, the Mother appeared at her balcony and gave *darshan*, 'holy audience'. Hindus believe that *darshan* (literally 'vision' or 'sight' of saintly personages) conveys the spiritual energy of grace and blessing.

Fascinated as I was by the Mother, and attracted by the ashram and Auroville, I had no choice but to go to Pondicherry. Very conveniently I got a car ride straight to my destination from Yeshwant Veecumsee, the owner of the Silversands holiday center in Mahabalipuram, south of Madras. The official tour had brought me to his inviting seaside resort which offered modern comfort in natural tropical surroundings. For several nights I had lodged in a thatched hut right on the beach. Seeking an instructor for sunrise yoga classes, Yeshwant had an appointment in Pondicherry with the yoga expert Swami Gitananda, who would present one of his students for the position.

Once I had installed myself in a guesthouse of the Sri Aurobindo Ashram, I had to adjust to yet another completely new world. On one wall of my room hung the photos of Sri Aurobindo and the Mother. On another was a very clear message: 'No smoking, no alcohol, no sex.'

In a conversation with Chunilal, the guesthouse manager, I found out more about Sri Aurobindo. Students of politics know him as an early leader in India's freedom struggle. Born in Calcutta in 1872 and educated at Cambridge in England, he had been a dynamic journalist and newspaper editor who urged Indians to rise up against British rule. According to ashramites he introduced the boycott as a tool of political resistance even before Mahatma Gandhi.

During a one-year imprisonment by the British, Sri Aurobindo experienced a life-transforming vision of Lord Krishna. They had 'oneness of consciousness,' he said. An inner voice told Sri Aurobindo that, the liberation of India being certain, he should prepare for the next step: liberation of the human race.

Two years later, in 1910, Sri Aurobindo settled in the French colony of Pondicherry. There, retired from active political life, he devoted himself to meditation, yoga and writing his main works on transcendental matters as well as poetry.

Around Sri Aurobindo gathered a group of people. His system of spiritual philosophy and discipline, that he named Integral Yoga (*Purna Yoga*), formed the budding community's ideological base. Yoga is essentially a generic name for the processes by which we grow from a limited awareness to a greater consciousness. The insights gained from this development are applied to our daily activities.

When Sri Aurobindo retired into permanent seclusion in 1926, he made the Mother head of the ashram. His disciples were now to be guided in their spiritual progress by her.

From my first breath in the ashram, I sensed a powerful energy permeating the very atmosphere of the place. In this heavenly clime I was swept along from one magical moment to the next, and meaningful occurrences abounded. Almost immediately, in the ashram dining room, I saw a woman who resembled me, even wearing her dark hair braided up like mine. As I went to wash my dishes, she returned from already having done that. Our eyes met and we exchanged smiles.

Our paths crossed again. I was walking up the library stairs, she down, a fact that amused us. We stopped and talked. Her name was Maxine, she also had grown up in New York City, and she was the same age.

The library being closed, she suggested we go for a tea, acquainting me with the surroundings as we strolled. The ashram, rather than self-contained in a separate compound, consisted of many white and pastel-colored buildings scattered throughout lovely, sun-drenched Pondicherry. It was a scorching South Indian day, but a cool breeze blew in from the Bay of Bengal.

Maxine very quickly opened herself up. 'I came to the ashram to find myself,' she stated. Although traveling with a male companion, they were 'off sex', attempting to 'develop higher consciousness, thwart desires and listen to the True Self within'. They were fighting ego and the temporal, physical self. Now consciously on the spiritual journey, Maxine let 'what happens, happen', never worrying, because there is a 'Master Plan'.

'When you truly believe in God,' she explained at a teahouse frequented by ashramites, 'you release your energies to be used by the divine, and all works out the way it should.' Maxine's words sounded like esoteric jargon.

'Well, we'll meet again if it's meant to be,' Maxine said as we parted in the spacious courtyard of the ashram's central building. In front of me I saw the *samadhi*, the burial place, of Sri Aurobindo who died in 1950. Beautiful flowers arranged in a symbolic design covered the marble tomb. I noticed people sitting, a few standing, in silent meditation.

The scene was other-worldly, but the environment remained South India, and how hot it was! The coolness emitted by the marble and a profound atmosphere of peace bade me approach. Kneeling down, I brought my forehead to the refreshing stone. I knew very little of Sri Aurobindo, yet impulsively I thanked him for having taken birth.

Someone was watching me, I sensed. Instinctively, I looked up to a window which faced the courtyard, but saw no one. That window, I later found out, belonged to the room of the Mother.

Soon afterwards I entered the office of the ashram secretary, Madhav P. Pandit. Introducing myself, I requested printed materials on Auroville for an article I intended to write. Sri Pandit surprised me with his declaration: 'We don't work that way. Find out by experience. That's the best.' He obviously had no time for me.

In the evening I attended the ashram's twice-weekly group meditation, held outdoors. Most people sat cross-legged on the ground. I did the same. From loudspeakers streamed ethereal music and I asked my neighbor what it was.

'The Mother improvising on the organ,' he replied.

Then came a voice. So low, was it a man or a woman? Garbled, unclear, was it English? My neighbor leaned over: 'That's a recording of the Mother, reading from *Savitri*.'

When I looked at him blankly, he told that *Savitri* was Sri Aurobindo's magnum opus, a 24,000-line epic poem in English describing the spiritual journey of the human soul. It had taken him over 30 years to write as he kept reworking the text from each higher level of consciousness he attained.

As much as I appreciated this information, my interest was lured away by the voice from the loudspeakers. It resonated inside me, like inner music. I shut my eyes and glimpses of my life passed before me.

I saw myself as little Norma, since the age of six so busy making stories and poems, at 11 editing a school magazine, at 13 publishing a weekly teen column in a neighborhood newspaper in Queens, New York City, where I was growing up as the elder daughter in a middle-class family.

With the emergence of my first childhood poem, I loved words and wanted to express myself in them, be a writer, a foreign correspondent, travel and see the world. I knew that one day I would write a meaningful book. At nine I won the first prize in a slogan-writing contest for Brotherhood Week. 'Hand in hand to make this land a better world to live in' stood out among 10,000 entries. O, those days of childhood innocence, when dreams and visions seemed so easy to fulfill.

The Mother's voice increased in volume and I let myself flow into it. Deep chords were touched within me.

After the meditation came her voice again, but this time not from the loudspeakers. It was in my mind that I distinctly heard her say: 'Come to me.'

Was I in my right senses? The Mother was calling me! Back at the guesthouse I ran into Sivadass, the Malaysian journalist living across the hall. At our first meeting we had both been surprised to find out we not only had the same profession, but also shared the same May birthday. 'See how the divine works?' he had remarked with a smile.

Noticing my excited state, he started to inquire. Regarding the voice, he said: 'We can feel her force, receive her guidance, whether we are near or far. She influences you even if you don't see her. We believe people are brought to the ashram by their soul, seeking divine truth.'

'You speak about the Mother as if she's God!' I exclaimed.

'Not God,' he responded, 'but one of His highly-realized instruments.'

Considering her a completed soul reincarnated with the mission to help others, ashramites referred to the Mother with great devotion and reverence. Frequently they cited examples from her life and quoted her writings. I was becoming convinced that I could not leave Pondicherry without meeting this remarkable woman.

The next morning, in the ashram embroidery shop, I was regarding a long row of display cases when an urge to look up overpowered me. On the wall hung a picture of the Mother, the foreground illuminated by a candle. Her eyes were fixed on me! I kept staring back. The photograph seemed eerily alive.

Why did I look up? ('You can feel her force. ...') Was it really her power? ('She influences you even if you don't see her. ...') And again I heard: 'Come to me.'

Oh yes, I wanted to go to the Mother. If she was inviting me, then surely she would also arrange the meeting. It had to be soon, though. Any moment a telegram could arrive from New Delhi setting an appointment to interview the Minister of Tourism as a delayed part of the official program.

My experience the following morning was even stranger. Before dawn I woke up for no apparent reason. Lying there in the dark, I realized with a startle that I was not alone.

Turning on the table lamp, I noticed nothing unusual and switched it off again. The sensation persisted that somebody or something was in the room. What force had entered here? A powerful presence, invisible but ever so real, surrounded me.

On all sides I felt an extraordinary calm which, at the same time, was alive with such an intensity it became virtually tangible.

It embraced me, revitalized and uplifted me, letting me recognize my own smallness, a tiny piece of a much larger whole. Here was another intimation that beyond what we see with our eyes there exists a greater reality.

Totally awake, I was directed by a wondrous impulse to go outdoors. Quickly making myself ready, I left my room. In the street I wondered where I was heading at that early hour. What was I doing? A bright light flashed in the darkness. It happened so fast. What was it? The afterglow stayed at my third eye.

My feet started to move as if they had a mind of their own. Breathless, I hastened through the pre-sunrise streets while around me swelled a chorus of birds, greeting the new day. Aah, now I knew where I was being guided. Turning a corner I saw, spread out in front of me, the sea.

By the water, an unusual high-pitched tone seized my attention. At that very second, the first ray appeared. Has the sunrise a sound? The rays multiplied as the sun rose magnificently into full view. My excitement mounted while the brilliant disk grew with awe-inspiring beauty.

As I continued looking, engrossed in the glorious spectacle, the sun took on the features of a face! Transparent, all radiance. Then the sun became a mirror, for the face now looked very much like my own, only infinitely more luminous. Light flooded me and joy pulsed through every cell of my body.

There had to be a meaning to this and a purpose, a firm conviction assured me. Were answers to my lifelong questions finally being supplied? I was so grateful.

At the guesthouse, just as I was about to enter my room, Sivadass came out of his. I always encountered him when I needed to talk.

'You look radiant,' he remarked.

'I've just had a meeting with the sun!' I blurted out.

Recounting my latest experience, I stressed that I had to see the Mother, it was urgent, imperative, nothing else mattered. He advised me to tell the whole story to Sushila, secretary to Sri Navajata, and I hurried to her office.

The rest happened very quickly. In the afternoon she presented me to Sri Navajata, general secretary of the Sri Aurobindo Society and treasurer of Auroville. Ashram and Auroville tasks brought him into close contact with the Mother.

The Mother was sending me messages, I told him, relating the details without holding anything back.

To my relief, Sri Navajata took me seriously. With full attention he listened, then asked me to come with him at the first opportunity, the next morning, when he would have his daily meeting with the Mother.

'Oh thank you!' I cried out, but he cautioned me not to be disappointed if the Mother could not receive me. More than 50 people visited her every day, sometimes having waited months for the appointment. He would try it. 'Otherwise, another time.'

That evening, the third in the ashram, I took my dinner with Sri Navajata and his family. During the meal I learned he had been living in Pondicherry already for 20 years. A prosperous Bombay businessman before giving up that life to resettle in the ashram, accompanied by his wife and two children, he had offered all his property to the Mother. From then on she assumed material and spiritual charge of him.

Afterwards Sri Navajata let me record an interview with him for my projected article on Auroville. Intrigued to know the circumstances of his transformation, I began by asking some questions about his background.

'Sri Navajata, may I ask you what is your full name?'

'*Sri* is a respectful title of address, and *Navajata* is the name given me by the Mother, my *guru*, my spiritual guide, when I joined the ashram. My old name is different, dropped off with the past. No use thinking about it.'

'Why did you receive the name *Navajata*?'

'*Navajata* means "newborn". The Mother gave me some inner experiences, and also this outer name.'

'Could you please tell about them?'

'I am sorry. In yoga we are not allowed to tell experiences.'

But he did not have to tell me. An inner experience, I too had received one. I also felt newborn. The sunrise had been an initiation into a higher understanding and a bestowal of blessings.

The interview continued until Sri Navajata said it was nearly his bedtime. He usually retired between nine and nine-thirty because he arose by three. Sri Aurobindo taught that between three and four, when all is silent, is the best hour for meditation.

'Every morning, before a little exercise and a long meditation,' Sri Navajata said, 'I dedicate myself unto the Lord, so that every moment He may use my mind, body and life as He wants.'

Telling me that he began his work around seven, Sri Navajata requested me to be in his office early the next day.

Back at the guesthouse I reflected on my sojourn in Pondicherry, noting that for me everything here flowed easily and naturally. Without my having made any conscious efforts, each of my steps seemed to be carrying me towards a spiritual destination which, before India, I had known only from books. All signs indicated a journey to higher understanding and I was apparently already on it.

Now that I had become aware of this process, how to participate actively in it?

'Don't worry,' came a voice.

There definitely seemed to be a guidance. I vowed to remain open and accept whatever would happen.

Life became simpler.

Meeting the Mother of Pondicherry

The next sunrise heralded an unforgettable Sunday, 12 November. Soon after breakfast I was sitting in Sri Navajata's office while he prepared his papers. The Governor's wife phoned, wanting to see the Mother, and Sri Navajata agreed to arrange it.

Although I had no high rank, he was working out my visit too, and this already on my fourth day in the ashram. But whether the *darshan* would take place immediately or 'otherwise, another time', was up to the Mother. I remembered Sri Navajata telling me the evening before that she always made the right decisions: 'Knowledge comes when you have no preferences and no desires, she says.'

Taking this to heart, I affirmed to myself: 'I will be happy if the Mother can see me and I will be equally happy if she cannot.'

At a certain moment Sri Navajata invited me to accompany him and Sushila. Nervously I followed them. Just past the office of Sri Pandit we approached a building where a sign requested 'Silence Please'.

Eventually we arrived at a long room where many people, all holding flowers, sat on the floor. No one spoke. Sri Navajata withdrew and Sushila led me to a man who wrote my name into a book. Ascending a long staircase, Sushila and I reached a roof terrace. The early morning sun welcomed us. About 30 men and women were waiting, all in silence.

Sushila handed me a large white flower and some smaller ones.

'For the transformation from the physical to the psychic,' she said, looking luminous with her white sari reflecting the sunlight. She guided me to a spot where Sri Navajata sat cross-legged on the ground, emitting an air of contemplation. In his clothing of fine white cotton, he too shimmered.

'May I take a photo of you?' I asked.

He shook his head, saying kindly, 'Better not. It's not right here. Better sit and be silent.'

'Try to relax, be calm, no excitement,' advised Sushila. 'Just like a child going to its mother, something natural, no nervousness.'

Sri Navajata got up and disappeared again. Sushila also had to depart and placed me in front of a door. The room of the Mother!

'Wait here,' Sushila said. 'If Mother will see you today, Navajata will call you. Watch for his signal.' She took my heavy bag containing tape recorder, cameras, notebooks and pens. A burden removed, I felt lighter.

Before she left, Sushila told me: 'Upon entering, you will see Mother with her back to you. Go to her right side and kneel down, putting your head on her right knee.'

I stayed in the doorway, all alone, the flowers in my hand. Then Sri Navajata appeared. In anticipation, I could hardly breathe, but my tension dissolved instantly when he said, with a smile: 'Mother will see you.'

Entering, I found the Mother not with her back to me but in profile. Her body was bent forward, half folded, sunk down into the chair. Lifeless, without energy. Quite affected by this first sight, I forgot Sushila's instructions. Sri Navajata came to my rescue, gently placing me on my knees at the Mother's right side.

I looked up at her, she down at me, our faces ever so close. The Mother! As I stared into her eyes, I knew why Sri Aurobindo had given Mira Richard this name. The source of All, he said, can be symbolized by a mother, out of whose womb comes all creation. In Mira Richard he recognized the qualities of the celestial energy which gives birth to the world and all beings.

But here in front of me she seemed to be merely another soul in a human body. Her stomach rumbled, or was that my stomach? I heard a heartbeat, hers or mine? I put my hand on her knee, she reached down and held it. When I placed my other hand close by, she squeezed it. I looked carefully at her hand, examining it in detail. The skin appeared translucent, light glowed through it. Dark veins stood out like a long range of mountains.

We alternated between looking seriously at each other and smiling, laughing even. I saw flickering blue-grey eyes. My remaining nervousness evaporated, it was good being with her. 'Something natural, like a child being with its mother,' just as Sushila had said.

The Mother gave me a pat, then another squeeze. As weak as she appeared physically, as powerful was her energy passing to me. The strong current caused my body to quiver involuntarily and for a moment I lost my ease.

Another pat on my hand gave reassurance, helping me to relax even more. My whole body softly tingled, as if caressed. A wave of happiness arose in me and I released myself totally into a state of exhaltation.

A pain in my knees called me back to earth. I wanted to say something to the Mother, not knowing yet what. Very slowly, as clearly as I could pronounce, I repeated to my own astonishment a statement dictated from inside: 'I want to change.'

Mysterious, deep-throated words emerged from the mouth of the Mother. Whereas I could very well understand the transmissions from the Mother to me on inner planes, I had difficulty comprehending her outer speech. Her words sounded garbled, as over the loudspeakers. A long-bearded man whom I later learned was Champaklal, her personal attendant, announced very loudly as if the Mother was hard of hearing: 'She says, this will help.'

Into my hand she put two envelopes, each the size of a large postage stamp. One bore a picture of Sri Aurobindo, the other her own. Then she presented me with a white rose.

Later, after having walked in silence with Sri Navajata back to his office, he said to me: 'You had a very good darshan. You are very fortunate. Mother gave you a long time. She was very responsive to you. She saw you were very receptive, ripe, ready. She gave you two blessing packets; usually she gives only one. And she held your hand.'

He also told that a new regulation had come through from the Mother. From now on she would see only people already known to her. I had reached her just in time, thanks to my sense of urgency. I took this as a sign.

After having been with the Mother, I felt different, rearranged.

'It is the impact of realized consciousness which changes you,' Sri Navajata explained. 'In her presence your physical and her physical, your mind and her mind, your soul and her soul, come into contact. It is infinity touching the little human being and giving a taste of infinity.'

Lunching alone in the ashram dining room, I remembered the words of Sivadass the first evening in the guesthouse: 'Meeting the Mother can change your life.'

Looking up, I noticed that a young man across the table regarded me intently. After a while he asked: 'Did you see the Mother today?'

Taken by surprise, my hand automatically went to my blouse and to the flower pinned there, the white rose handed me by the Mother.

'Yes, but how did you know?' I exclaimed. 'From this white rose? But couldn't just anyone have given it to me?'

He looked at me very thoughtfully and replied: 'There are some things you can't explain.'

In the afternoon, I longed for a landscape of vastness corresponding to the one encountered within me. Looking up into Mother's blue-grey eyes, an oceanic spaciousness had inundated me and still I felt unlimited. I walked down to the beach. Only the endless water, extending towards an equally boundless sky, could know my heart.

Strolling along the sea, in harmony with the soothing song it sang, a floating sensation slowly came up in me that I very well knew. I used to have it from time to time upon awakening in the morning, when I would recall only the sensation itself, never any details. Now all of a sudden they emerged.

I moved through a maze which turned around and around and spiraled upwards. I was led and pulled and wanted to hold onto my body but could not. I was squeezed and stretched and nothing else existed except the continually changing movement.

Eventually I came out of the maze into an immense open space, everywhere blue, turning to golden, and it vibrated. Everything in me purred. A great calm took over.

This dream had first come to me one night in my early childhood, at a time when I wondered if I were in the right place and if my father and mother were my real parents. Deep within I always had known about the existence of other surroundings, where was my true home. Meeting the Mother helped me see that I was a daughter of more than one mother alone.

Pondicherry had opened to me a world larger than my most daring fantasy could ever have imagined. Life's very purpose dawned upon me. I wanted to attune myself accordingly.

M. P. Pandit and the Ideal
of Perfection

The urgent need to be with the Mother had been fulfilled and my wish returned to visit Auroville, the utopian community she inspired. I decided to see again Madhar P Pandit. After all, there had to be some printed material on Auroville to provide orientation. Or would he once more ask me to find out by experience?

In the meantime I learned that Sri Pandit had been a close disciple of the Mother for almost 30 years already. Entrusted with diverse responsibilities as ashram secretary, he had tasks which brought him to her daily. Besides being one of the main authorities on the philosophy and yoga of Sri Aurobindo and the Mother, he was a respected lecturer in his own right and a noted author on diverse spiritual themes.

When I entered his office, Sri Pandit greeted me, this time with a smile, remarking that I looked different.

Mother gave me her blessed *darshan*, I told him. He nodded and said that during his own first *darshan*, many years ago, he recognized divine love in her.

'I totally melted and ceased to be an individual,' he stated. 'I found a hundred births worth that moment.'

Sri Pandit's openness surprised me, and I gladly took the opportunity to tell him that in Pondicherry remarkable things had happened to me, without my seeking them.

'Yes, therefore I don't plan,' he responded. 'With me, thoughts come. Some have a certain authenticity which cannot be denied.'

'How do you determine between an authentic message and a thought not to be followed?'

'I wait,' he replied. 'If it is not genuine, it wears out quickly. Otherwise it persists and all things get organized to suit that.'

Because he was taking time to converse with me, I asked him to give me a brief idea of the teachings of Sri Aurobindo and the Mother.

Without having to reflect, he answered: 'The central thrust of their work is that the human being is not the last stage in evolution but only a transitional form, heading towards a new illumined species. This higher form will not be endowed with a mind characterized by our imperfect reasoning intellect but by direct connection with the divine.'

'So those beings will not have to practise yoga', I said, 'because their entire life will be yoga.'

'Correct,' affirmed Sri Pandit. 'Yoga is union, of our individual mind with the Ultimate Reality. Its very essence is the raising of our individual consciousness so that it comes into contact and eventually to oneness with the divine, transcendent, unnameable source and support of all things, from which we have become separated.'

'Suppose someone doesn't believe in the divine?' I asked.

'Then the effort for such people is to unite themselves with the source of their own being, their own truth. They may not believe in God, but they can surely believe in their own self and in their highest human qualities and virtues.'

'What exactly is Sri Aurobindo's Integral Yoga?' was my next question.

'It can be defined as a coordinated development of all the parts of our being, along with an integration on each plane of existence,' he explained. 'The aim is to attain the highest spiritual power, but not for the purpose of escaping life. The idea is to bring that power into the world, in order to enlighten, purify and perfect our functioning.'

Sri Pandit summarized: 'The goal is to bring about the life divine on earth.'

'That seems a remote dream,' I commented.

'That dream is the very purpose of evolution,' he went on. 'Perfection in life, in the art of living, will result in harmony, joy and delight in all our relationships: with the divine, with our planet, with each other.'

'What do you mean by perfection?' I asked.

'Not the general concept, which sees perfection as a summit to be reached one day. According to Mother, perfection is the maximal harmonization of all the elements present in any given situation. Such a state is within our reach. Today's perfection will necessarily be exceeded by tomorrow's. Perfection is a moving ideal, at every moment there is a perfection to be attained.'

'If the perfection of the individual life is possible,' I said, 'and if each individual, when illumined, contributes towards the creation of a perfected collective, how can we proceed to attain this peace-on-earth state?'

'Each person has to work for it within himself,' answered Sri Pandit, 'by putting his weight on the side of truth and harmony. When you actively try to develop the godly qualities in yourself, you automatically deter the ungodly ones. Our yoga is a practice to elevate, expand and deepen, in a deliberate effort, the workings of consciousness. This adds to the cosmic balance of the divine.'

'Then the key lies with the individual.'

'Precisely, and with like-minded people associating and working together to create what we may call "islands of light". A changed collective consciousness has to proceed from such little islands, coming closer and closer to each other.' He made a joining movement with his hands. 'There is not going to be a miracle, a sudden transformation of humanity.'

'Thousands of years ago,' I remarked, 'there was a mass revelation at Sinai, when many people together heard what was termed the voice of God.'

'Well, in those days the voice of God manifested in a particular way,' replied Sri Pandit. 'In our time it comes as an inner voice to individuals. This can happen as well to someone who never before had an ear for such things.'

'What does one have to do as a preparation?'

'The basis of perfection, and of all true yoga, is simply peace within,' he pointed out. 'While we still hang on to certain habits, we cannot enjoy this marvelous peace.'

'Which habits?' I asked.

'Ego, desire, preferences, attachment.'

'We cling to these tenaciously, don't we?'

'To discourage them we can observe three things,' responded Sri Pandit. 'You will find them mentioned in here,' he said, taking papers from a cabinet. Aha – so he did have informational material!

Indicating one of the brochures, he said: 'The ashram expresses the ideals of Sri Aurobindo and the Mother. Auroville is the hard reality of putting these ideals into practice as a cooperative human unity.' He handed the papers to me.

Aspiration, rejection and surrender, I read later in my room, were what helped develop the proper climate conducive for the soul's growth. We aspire to the divine, rejecting everything which prevents this, and we surrender completely, giving all that we are. This attitude certainly appealed to me.

Onwards then, enriched with the new moving ideal of perfection!

Auroville, City of the Future

From the materials given to me by Sri Pandit I learned that the name *Auroville* literally meant 'City of Dawn' while also referring to Sri Aurobindo.

In those days the experimental township, growing out of a rugged stretch of desert-like coastal land a few miles north of Pondicherry, consisted of nine settlements. Several hundred pioneers, the majority from France, Germany and Italy, lived mainly in small thatched huts which combined Indian tradition with Western facilities. The average age of the settlers, excluding children, was about 30. It was the Mother's dream that the city would eventually house 50,000 people, from all areas of the world and every walk of life.

Auroville was inaugurated with an impressive ceremony on 28 February 1968. Children from 124 different nations and each state of India placed a handful of earth from their native land into an urn shaped like a lotus bud. This represented Auroville's aim to become the 'cradle of the new world'.

It was not necessary to embrace Sri Aurobindo's philosophy to live in Auroville, said the Mother. The only condition was 'to believe in the essential unity of mankind and be determined to work for it'.

I got my first impression of the project on a gratis, all-day bus tour. Our guide, ashramite Govind, prepared us before we started out: 'Auroville is based on offering, not on taking,' he said. 'Try to catch the vibrations there.'

Our excursion took us past the community's grain fields, vegetable gardens, orchards and dairy farms. Among the several small-scale industries we visited were Aurofood, producer of wholegrain bread, and Auropress, which turned out informational material.

In the paper factory, watching Aurovillians boil, beat and color old, discarded clothing and transform it into beautiful, smoothly-finished or linen-like handmade paper, I thought of all the trees spared by this alternative papermaking process.

'Business is not our business,' said the young man from Germany who was hanging up large sheets of the wet paper to dry. 'Since Auroville provides for all our needs, we don't work for money. We work to develop consciousness. The Mother said that to work for the divine is to pray with the body. With this spirit, values change about one job being better than another.'

When we came to the Last School, rather a sculpture than a building, Govind told us: 'The first educational principle here, as in the ashram, is Sri Aurobindo's maxim that nothing can be taught. Education is based on what we hope to receive from the future, not what we know about the past.' Traditional methods were dismissed, as was reflected by the names of Auroville's planned schools: After School One, After School Two, Super School One, Super School Two, No School.

'Emphasis is on knowledge of the Self, in harmony with knowledge of the outside world,' Govind continued. All life is our school, I interpreted.

The next day I went back to Auroville on my own and spoke with people in the settlements significantly named Promesse, Hope, Aspiration and Peace. There was no private ownership and Aurovillians worked collectively in the community's various projects. Residents contributed their skill and labor in return for 'Prosperity', their upkeep. Freed from the problems of a money-based economy, settlers were expected to devote some of their time to spiritual studies, though there were no compulsions.

After my experiences at the ashram, I easily recognized that Auroville was more than a city in the making. It was as well a process of consciousness unfoldment expressing itself through the residents.

In the settlement of Aspiration I chatted with Paride, from Italy, who was supervising the construction of a hospital. When I asked him when the building would be ready, he replied: 'Maybe in three months, three years, maybe never. The most important thing here is the growth inside us.'

Near the workers' camp named Peace I witnessed the early stages of the construction of Matrimandir, a temple to the Universal Light, seen in a vision by the Mother as a temple 100 feet in diameter. Through a circular opening in the roof the sun would shine onto a large spherical crystal located in the center of an all-white 12-sided chamber.

To the Mother the sun represented the divine Lord, smiling down on us, and its union with the crystal stood for the future realization of humanity.

The symbolism of Matrimandir is very well expressed by the Dutch-born Aurovillian Ruud Lohman: 'Matrimandir in its simple symbol shows His Presence as a continuous outpouring of Light, and it only depends on our individual and collective receptivity how much of Him we can absorb.'[4]

The first part of the Matrimandir project called for digging down 150 feet into the earth, then laying a cement foundation and building four pillars. On the site I met Roger, from the United States, who told me: 'The construction work is a symbol of our yoga. We're digging deep into ourselves to make Auroville a reality.'

Yet Auroville was not all harmony and light. At Aspiration I saw a telling notice on the community bulletin board: 'We say we are progressing but we are becoming more and more intolerant of each other's opinions, and more and more we are not signing our name on comment sheets. These two traits do not fit in here.'

When I mentioned my impressions of the future city to Sivadass, he aired his view that the Auroville approach needed to be more practical.

'There is no place in Auroville for money,' he declared. 'How can that work?' He went on to criticize the way donations were spent. According to him, there was a growing disagreement with the financial administration of the project.

'But Auroville is a project sponsored by the Mother,' he said, 'so no one can openly oppose its workings.'

Sivadass pointed out another problem. Auroville had to avoid the situation that existed in Pondicherry, where the locals showed hostility towards the ashram, which in turn kept aloof from them.

'The relationship reveals traditional north–south alienation,' he explained. 'Sri Aurobindo was a Northerner who settled in this French colonial town when it offered him refuge from the British. Those who followed him were also North Indians and most ashramites still are. Auroville tries to avoid the mistakes of the ashram by integrating local villagers into the community rather than driving them away.'

Later I reviewed my notes and came across Sri Aurobindo's statement that the ashram had not been created to renounce the world, elsewhere a common objective of such institutions. In his mighty vision the ashram was a center and a field of practice for the evolution of another kind and form of life, moved by a higher consciousness.

This ambitious goal was already difficult enough to reach through the ashram with its homogeneous population consisting mainly of North Indians of similar upbringing. But to the Mother, nothing less would suffice than creating with Auroville the prototype of a world community made up of people comprising all nationalities and cultures, all backgrounds and professions. This, evidently, could not be realized overnight, and not without considerable growing pains.

When I visited Auroville in those earliest formative years, it represented the harsh down-to-earth reality of many pioneering idealists together grappling with a multi-lingual, multi-cultural challenge in a rough tropical terrain which lacked even topsoil and trees. I was not surprised that problems abounded. It is usually a far distance from our high aspirations to their actualization. But it is certainly better to participate in a project aimed at the improvement of human existence and once in a while to stumble, than to remain complacent and do nothing.

After my meeting with the Mother and the visits to Auroville, I could see myself remaining forever in Pondicherry. That, however, was not to be. The expected telegram from New Delhi finally arrived: 'Your interview with Dr Karan Singh fixed at 11a.m. on twenty-two November repeat 22 in Sardar Patel Bhavan Parliament Street New Delhi.'

Reluctantly, I prepared for my departure from South India. If I still looked the same as when I arrived, inside me a lot had already changed.

Dr. Karan Singh and the Politics of Global Consciousness

The Minister of Tourism and Civil Aviation, Dr. Karan Singh turned out to be a charming man of princely heritage who expressed himself in a most elegant manner while revealing a broad vision.

Born in 1931 in Cannes in France, Karan Singh was the only son of Sir Hari Singh, Maharaja of Jammu and Kashmir. With the end of the Maharaja ruling system after India's independence, Karan Singh was appointed the regent of Kashmir. Three years later, at the age of 21, the former prince won the first general election for this position.

After governing for 18 years, he was recruited into the national government of Prime Minister Indira Gandhi. At the age of 36 he became the Minister of Tourism and Civil Aviation, the youngest person ever to hold a post in the central cabinet.

Dr. Singh answered very precisely, with facts and figures, all my questions on Indian tourism. When I mentioned just having come from Pondicherry, he smiled and told he had earned his doctorate from Delhi University with the thesis *Prophet of Indian Nationalism*, about Sri Aurobindo's political thought.

We discussed Sri Aurobindo's philosophy – or more accurately, I listened to Dr. Singh eloquently discourse on its main themes. At one point he said: 'Each human being born on this planet carries within himself an unquenchable spark of divinity. Our destiny as human beings revolves around the fanning of this spark into the smokeless flame of spiritual realization.'

It sounded so easy, I thought, but how to do it? Does everything happen by itself?

Dr. Singh continued as if quoting from his writings: 'I believe that all political, economic and social activity should have as its ultimate goal the fostering of this divinity within each individual. Scientific and technological developments are counterproductive if they do not conduce towards this end.'

When he said, 'I find no real distinction between my work and my spiritual quest,' I asked: 'Didn't Mahatma Gandhi once say that people who maintain that religion and politics don't mix know little about religion? What do you think he meant?'

'I think he was telling us that true religion is not what many people take it to be, that you must go to church or temple on a certain day. This just represents an outer conformism. I think he was referring to religion in the deeper sense, as a guiding principle which has to permeate all our activities. Since politics is an important and pervasive activity, you cannot isolate it from religion.'

'Can a person whose main interest is the pursuit of the spiritual, play an effective role in politics?' I next wanted to know.

'Indeed, yes!' he exclaimed. 'The prayer, the silence, the meditation and the contemplation are one way to the divine. There is another way: through activity. Politics, for instance.'

'What do you think is the main prerequisite for a national political leader in a democratic nation?' I asked.

'To get elected!' he said, laughing. 'There is no other qualification laid down.'

'True, but once someone gets elected, what is the main prerequisite to stay in office?'

'What you are asking is whether great spiritual, intellectual and moral stature is required in a democratic leader. Ideally, yes. But in fact, no. People are not elected on the basis of their spiritual, moral or intellectual caliber but rather because of the contours of policy in a given period. One can hope that the great leaders of the world are men and women of compassion, understanding and wisdom. I'm afraid it is very much of a lottery.'

'What quality, if you could pick out only one, would you ideally want every politician to have?'

Without any hesitation Dr. Singh replied: 'Global consciousness. The consciousness that they are not only leaders of their own nation but belong to a newly developing global consciousness.'

'What is global consciousness?' I asked.

'The view which considers the welfare of the whole planet before its individual parts. Some concepts belonging to it are the spiritual interconnectedness and interdependence of all that exists, the divinity inherent in each individual, and the human race as a single family.'

'Could politics really serve as a vehicle for transformation?' I inquired.

'Certainly,' he affirmed, 'at a certain point in time. We live in an age of politics. And how do we transform consciousness? Through using the predominant mode, which today is politics. Then surely it is through politics, correctly understood and articulated, that we can hope to awaken the consciousness of people.'

'What do you mean by consciousness? I always like to define basic terms, to ensure we are talking about the same thing.'

'Consciousness is what in Sanskrit we call *chetana*, the awareness of being,' he responded. 'Exterior objects are pleasant or unpleasant. Somebody may like one thing, somebody else may like the other. What makes life worth living is the inner power which gives awareness of Self and the universal forces.'

The conversation having taken this turn, I spoke about my visit to Auroville, saying it had struck me as a process more than as a place. 'The buildings constructed there are not as significant as the inner growth of its dwellers,' I commented.

He understood completely, and we discussed the future city for some time. Dr. Singh knew much about Auroville because, aside from his own personal interest in the unique experiment, he was connected with it through his work. As Deputy Leader of the Indian delegation to the United Nations Conference on the Human Environment in Stockholm five months before, he had introduced an official paper before the Committee on Human Settlements. Of course! That was the paper, 'Auroville – Search for a Total Environment', that had contributed to my interest in Auroville, the Mother and Sri Aurobindo.

Dr Singh went on to elaborate that, at the moment, the divine was apparently using him as a vehicle on a national level for developments connected with Sri Aurobindo and Auroville. After a meeting he had called to discuss the centenary of Sri Aurobindo's birth, a national committee had been formed with Prime Minister Indira Gandhi as its head. A special edition of Sri Aurobindo's published works, a bust of Sri Aurobindo installed in Parliament House, the purchase of the Calcutta house where Sri Aurobindo had been born and its conversion into an ashram – these were just a few of the results of his original initiative.

Also in conjunction with the centenary celebrations, 33

world-renowned philosophers had been invited to India. One of
them was R. Buckminster Fuller, the American futuristic thinker,
inventor, engineer and architect. He would also be arriving in New
Delhi in his function as advisor to the International Airports
Authority of India. Dr. Singh suggested I try to interview him.

Reviewing my notes later in the day, I thought over Dr. Singh's
statement that he found no real distinction between his work and
his spiritual quest. After having heard about some of his activities,
I understood why. The encounter with this inspired politician left
me wondering whether my present occupation, that of travel trade
journalist, could further my inner development, let alone
contribute to the awakening of people's consciousness.

The Jet Age Guru

Full and fulfilling my experiences in India had been. My last scheduled interview, with Dr. Karan Singh, had made me realize anew that I was being led from one inspiring person to another. All served as teachers to me, on different levels, directing me ahead towards a not yet clearly defined destination. To whom would I next be guided?

Although no further commitments bound me and no sightseeing desires asked me to stay, I felt it was not yet time to return West.

I decided to phone one of the New Delhi contact people suggested to me by friends in Amsterdam. Heading the list was Sri Sinha, an Indian journalist who was India correspondent for several European publications. He had been recommended by Jan van der Pluym, editor-in-chief of *de Volkskrant*, one of Holland's national newspapers.

When I called Sri Sinha, he spoke to me in an intimate tone as if we already knew each other.

'So, you're finally here. I have a letter from Jan to you. I'll be at your hotel in two hours. We'll go to the Press Club and then have dinner.'

Promptly at eight he arrived, a well-dressed attractive man in his late thirties or so. Smart European-cut jacket and trousers, pin-striped shirt and silk tie identified him as a Westernized Indian.

At the Press Club, only a few people – all men – sat in the lounge. They looked up as we entered, acknowledging Sri Sinha with a nod or a few words. Declining to sit at anyone's table, he conducted me to a place in a far corner. When he offered me a drink, I asked for fruit juice.

'We don't have any here,' he replied, and proceeded to order two scotches. During the next hour he extolled his position as foreign correspondent, claiming to be one of India's highest-paid journalists. He even mentioned his salary. His boastful monologue about having a private office and secretary had an effect on me rather opposite to what he undoubtedly intended. When he related his difficulties in trying to import a Mercedes, I mentioned I would probably sell my car, because it created so much pollution. He hardly listened, interrupting me to add that he traveled often and would soon be leaving on assignment for Bangladesh.

Eventually he began asking me questions, as if making an interview. What were my impressions of India, what had I experienced? Fresh from Pondicherry, my enthusiasm prevented me from restricting my answers to journalistic fact. Like a new convert, I described in flowery language my trip as a series of revelations, the fitting together of the pieces of a huge picture puzzle called Life. I even told him I realized there was a Master Plan. He made no comment, except: 'Finish your drink. We've got to get some dinner now, before the restaurants close.' I feared I had talked too much.

As soon as we were in the car, Sri Sinha asked my place of birth. When I answered 'New York', he said he had thought I was American but wanted to make sure. Then he asked the month of my birth.

'May,' I replied. 'You?'

'May, Taurus. My ascendent sign is Aquarius.'

'Mine too.'

'Ooooh!' he cried out, bringing the car to a screeching halt at the side of the road. 'Now I'm sure!'

Grabbing me by the shoulders, he pressed his lips to mine, forced them open, and breathed strange-sounding words into me in mouth-to-mouth-resuscitation style. I was too stunned by this sudden crisis of passion to be able to push him away. The unexpected assault lasted only a few seconds. After his excitement had disappeared as quickly as it arose, he appeared exhausted. Leaning back, he declared with a serious voice: 'I am your guru – the one you've been searching for.'

I was quite amused, regarding his behavior as a novel version of the classic male seduction tactic. Had I known more about Indian society, where a woman does not allow any physical nearness with a man not her husband, I would immediately have stepped out of the car.

'I am your guru. That is why you have come to India,' Sinha continued, undaunted by my increasing hilarity. He topped his singular performance with the wondrous revelation: 'I have been waiting 13 years for you.'

'I thought an Indian guru had to have a beard, long hair, and live ascetically,' I said to provoke him.

'I am a jet age guru,' Sinha replied, focusing his black eyes piercingly on mine. 'You are nearly 12 months late,' he said. 'Thirteen years ago a vision revealed I had 12 years to get ready for the arrival of an American woman, whom I would help with her spiritual development as well as her work, which had to do with writing.'

Listening sceptically, I nevertheless remembered that my journey had indeed been delayed by the endemic slow grinding of the Indian bureaucracy. And, since I had suspended disbelief after my experiences in Pondicherry, how could I reject this latest turn of events? I decided to remain open, as I had vowed to do, and let happen what would, just like Maxine. Yet when I showed no real interest in Sinha's guru role, he dropped the subject.

After the dinner, which passed with more bragging about his journalistic coups, he delivered me back to my hotel. Sure enough, he wanted to come up to the room 'to give more details of the vision 13 years ago'. When I burst into laughter, Sinha indignantly remarked I had much to learn about how to treat a guru, and left.

A very early phone call the next morning let me know that, despite my indifferent attitude, Sinha would maintain his guru stance. Assuming my agreement, he instructed me to be ready by eight. He would bring me to someone special who could help me understand more.

Much concerning Sinha caused me to wonder about his intentions, and my rational mind warned me to stop seeing him immediately, yet something made me feel I had no choice but to continue. He seemed a necessary part of the process that was carrying me along.

When he picked me up in front of my hotel, he announced we were on the way to the home of a friend, the painter Elizabeth Brunner. In 1930, at the age of 20, she had accompanied her mother, also a painter, from their native Hungary to India for studies with Rabindranath Tagore, the Nobel Prize-winning writer, mystic and educator. The mother had died and Elizabeth lived alone in New Delhi.

The moment we rang her doorbell a dog began to bark, madly and furiously, drowning Elizabeth's welcome to us. She waved us in, shouting above the din that she would hold the dog back as we entered. What a death-defying operation to maneuvre past the crazed beast!

As we rushed into the living room, he snapped menacingly while trying to pull himself free from the heavy metal chain which secured him. When Elizabeth apologized profusely for her pet's behavior I commented, none too diplomatically, that his face reminded me of a demonic being.

'Could be,' Elizabeth said quite calmly, telling us that Bingo had wandered into her yard three years ago and never left. He was a reincarnated soul, come to protect her.

To ensure that Bingo got no wrong ideas, I chose a seat distant from his mistress and certainly as far away from him as possible. He was still straining at his chain and snarling. While Elizabeth served tea, I looked around the room.

The floor was a veritable chaos of papers and books piled up everywhere, as if Elizabeth had not space enough for all her belongings or could not bear to part with anything. But when I looked up, I saw on the walls the serene and sublime expressions of swamis, yogis and other spiritual personages, as well as many canvases connected with Buddhism, one source of Elizabeth's inspiration.

When I admired her portraits of Mahatma Gandhi and the Dalai Lama, Elizabeth said she had attended many of Gandhiji's prayer meetings and she knew the Dalai Lama well, having painted him several times. He was an enlightened soul, descended to teach others.

Her own task was to paint. She had never married and lived very simply. A complete vegetarian, she did not drink alcohol or coffee nor smoke cigarettes. Dressing plainly, she usually wore a handwoven cotton *lungi*, the Indian style I enjoyed, and a matching *kurta* top. She did not follow any specific spiritual practices but visited temples and gurus without binding herself to any particular one. Her experiences she tried to convey through portraits of India's great leaders, intellectuals, artists, saints, and even simple villagers.

Elizabeth's art stimulated me. In her presence I noticed that I too had a desire to express myself on transcendental themes. She painted; I aspired to write. Moreover, she exemplified the unpretentious lifestyle to which I felt attracted since being in India. My inner guidance not to dismiss Sinha had been correct. This had brought me to Elizabeth, who was indeed special, just as promised. While I was thinking all this, the doorbell rang. Sinha announced to me: 'Here is the person I told you about,' and Elizabeth added: 'He reads faces.'

Whoever this person was, he preferred not to come in. Apparently he was well acquainted with Elizabeth's sentry. Over the dog's renewed frenzy, our hostess gestured that we should run past Bingo into the garden while she held him back.

Outside, I was introduced to Panditji, the respectful address for a Hindu appreciated either for his scholarship or his wisdom. Contrary to what his title implied, Panditji's almost completely black outfit, from his cap down to very pointed slippers, indicated he was a Muslim. As the three of us took places around a lawn table, his self-assured solidity created a sober atmosphere. Small talk seemed out of place.

With a matter-of-fact attitude Panditji began by requesting me to take down my braids and push my hair away from my face. Since he spoke only Hindi, Sinha served as translator. I had to look directly at Panditji, and then turn my head slightly to the right, and then to the left. He wanted to examine, of all things, my ear lobes! After gazing at them at length with great solemnity, he asked my name and birth date, and drew lines and numbers on a pad.

When he produced my 'lucky number', I noted that its three ciphers added up to a figure which had indeed had special significance to me in the last years. The sun governed my mental attitude, he continued, stressing that everything to do with the sun would bring benefit. I started to listen more attentively. When I heard that the number of the sun is 12, it flashed through my mind that I met the Mother on a Sunday, and it had been the twelfth day of the month.

Elizabeth's servant brought a pot of tea, but no one touched it.

Then Panditji narrated my past fairly accurately, reading my ear lobes as if they were miniature chronicles of my personal history. He saw I had come unconsciously to India, but it was destined, in order to form an association with someone who would have a very good influence on my life. This attachment already existed and would last many years.

At this statement Sinha looked triumphant, winking at me. I

myself was thinking of the Mother. Besides, I started to wonder whether Sinha was translating Panditji's findings accurately or if he was changing and coloring them. Normally I do not have a suspicious nature, but Sinha with his strange behavior brought up this idea in me.

Panditji predicted a meteoric rise for my career. I would write books that would enrich society.

'And what do I have to do to get ready?' I questioned, quite intrigued by now. What an anticlimax when he replied I did not have to do anything!

'You will develop with the influence of someone external,' translated Sinha, winking again. 'Your Indian guru will guide you.' My scepticism returned. 'The future will unfold in a natural manner,' he added.

Panditji's advice was simple: 'Do not make any effort to set things into a pattern. Everything will come by itself. All will happen automatically, naturally, spontaneously. The main thing,' he emphasized, as he had several times, 'is the influence of the sun.'

Suffice it to say that many of Panditji's predictions fed my lifelong wish to contribute meaningfully to society and showed me a new future, on the spiritual path. Others I considered totally preposterous.

What to think, for instance, of his forecast that I would marry and have five children? I silently dismissed this as ridiculous. Panditji even specified the marriage would be with an Indian. 'But after 35, it will be secondary to your work. Then the writing will be more important.'

Precisely. But, I wondered, how much of this reading was accurate? Referring to the five children, I questioned him whether he really was certain about this. Panditji got angry. 'The whole reading is off,' came the translation, and Sinha asked me to apologize.

'I'm sorry!' I burst out. Sinha jumped up and rushed after Panditji, who was already walking away. I watched anxiously as the one ardently pleaded while the other kept firmly refusing. Finally Panditji relented and took again his seat. Sinha quickly informed me my unsuitable behavior had been excused because it came from ignorance, not disrespect.

The reading resumed with Panditji's warning that some evil influences were focusing on me. They were destined, 'due to the stars'. A time of trial was coming – from March to May would be a particularly difficult period. He gave a good amount of advice, including not to wear black when I returned to Amsterdam. I saw his point, since I connected this color with death and negativity.

To counteract the obstructive forces, he had to make a talisman, an object charged with a specific task. By the evening he could create one, in the form of a small ornament, to protect me from evil. It would be infused with *mantras*, holy chants, and for seven additional days he would 'offer prayers in absentia' to ensure its power. I could collect the energized talisman tonight, and had to wear it until no longer needed, which would be clear at the time.

An additional aid appeared from Panditji's briefcase, a piece of bark. It came of course from a sacred tree in the Himalayas. After drawing hieroglyphic symbols on the surface, he handed it to me. I was supposed to place the bark in a protective plastic cover and look at it occasionally.

'Seven days of chanting the mantra will mean many expenses,' said Panditji, stating a figure which in those years was quite an amount.

Doubts assailed me, and who would not condone them? My tendency to have faith in the goodness of people won and I placed the money on the table.

When I inquired about my past lives, Panditji muttered something but then said, slightly irritated, 'There's no point in asking this.'

'But can't we advance more speedily through researching our previous incarnations?' I pressed on. 'Doesn't consciousness progressively develop, from one life to the next?'

Panditji advised me not to concern myself with the past. 'Take what I give you. That is your guidance.'

Then he declared: 'Change Norma. The name has elements of "no", of negativity.'

'I cannot,' I protested, explaining that I had built up a professional reputation with this name. 'To drop it would be very difficult.'

'If this is so,' answered Panditji undisturbed, 'keep the name and the talisman will help you.'

Panditji surprised me with the news that I would leave India the following month, 'but conditions will develop that you keep returning, because you have met your guru here.'

What were my plans for the remaining weeks, he wanted to

know. I admitted I had none. Sinha right away suggested a visit to Benares. After consulting a long, narrow book of astrological signs and numbers, Panditji approved this advice.

I should be in Benares on Sunday, said Sinha, and proceed immediately to nearby Sarnath. There Gautama the Buddha delivered his first discourse, 2,500 years ago. On Sunday 100,000 low-caste Hindus would convert to Buddhism. Ambassadors and representatives of several neighboring countries would attend the initiation ceremony.

'A colorful story,' Sinha said. 'Go there.'

Panditji approved my flying to Benares on Sunday; Saturday was inauspicious. Requesting me to return in the evening when the talisman would be ready, he left the garden.

'Like some tea?' asked Sinha, pouring from the pot. 'Cheers! You have found your guru,' he toasted, clinking my cup. I scented brandy.

'Drink,' he commanded when I pushed the cup away. 'Good for you now. You must do everything I say, but everything will happen by itself.'

That evening Sinha phoned saying he was ill and had to stay in bed for 20 hours, on the doctor's advice. I should go on my own to the earlobe-man.

'Have a good time in Benares,' he added. 'There further teachings will come.'

Impressions of Benares
and Seeing J. Krishnamurti

In India I learned that life had its own flow, in harmony with a much greater current. If this was so, why did we need a guru? The answer seemed clear: to guide us more safely, perhaps also faster, over a path the guru had already journeyed.

The Mother of Pondicherry felt like a spiritual mother to me – did this make her my guru? What really was a guru? Despite the unexpected image of Sinha and his unusual behavior, something about him caused me to reconsider his self-proclaimed role in relation to my further development. Had my conception of a guru been too limited?

In any case, I liked Sinha's idea that I visit Benares, described by my guidebook as the holiest city of Hinduism, its thousands-of-years-old spiritual capital. Situated midway between Delhi and Calcutta, so I read, Benares curves for over three miles along the western bank of the mighty river Ganga, the Ganges, face to face with the rising sun.

At the airport of Varanasi, the official name for Benares, the only public transportation was a bus to the outlying Cantonment area, where most tourists stayed. From there I continued to the old city, by the river, in accordance with my determination to mix with the local people. I engaged a bicycle rickshaw, a three-wheeled open carriage pedaled in front by a driver, the most convenient way to get around in Indian towns.

During the ride an excess of impressions overwhelmed me. On my seat, not separated from the surroundings, I found myself in the middle of the chaotic and noisy outdoor life of an old North Indian city. The streets were jammed with countless other rickshaws, furiously honking cars, buses packed to the extreme, overloaded oxcarts, horse-drawn wagons, pigs hunting garbage, wandering holy cows, scraggy stray dogs, an occasional elephant, and of course absolutely everywhere an endless mass of people moving in all directions.

In the streets of Benares, where private is public, I saw people sleeping, cooking, eating, washing their clothes or themselves, selling or buying merchandise of all kinds, dentists pulling teeth, cobblers mending shoes, men urinating, shaving or getting a haircut, tiny children carrying babies around like rag dolls, corpses being transported . . . the whole life span from birth to death.

There is no Hindu who would not wish to die in Benares and to be burned at its 'holiest cremation site, Manikarnika Ghat', my guidebook had informed me during the morning flight. For Benares was the earthly abode of Shiva, the all-powerful god of both destruction and re-creation. In this city, Shiva himself whispered into the ear of the dying to impart the secret wisdom which ensured *moksha*, freedom from further births and rebirths. The final blessing was to have one's mortal remains, the ashes from the cremation fire, placed into 'the holy Ganga, holiest of India's rivers'.

According to my holy-oriented guidebook, whose colorful text betrayed an Indian hand, Benares had a sacred mystic center. After I read this, no other area would do for me. I was heading for the KVM Hotel, recommended by an Indian Airlines representative at Varanasi airport.

No rooms were free, and I was directed to the Central Hotel. A dingy and filthy room was offered for much more than I had paid at the pleasant and clean hotel in Ernakulam.

When I returned with a long face to my waiting rickshaw driver, he said: 'International Hotel, very nice, Madam.'

'Is it near the Ganga?' I asked.

He shook his head, as if the chances of my finding an acceptable room close to the river were impossible, at least for me as a woman traveling alone.

The International gave me a good-sized room with a modern, Western bathroom. It probably had not been scrubbed in months and the plumbing needed every possible repair, but desperation caused me to sign in. There was the Buddhism conversion ceremony in Sarnath to attend.

Besides, I assumed that hardly anything better could be found in the budget category. The lack of clean, low-priced hotels in

India was known to me from my conversation with the Minister of Tourism, Dr. Karan Singh.

After dismissing the rickshaw driver, I suffered through a greasy lunch in the International's dining room, to my amusement called the 'Paradiso Restaurant'. When I got up to leave, the manager walked over to me.

'Madam,' he said, 'may I be so bold to tell you, the great Krishnamurti will be speaking this evening? Your orange lungi, in the color our holy men wear, made me think you are interested in things of the spirit.'

I appreciated the information and noted address and time.

Out in the street, I looked for a taxi to Sarnath, five miles to the north. No metered cars were available, and a non-metered one would have cost as many rupees as I paid for my hotel room. This was evidently an inflated tourist price. A bystander, seeing my frustration, suggested I take a bus.

With much difficulty I located the unmarked bus stop, not so far from the hotel, but no one knew when the next bus would come and whether it would come at all. Suddenly the driver of my rickshaw, who had apparently observed my tribulations, came running over.

'Madam,' he said in English, 'Sarnath, me take you, Madam. Good price.'

In the first minutes of the ride I was worrying if I would reach the Buddhist event before it was over. Had I known beforehand the rickshaw trip would take one hour, I would have opted to lose rupees to the taxi driver rather than precious time, anxious as I was not to miss the conversion ceremony.

After a while I stopped thinking about the future, and just sat back to enjoy the captivating scenes of vibrant life all around. Finally, I could not have been happier that circumstances had made me take a rickshaw.

At Sarnath, one of the foremost Buddhist pilgrimage centers in India, the ceremony was just about to begin. A high priest from Thailand, Bhikhu Srakhru Prakash Samadhigun, had flown in from Bangkok to conduct the proceedings. Not 100,000 but only about 1,000 converts participated. They all looked like poor villagers, from the lower Hindu castes, who hoped in this way to escape restrictive social customs.

Immediately afterwards I asked my rickshaw driver to bring me to the place where Krishnamurti would speak.

I remembered Jiddu Krishnamurti from his talk in Amsterdam a few years earlier, when he had included Holland in one of his country-to-country speaking tours. A kind of modern-day Socrates with a highly original approach to life's problems, he departed from the ancient Indian tradition that a guru is needed to attain wisdom. He did not believe in gurus and was not one himself, so he always stressed.

Curiously enough, J. Krishnamurti's unique career as a non-guru began when he was chosen for the role of 'World Teacher' by the Theosophical Society. Headquartered in Adyar in Madras, the international esoteric organization advocates a universal mystical approach based largely on the eternal wisdom underlying all religions.

In 1911, at the age of 15, J. Krishnamurti was taken from his native South India to England where he received further education and grooming for his singular mission.

Although for many years Krishnamurti accepted the destiny thrust upon him, by 1929 he saw his life differently and was ready to set out on his own path, one of rebellion and iconoclasm. Giving up all the pomp and circumstance afforded to him as the savior of our time, he dissolved the organization formed to prepare the people for his coming, and dissociated himself from all ideologies, doctrines and gods.

In Ommen, in Holland, in 1929, he delivered a memorable speech ending his messianic career. Truth, he declared, could be perceived only directly, not through another person. The discovery of truth was purely an individual matter and no organization, religious or otherwise, could assist towards this end.

Since then Krishnamurti had traveled the globe as a spokesman for the personal revolution which leads to fulfillment through looking within. One of his messages was that we reach truth only when our mind is free of all conditioning. Then we can perceive what is, just as it is.

Having already heard Krishnamurti from afar, from the balcony of a large and very crowded Dutch auditorium, I was pleased to be sitting now in a small group of Indians and a few Westerners forming an intimate assemblage.

An excitement permeated the atmosphere while we all anxiously awaited the arrival of 'Krishnaji', as admirers called him.

Close up, Krishnaji was a striking man. Dressed in a fine silk *kurta*, his white hair combed immaculately, an air of elegance about him, he looked stunning. What a correct and proper bearing! His opening words, however, smacked me in the face.

'Why are you here?' he snapped at us, almost contemptuously. I felt embarrassed, caught doing something foolish. He continued in a harsh, ego-slapping style. His remarks hurt, filled with truth as they were, yet they roused me out of any mental torpor.

Then a man asked a question that caused Krishnaji to order him from the room. He belittled him further by explaining the expulsion with: 'Because, Sir, from your question I see you have not understood anything I have said.'

In Krishnamurti's discourse were several points I would have liked him to elaborate upon but, aghast at his attacks on the audience, I dared not make any request and could not help but withdraw from him. Nonetheless, his unorthodox approach, creative and free of patterns, stimulated me to a certain extent. He required from us a pure awareness, which saw everything just as it is.

Krishnaji's talk covered many topics. I did not write down everything he said, but ten years later I recorded his words with a tape recorder, during a private interview in Bombay, four years before he passed away. In Benares I took only a few notes, probably the thoughts necessary for me at the moment.

I jotted down: 'What are we seeking? And, when we find it, how do we know it is true? When you have found it, you must recognize it . . . according to your circumstances . . . .'

What a warm feeling, as I came out into the dark of the Indian night, to hear the familiar voice of my rickshaw driver: 'Over here, Madam.'

Benares, Earthly Abode of Shiva

In an unexpected way, the rickshaw driver and I had developed a kind of friendship during our Sunday journey. To all appearances his concern and helpfulness were genuine, not only motivated by the desire for rupees.

When I entered the hotel lobby on Monday morning, there he was, waiting for me. This simple man intrigued me because, like quite a number of poor people I had seen in India, he was so cheerful and seemingly content with life. I wanted to interview him. Upon his acceptance, I found it only natural to invite him first for breakfast. The hotel manager came over to see if anything was wrong. From his attitude I concluded that a middle-class person did not sit at the same table with a laborer.

Obviously the Indian practice of separation between the various social groups implied much more than the griefs of the low-caste villagers I had seen converting to Buddhism the day before. As a foreigner, however, I had more freedom to break rules of social convention. Hearing the quasi-official reason for my sociability, the hotel manager surprisingly became very supportive and offered to serve as interpreter.

The rickshaw driver's name was Sawat Sakhawat. A 50-year-old Muslim, he was born in Benares to poor parents who died when he was a baby. He attended school until the age of 13 and married at 20. After 22 years of marriage his wife died.

'Had no good body, finished,' he said to me in English, interrupting the hotel manager's translation. His only child had died six months before his wife.

Sawat lived with his brother, his brother's wife, their six children and his maternal uncle in a joint-family arrangement. Together they rented a five-room house, his share amounting to one fifth of the total cost. A year before he had married a sickly 16-year-old girl, at her brother's request. She was poor, had no parents, and needed regular medical care.

'Without wife, no charm in life,' added Sawat. He was hoping to obtain a child through her.

'Due to circumstances' Sawat drove the bicycle rickshaw, which he had to rent. By Western standards he earned next to nothing, especially after deduction of the rental fee. His income did not allow him to put any money aside.

Before driving a rickshaw, Sawat sold fruit at the railroad station but stopped because there was too much competition. Previously he had been a soldier in the Indian army for nearly six years. Despite the fact that he got every facility there, the lack of freedom made him leave.

'What is freedom to you?' I asked.

'Freedom is that he can work, or not work, wake up when he wants, sleep when he wants, eat when he wants,' translated the manager.

'What is the most important thing in life to you?' I wanted to know.

'Labor,' Sawat answered me directly.

'Why?'

'Because due to labor his health is good,' came the translation. 'If he didn't work he would get lazy and lose his health. He doesn't know any other profession and cannot read or write. He learned some English in the army.'

'Does he enjoy his life?' I asked.

'Enjoy life?' repeated Sawat. 'Yes, me happy.'

Again I had to ask why.

'Good health, wife, eating, dress, enough money, me like,' answered Sawat.

Sawat's main ambition? 'Never to feel any problems with the things he just mentioned,' said the hotel man.

'And if he could have one wish in the whole world, what would it be?' I inquired.

Sawat could not reply to this question, saying he had no wish and never thought about this. When I persisted, he explained: 'Me good house, business, health, money, wife, me like. Me no need other money, other things. Whole day work, eat, dress, me like. Me very poor man. Not much money but me like my life.'

An enviable attitude, I thought. Despite his material poverty, Sawat was actually quite a rich person.

When breakfast and interview were finished, I set out on my explorations of Benares. For one of the few times since Agra I was wearing the matching kurta top to my orange lungi. Until now I dared not often put them on together, such a blazing effect they caused. Today I had chosen them without hesitation.

I asked Sawat to take me shopping, as I urgently needed a warm shawl for the evenings, which were getting cooler now that the winter approached us in North India.

No longer could I wear the black woolen cape crocheted for me by my dear sister Bonnie. I loved it, but the earlobe-man had cautioned me not to wear this color. Before leaving Benares I gave it to Sawat, for his wife. Many Muslims wore black, I noticed.

In the centre of town, near the hectic Godaulia crossing not far from the river, I bought a white woolen shawl embroidered with orange flowers. Then we continued towards the Ganges, the mighty Ganga, as far as rickshaws were able to go. From there I proceeded on my own to Dashashvamedha Ghat, one of Benares's most sacred *ghats*, the stairways that descend into the water.

A continuous stream of Hindu pilgrims moved towards the river. Along the way a myriad of sights, sounds and smells delayed my progress with fascinating distraction. Suddenly I was accosted by a bright-faced older man, wearing the saffron-colored robes of a *sadhu*, a Hindu renunciate.

'I am a holy man!' he shouted out jubilantly. I stopped and grinned, captured by the sadhu's bouncy exuberance. His appearance seized me, with his weather-beaten brown skin and scraggly grey beard under an attractive gold-colored turban.

My assailant announced his name as Shankar Baba, 'Shankar, name Shiva; Baba, sweet title holy man.' Then he narrated, rattling along and never stopping, in loud scanty English, the broad outline of his life. Before renouncing the world to become a Shiva-worshipping monk, he had studied Sanskrit at Calcutta University.

When a small audience of curious Indians gathered, I imagined us as comedy characters in an American TV series, parodying the spiritual search. My sadhu, however, was real and appeared indeed to have given up the settled life of home and family to wander India's pilgrimage trails.

'Visit temples yet?' he inquired. 'Many thousand temples! All very holy. See the Golden Temple of Vishvanatha? Holiest. Shiva, most holiest.'

The man's guru, 100 years old, had told him to come to Benares. 'What my guru tells, I do.' I laughed to myself at the coincidence, thinking that I had also journeyed here because of a guru, or rather a would-be guru.

'Why did he want you to come to Benares?' I asked.

'Bath Ganga six o'clock morning. Everyday bath, worship Shiva.'

Was this what my guru wanted as well?

'What's so special about a bath here?'

'Aaaaah!' Shankar Baba's face broke into a vast smile before he said, 'Verrrry verrrrry holy.'

'You get a holy feeling?'

'Clean, pure inside, good for the mind, more energy.'

I told him I had read that the Ganga water was brown and dirty, and that all kinds of garbage was thrown into it, including human and animal wastes, diseased dead bodies and cremation ashes. The old man nodded, understanding English much better than he spoke it, and then asked invitingly: 'You come Ganga bath?'

As he started walking, I automatically followed, down to the riverside. Every other moment a beggar leaped into our path, asking for rupees. The sadhu waved them away, advising me to give small amounts only to the old, sick or disabled.

Approaching the ghat I saw men, women and children on the steps or in the water. Some stood with clasped hands reciting prayers, some gently placed flowers into the river or floated burning oil lamps in miniature leaf boats the size of a teacup. Others more mundanely washed their bodies and their clothes. Millions of Hindu pilgrims bathe in the Ganga annually, believing that the ritual ensures liberation.

Shyness arose in me, for I was witnessing here some very private acts. The people looked so devout and sincere. This was no performance, nobody watched them except a few foreigners like me.

Chattering in his friendly manner, Shankar Baba led us towards one of the rowboats. A long harangue developed with the boatman about the price I had to pay. Finally the baba waved me into the boat and we pulled away from the ghat.

From the perspective of the Ganga, the city looked other-worldly. Temples with high spires and other ancient buildings crowded the skyline. This was then the sacred place where the great Shiva settled with his wife Parvati after he left yogi life in the Himalayas.

In contrast, the opposite shore presented an empty, desert-like landscape, reminiscent of biblical times. The boatman stopped and indicated we could bathe.

The first touch of cold River Ganga induced shivers.

'Go down!' shouted Shankar Baba.

I plunged completely into the water and all of a sudden saw Shiva in my mind. In fact, the river itself seemed to be Shiva, and an urge to be One with him overcame me. Unhampered by earthly gravity, I let myself flow with the water, wanting to merge, dissolve entirely, nothing else mattered.

'Come up, come up,' commanded Shankar Baba. I had to struggle to leave the all-absorbing embrace of the Ganga.

'You drown!' he exclaimed while I was gasping and coughing.

'Ooooh Shiva,' was all I could think when I was sitting once again in the boat.

As we rowed back to Dashashvamedha Ghat, I told Shankar Baba I would like to have a shawl like his, indicating the headcloth now drying in the sun. The fine cotton was covered with Indian writing.

'*Om Namah Shivaya*, holy chant Shiva,' he explained, pointing to the red letters printed on the material. 'Only few rupees in market place.'

'I would rather have yours,' I said, considering the cloth worn by a holy man and washed in the Ganga as a sanctified object. 'I'll buy you a new one.' To my delight he agreed.

A little later Shankar Baba mentioned he had troubles with his eyes. Among his few possessions he had several holy books, which he could not read because he had no glasses. He needed a pair badly, but they were too expensive.

I said it would make me very happy if he would accept some money from me to buy eyeglasses. 'Oh yes, yes,' he exclaimed.

On the shore the baba asked me, 'Come Shiva temple? Vishvanatha, most holiest.'

We squeezed through a mass of people into the Vishvanatha Lane, the narrow, winding shopping alleyway which leads to the temple. Merchants offered a multitude of exotic wares from small stalls tucked into the walls of the passage. Diverse sounds abounded, including the sugary Bombay film music one hears everywhere in Indian cities. The incredible abundance of attractions invigorated my senses to an extreme.

Suddenly a pair of sandals, dangling on display, attracted me like a magnet. Shankar Baba shouted out gleefully: 'Holy shoes! Holy ones wear.'

The shoes were nothing but flat pieces of wood, cut in the shape of a foot, with a strap of rough cord fastened over the top. I knew immediately they were for me. The size was correct and I stepped into them with a familiar ease, as if I had done so before. My evolving appearance as a self-styled *sadhwi*, female renunciate, certainly received an authentic touch.

Shankar Baba also helped me purchase a *mala*, prayer beads, made of brown *rudraksha* 'eye of Shiva' berries. I looped the mala around my neck, next to the earlobe-man's coin-shaped talisman bearing the image of a moustached face.

As if by chance had my new look developed, since the fateful day in Agra when I found out my suitcase was missing. To walk around like this had never been my intention. At any rate, here in Benares my attire was perfectly in place.

'Orange, Shiva; yellow, Krishna,' Shankar Baba had said when we met, regarding me with approval.

The further into the crowded Vishvanatha alleyway we progressed, the more into the past I was transported. Not because of the ancient surroundings. It was an unknown force, a mysterious energy perhaps, from times immemorial, that led me. My heart throbbed expectantly. A vendor thrust flowers into my hand. The baba smiled. 'Give Shiva. Monday Shiva day.'

Disappointment clouded my joy when we reached the Vishvanatha Temple and I saw a sign barring entrance to non-Hindus. I wondered how this could agree with Hinduism's tenet of Oneness.

'No problem,' assured Shankar Baba. Suddenly the sadhu began to walk away from the entrance very quickly, so that I had to rush to keep pace with him. We went into a side lane and he led me to a small opening in the wall which looked into the inner sanctum of the temple.

'Shiva, most holiest,' he said.

Peering through the hole, I got a good view of the main object of devotion for every Hindu coming to Benares: the *lingam* of Vishvanatha. It was a large stylized stone phallus – and indeed the Sanskrit word *lingam* actually means 'phallus' and 'emblem'. All over India there are countless numbers of these round, vertical shafts which symbolize Shiva, but few are so venerated as this particular one.

While I watched, worshippers bent down to touch the lingam and reverently covered it with flowers, leaves and water. Cries of 'Om Namah Shivaya!' and 'Jaya, Jaya Vishvanatha Shambha!' ('Victory, Victory to Vishvanatha Shiva!') further enlivened the scene.

Oh, how I too wanted to touch the lingam! This time I had to content myself with seeing it from a distance. Ten years later, while living in Benares, I entered Vishvanatha many times and then my hand finally had its wish granted.

Shankar Baba had trouble pulling me away. At the back of the temple complex, in the courtyard, accessible to everyone, he bade me drink from the so-called Well of Wisdom.

'Verrrry verrrrry holy!' he said. As I filled my mouth with the water, I imagined I was swallowing a divine fluid.

Then, bubbling like a playful child, Shankar Baba started sounding a large bell in the courtyard. 'Now you!' he invited me, and I followed his spirited example. In this mood we left the temple. The baba accompanied me through the maze-like twists and turns of the narrow lanes back to Dashashvamedha Ghat, where we took affectionate leave of each other.

When I returned to the rickshaw, Sawat almost came to blows with a tout who badgered me by endlessly repeating he had 'a very good silk shop' and I could 'visit it as a friend'. He would give me a 'good Indian price'.

'No good,' Sawat said to me. 'Cheating place.'

I managed to escape and, requiring a pause from the intense atmosphere around us, we left the commotion and confusion of the center.

'Durga temple, many tourists go,' Sawat suggested.

Very quickly I learned why this impressive place of Hindu worship was commonly called the 'Monkey Temple'. Scores of these mischievous creatures freely roamed the premises, jumping and snarling at visitors. To ward them off, Sawat used a long bamboo pole. Afterwards I asked him whether I could have it, as a walking stick. My colorful Benares outfit was complete.

The Monkey Temple hardly provided the calm surroundings I had sought, so by then I wished for nothing else but to stroll leisurely on my own through a quieter section of town. Eventually

I found my way to the Ganga. My feet, sore from the new wooden sandals, recovered in the cold, refreshing water while I rested on the steps of a ghat.

A herdsmen and his group of buffalos passed directly behind me, on their way into the river. The large animals came very close but I was not frightened, feeling friendship for them. In a very relaxed manner they took their bath, as did several persons near by. Set within the grand sweep of the expansive Ganga, the scene seemed apart from the rest of the world, one with a greater nature.

When I got up, something made me turn around. There, on a stone terrace, high above the river, stood a figure dressed completely in golden-orange. We looked at each other for quite some time until he motioned me to climb the steep stairway leading up to him. Getting closer, I saw he was a young Buddhist monk, apparently from the Far East. Suddenly he descended towards me, took my hand and examined the palm quickly.

'Come with me,' he said. Getting accustomed in India to mysteries of all sorts, I followed him higher up, through a stone archway, into a courtyard. There I saw other young men, as well in golden-orange robes and with shaved heads. We entered into a building and sat down in an alcove of carved stone. The view over the Ganga was breathtaking.

Another young monk joined us, and they served tea. Khai Ratchavong, my monk from the steps, was studying philosophy and religion at Benares Hindu University. He was 23 years old and from Laos. At 11 his parents had given him to the monastery. It was an honor for them that he became a novice monk. He liked Buddhism because it taught people to act nobly.

'We believe in *karma*, action, deed,' he explained. 'Do good, get good; do bad, get bad.'

In a serene mood we conversed about Buddhism, their lives, my life, and exchanged addresses before I departed.

Back in my hotel, I recollected the events of this unusual day. Too much had happened for extensive recording in my notebook but, I was sure I would never forget my bath in the Ganga, the sight of the holy lingam and the taste of sadhu life experienced in the company of Shankar Baba. I retired early, visions of Shiva dancing in my head.

Kashi and the Sun God

In all, I stayed in Benares hardly one week, if I went by the calendar. But the normal reckoning of time was not allowed me in the ancient city. Unexplainably, my watch stopped working and I saw no public clocks. Caught up in a continuous flow of events, I had to adapt to the Indian situation where people do not bind themselves to time, with the result that I lost track of the days.

The amount and intensity of the impressions which crowded in upon me took care that I lived in the moment, giving up my thoughts about what had just happened and what was going to come.

On several occasions I ran into Shankar Baba, at Dashashvamedha Ghat where he could usually be found. We viewed Benares again from the river, had more chats in the courtyard of the Vishvanatha Temple and went to his favorite tea house. There, in a small room painted in vivid blue and adorned with bright pictures of Hindu deities, frequented by very poor people and beggars who received free food, the baba told me more about his existence as a *sadhu*. He too was content with his life, although by usual standards he was even poorer than Sawat. He had absolutely no money at all, as a renunciate having vowed himself to voluntary poverty.

One day he rushed up to me and happily displayed his new glasses. I was really glad, as I had not excluded the possibility that his eye troubles had just been a pretext to obtain money. At the same time I felt ashamed of my mistrust. It was my mind that was impure, not his.

In my hotel, several nights in a row, my precious sleep was shortened by one of the guests tapping and making noises outside my door. He could not be traced and I preferred to leave the International.

Sawat brought me to the calm Cantonment area. At Clark's Hotel I was welcomed by a British colonial atmosphere and the stares of Westerners, who did not take my exotic costume in quite the same way as did the Indians. Here, to my relief, I could catch up on the night rest I had missed.

Already before the next morning's dawn my eyes opened, as they were getting accustomed to do in India. An unexplainable urge compelled me to leave the bed, as in Pondicherry, when I was guided to that remarkable sunrise over the Bay of Bengal. In Benares I was led to the window.

The first light of day appeared. Watching the sun rise, I had the quite improbable sensation that the brilliant red ball was alive! Furthermore, it was calling me. I started breathing deeply and with each intake sensed that a very subtle energy entered my body.

'Light is your food,' I heard. 'Inhale it daily, consciously, through your third eye.'

Could this be the voice of – the sun!

'Who are you, O great one, that is speaking to me?' I inquired.

'Trust,' came the answer.

What could I do? There was no Sivadass here to consult, no Sri Navajata, no Ahalya, not even a Sinha. I could look for Shankar Baba, but his limited English frustrated my mind which was seeking to understand.

Then I remembered that here in India my searching beginner's questions had always been taken seriously by the official tour guides. I therefore went to the local Government of India Tourist Office in pursuit of clues to my unusual Benares experiences. I was still wearing the orange outfit, the wooden sandals and carrying the bamboo walking stick.

Sri Ganguli, head of the office, listened to my request for a guide familiar with the mystical meanings of the old city and called on Hari Singh, an articulate university graduate of philosophy. Within a short time Hari and I were walking through the narrow, winding shopping alley leading to the Golden Temple of Vishvanatha. The temple spire symbolized the upward flight of illuminated consciousness, Hari explained.

I tried to gain some understanding of the past days by asking: 'What is the philosophical basis for Hindu worship of the *lingam*?' I hoped he knew I was asking a question of scholarly interest.

Hari responded that the *lingam* was not merely a phallic emblem, as most Westerners thought. It symbolized the creative powers and was usually set into a circular base, the *yoni*, a stylized female organ. The lingam stood for the consciousness of the universe while the yoni represented *shakti*, the divine energy, which activated it.

During our conversation we passed several small stalls selling lingams and paused in front of 'Ram's Shop', built into the wall approximately one meter wide and two meters deep.

'The *lingam* is an outward symbol,' said Hari as I chose a small soapstone model. 'See Shiva as an energy rather than as an individual,' he advised, and I recalled that Sri Aurobindo saw the Mother in this way.

'What exactly does *Om Namah Shivaya* mean?' I asked him.

'You can consider *Om* to be the Sanskrit word for God,' he replied, 'and *Namah Shivaya* stands for "salutation to Lord Shiva". But the true significance of this very powerful mantra can be understood only through constant repetition of it.'

A mantra is a particular syllable or word, alone or in series, of which the vibrational frequency and sound is designed, among various purposes, to help a person attain spiritual maturity. The chanting of the mantra, aloud or silently, concentrates the mind and directs it towards higher states of consciousness.

After I had purchased the lingam, I mentioned my visit to the Well of Wisdom. Hindus believe that the well, *Jnana Vapi*, was dug by Shiva himself, Hari said. Its water they regard as a liquefied form of *jnana*, the higher knowledge which has a transforming effect. It was good I drank from the well, he commented.

As we continued our walk Hari said he appreciated my interest, because a Hindu's aim in life is to gain wisdom.

'We Hindus say we cannot know God but we can know our Self. To know one's Self goes beyond the mind's comprehension. Such knowing comes through enlightenment, not by thought. To know the soul is to know the divine. Soul is God. Knowing is becoming. To know the Self is to become God.'

After a while we entered a tiny snack stall for a glass of steaming *chai*, sugared milk tea. Hari talked animatedly about Benares and its sacredness. Scholars traced the origins back at least 3,000 years, but Hindu pilgrims considered it 'the timeless city'. If any place might be called the heart of India, it was Benares.

'Pilgrims travel here to worship Lord Shiva, believing he will surely grant them whatever they wish,' Hari said. 'Their faith in

Shiva is without limit. Every Hindu longs to come here, just as Christians, Muslims and Jewish people wish to see Rome, Mecca or Jerusalem.'

'If sadhus have renounced all temporal, worldly ties, why is Benares so important to them?' I questioned.

Hari declared, as if delivering a lecture: 'The yogi of Benares practises yoga on the banks of the Ganga while the sun rises on the horizon. He concentrates on the divine energy, wanting to feel a sense of unity. This city, as you know, is the home of Lord Shiva, who settled here after he left ascetic life on Mount Kailasa in the Himalayas. Shiva was the original yogi who taught yoga to humanity.'

Our lesson was interrupted by the arrival of the tea, which was almost too sweet for me to drink.

'In Indian metaphysics,' Hari explained, 'Shiva as a meditating yogi represents the human soul in silence and withdrawal. Krishna, on the other hand, is the human soul in love and action.

'According to Hindu mythology, the ancient name of Benares is Kashi, from *kash*, "to shine".'

Hari took out a paper, drew the crescent shape of Benares on it, then ripped the sheet into shreds. My perplexed expression amused him.

'Kashi does not indicate the ancient city which curves along the Ganga, face to face with the rising sun,' he said, indicating the torn paper. 'Kashi is a symbol, a cosmos, not part of our earth. It exists in the ethereal spheres.' His eyes sparkled. 'Kashi is a luminous transcendent reality, having no physical existence.'

I was taking notes by hand since my tape recorder had broken down.

'Kind-hearted Lord Shiva could not tolerate the miseries and the injustices of this world, so out of compassion for the suffering humanity he constructed a transcendental city of deliverance on the center prong of his trident. Located on the invisible planes of existence, it radiates the most perfect light.

'This celestial city is reflected on earth as Kashi, facing the most glorious and powerful manifestation of the Supreme, Lord Surya, the Sun. Even today, simply by bathing in the Ganga at Benares and offering some of the holy water to Surya, any saint or sinner can be granted liberation from the cycle of birth and rebirth.

'Probably nowhere else', Hari continued, 'is the rising sun so reverently welcomed. At dawn every day people come down to the

Ganga to greet the Lord of Life. The whole riverbank becomes a living, outdoor solar temple.'

In Hindu mythology Surya, the Sun, is represented as a red-faced, moustached god who rides through the heavens in a chariot drawn by seven horses, one for each day of the week. What most people did not know, Hari said as if revealing a clue to a great mystery, was that Surya lived in Benares, or rather in the transcendental Kashi. Mythology was a reality here.

'Can you please be more specific?' I asked. I suspected that Hari's knowledge of spiritual matters might not be merely academic. His statements seemed to be based on empirical content as well.

He told me that Shiva once sent Lord Surya to Kashi to fulfill a certain task. Surya became so enraptured by the city's luminosity he vowed never to leave this divine place and took up residence. That luminous world, the invisible Kashi, is separated from our world by a kind of veil, sometimes so thin as to be virtually transparent.

I was thrilled to receive this sign from Indian mythology which indicated that perhaps my conversations with the sun had not been delirious imaginings. Still, I could not help but inquire: 'You claim that the sun is a living entity in other than human form, dwelling as a kind of permanent resident in Kashi. Is there any scientific or historical proof?'

Hari laughed, remarking that only a Westerner would pose such a question.

My background indeed obliged me to be realistic, I responded. He talked as if the mythological Surya, the Sun God, were a true being, alive and well in Benares. How could this be possible?

'That is the *kash*, the shining,' Hari replied cryptically.

His words were immediately clear, just as Sri Navajata in Pondicherry did not have to explain how he had become newborn. By my own experience I understood. I knew who made contact this morning, at my window, as outlandish as such an encounter might seem to the rational mind. I felt a close bond with the sun, perhaps from times and lives past. Deeply buried memory banks were opening to me.

Now I requested: 'Please tell me more about Kashi as the City of Light, and the connection with the sun.'

The sun was too vast to be covered in a few sentences, said Hari. Besides, he had never researched this subject. References could be found in various old manuscripts, and there existed a thorough documentation on sun worship in ancient India from its earliest beginnings. In fact, the largest Hindu temple in India, Konarak, was dedicated to the Sun God.

Conviction of the sun's divinity had been an essential element of the consciousness of the Indian people throughout their history. To the ancient *rishis*, the illumined sages who received and interpreted revelations about life, the physical sun symbolized the spiritual sun. The spiritual sun was to them the center of universal power and knowledge. At the same time it represented the Supreme Soul, the cause of all matter, the Sun behind the sun.

Although in the India of today very few sun temples were still in use, said Hari, devout Hindus address the Sun God daily. At sunrise, and preferably also at noon and sunset, they chant the Gayatri mantra, the most sacred verse in Sanskrit. It calls upon the Sun God Surya to confer his splendor upon worshippers and to enlighten their minds.

'The energy emanated by the sun is seen as the solar breath or *prana*, the vital life-force which acts and creates throughout the universe. When we breathe, we take in this solar breath, minute participles charged with the subtle energy emitted by the sun. Absorption by the body renews mental and physical vigor.'

I very much valued Hari's inspiring company and met him several times over the following days.

One morning we went very early to the Ganga and took a row boat to the cremation ghat of Manikarnika. Unlike elsewhere in India, where cremation grounds are shunned as polluted, in Benares they are regarded as the most auspicious of places. This holds especially true for Manikarnika Ghat, located in the heart of the city, at the river next to the holy bathing spots.

From a distance Hari and I watched the corpses being burned and discussed the cycle of life and death. To a Hindu, death is not a tragic and final ending but merely a transition to another birth. People live in Kashi hoping to die there for the liberation it brings.

Before we left the river, Hari served as interpreter for some questions I asked our rower, the same ones I had posed to Sawat.

His name was Dasu and he had been born in Benares, though he did not know when. From his appearance I thought him to be around 35. Continuing his family's hereditary profession, he rowed every day on the Ganga. What he wanted of life? 'Bread to eat, clothes to wear, bathe in the Ganga every day, worship Shiva every day.'

Like Sawat he was happy, but his explanation differed: 'Because I am a devotee of Shiva.'

Then I asked Dasu what he would choose if he could have one wish that would surely be granted. His answer surprised me. Such an answer I had not expected from the mouth of an illiterate man who, by my old standards, was very poor indeed. All he wanted was 'the highest blessing of God'.

Devotion has for a very long time shaped the image of Benares. Hari told me that for thousands of years seekers and sages had been coming here from all directions. Gautama the Buddha went to Benares after attaining enlightenment and gave his first discourse in the nearby deer park of Sarnath.

'Would you show me Sarnath?' I impulsively asked Hari, mentioning my prior, but very brief visit on Sunday for the conversion ceremony. He accepted, saying that he greatly admired Gautama the Buddha for the depth of insight that the Compassionate One represented.

As we traveled in a motor rickshaw to Sarnath, Hari explained that Gautama was actually the fourth buddha, or in another way of reckoning the twenty-fourth, the most recent in a series of buddhas who have appeared at intervals to help humanity develop in spiritual perception. The fifth buddha, Maitreya, the Buddha of Love, was expected next.

Born as Prince Siddhartha 2,500 years ago in Northern India, Gautama had a royal upbringing, married, and lived in luxury. He was sheltered from worldly woes until one day, outside the palace walls, he became conscious of the sufferings of illness, old age and death. Renouncing his wealth and position, he left the court in search of the answers to life's essential questions.

After years spent in strict asceticism, following spiritual disciplines and going from one teacher to the other, he sat down to meditate under a bodhi tree. Entering into ever deeper states, he attained full enlightenment, the final stage of the purified mind. He was freed from past karmas and ignorance, the cause of all suffering.

Omniscience was now his, barriers no longer existed between him and any knowledge. The mysteries of life were available, like an open book. He had reached his goal. At sunrise he declared he had attained the supreme light of wisdom, gained through the higher, intuitive mind.

In Sarnath, Hari began our tour at the Dhamekh Stupa, a

Buddhist memorial dating from the 3rd century B.C. This impressive construction stands on the spot where, around 530 B.C., the enlightened Gautama gave his first teachings.

Termed the Four Noble Truths, they assert that all life is suffering, caused by our personal desires and attachments, and that these can be brought to an end. The fourth Noble Truth imparts the Buddha's recipe to stop the suffering: his Noble Eightfold Path, which consists of eight virtues we have to practice until we reach perfection in each of them.

Hari pointed out that these teachings prescribed, above all else, self-reliance. We have the choice to work out our own destiny.

'Be unto yourself a refuge, seek no external refuge,' recited Hari, quoting Gautama Buddha. 'His emphasis on self-responsibility accords with our Hindu understanding.'

'You have much respect for the Buddha,' I commented as Hari led me inside a magnificent Buddhist temple. Near the entrance was a table covered with books.

'Ah, here is what I was seeking,' he exclaimed, picking up *Gotama the Buddha* by Ananda K. Coomaraswamy and I. B. Horner. He went quickly through the pages.

'Look here,' he said, and I read: 'Many of the Buddha's epithets connect him with the Sun or Fire and imply his divinity: he is, for example, "the eye in the world", his name is "Truth".'[5]

Outside the temple we headed for the revered bodhi tree, raised from a cutting of the original tree under which Gautama had meditated in Bodh Gaya, 200 miles southeast of Benares.

Hari expounded: 'We Hindus consider the Buddha to be the ninth incarnation of Vishnu, the god who maintains the universe and the cosmic order. When spirituality is at a low ebb, Vishnu manifests to overcome evil and reawaken people to righteousness. Now we are awaiting his tenth and last incarnation, Kalki.'

Although unfamiliar with the name Kalki, it seized my attention immediately. As we approached the tree, the two syllables kept resounding inside me.

A noticeable air of devotion encompassed the tree, and a mixture of respect and reverence caused me to bow my head. On the ground I noticed many fallen bodhi leaves. What a treasure! Bending down, I gathered a few. As they touched my hand, I flowed into an ecstasy.

When I opened my eyes, a small crowd had gathered. No one spoke. They were just standing, watching me. I wondered what I was doing here. Hari, where was Hari? My hand instinctively touched the earlobe-man's talisman.

For the first time it occurred to me that the moustached face on the talisman resembled the Sun God Surya, as portrayed in representations Hari had showed me in several Hindu temples. I got the thought to look at the sun and as I glanced upwards, I heard an inner voice: 'Breathe the light in deeply. Be the light. Abandon fear.' I smiled at this unexpected message, received here in public. Some people in the crowd started smiling too.

Back in Benares, where I had enjoyed timeless days, I felt the moment had come to continue my journey. An eternity had passed since my arrival.

I decided to return to Delhi via Vrindavan. There, Neem Karoli Baba – whom I knew from the book I had read in South India – had one of his main ashrams. Shankar Baba's high opinion of the saint certainly strengthened my wish to visit him.

'Verry great man, verry holy man. Ask to anybody in Vrindavan. Verry great man by the kindness of God. Not possible to be a great man by himself. Due to the kindness of God.'

During the long train ride, I vibrated with a joyous gratitude for all I had been given. Could I ever have imagined conversing with the sun! What Lord Surya had let me recognize in Benares, was it any less real than the world of frozen foods, six-lane highways and jet planes?

Similarly, my small glimpse of the renunciate path had been eye-opening. To my surprise, I was attracted by this lifestyle. Of course I had no idea that one day, returning to India, I would actually live in the company of *sadhus* and that Benares would become my home for several years.

Face to Face in Vrindavan

When the preserver god Vishnu took his eighth incarnation to rescue the world and appeared as the lovable Krishna, it was in Vrindavan that he grew up as the foster son of a simple cowherd couple. Engaging in all the mundane experiences of life, he seemed human and endeared himself to Hindus more than any other deity. His worshippers follow the path of *bhakti*, devotion to a personal god. Fervently the *bhakta*, or devotee, yearns for union with the divine.

In the pastoral environs of Vrindavan, known for its lush forests, the young Krishna sported in amorous games with Radha, his spiritual consort, and with the *gopis*, the enraptured cowherd maidens. Their passion for him symbolizes the love, longing and search of the human soul for its source.

I myself was graced to experience the magical vibrations of Vrindavan ten years later, on my return to India. Then I was captivated by the call of Lord Krishna's spell-binding cosmic flute, which invites all souls to rejoin God in never-ending delight. Repeatedly I spent months in Vrindavan sharing the Krishna-intoxicated company of the mystic Sri Pada Baba. I enjoyed heavenly dizzy adventures at all levels and discovered what Sri Pada termed the Transcendental Vrindavan.

But on my first visit, Krishna did not yet involve me in his *lila*, his joyful play, and my interest was not kindled to see any of the numerous temples dedicated to him and his Radha. I had only one aim: I sought the *darshan* of Maharaji Neem Karoli Baba.

As I was about to step off the bus that had brought me from the train stop in Mathura, the place where Krishna was born, a swarm of rickshaw drivers, shouting in Hindi, descended upon me. I pulled back, amazed at all the commotion over my person, or more precisely, my rupees.

Then, ringing out above the din, came the welcome phrase, 'Neem Karoli Baba?' I had no choice but to go with the rickshaw driver who pronounced these fateful words.

Within minutes I was seated in a bicycle carriage brightly decorated with side panels depicting Krishna. We roller-coasted along pot-holed country roads for perhaps 15 minutes before my driver dropped me off in front of a high fence, its spikes painted pink, its gate tightly locked. I stood there peering into a compound of ashram buildings.

Eventually a teenage boy appeared and looked me over. 'Closed, afternoon rest,' he explained. 'Come back two hours.'

Where to go? The afternoon sun beat down heavily and the rickshaw driver had already disappeared.

Luckily, there was a tree. Large branches spread luxuriously to form a most enticing shelter from the scorching sun. In fact, I even heard a soft, gentle invitation to come under the boughs. My ears discerned it very clearly, it was the voice of the tree! Although I had received other improbable communications here in India, it cost me some time to regain my composure. The story of Mira Alfassa and the talking tree in the Fontainebleau Forest assumed a new relevance in my expanding horizons.

I approached, gladly accepting the gracious offer, and settled under the cooling foliage. Taking some peanuts from my bag, one by one I shelled and ate them. Since Benares and my sudden identification with sadhu life, my food had become very simple.

Leaning against the tree, my closed eyes saw a shining circle of golden light. Then I heard, in a very melodious tone, *'Hare Krishna, Hare Krishna.'*

The young man from behind the fence, bare-chested and wearing only a thin cotton lungi, swayed before me. Stupified, I watched as he twisted and twirled, singing *'Hare Krishna, Hare Krishna, Krishna Krishna, Hare Hare.'* His arms followed the movements of his body as the chant carried him into a highly charged emotional state. The dancing became frenetic.

'Krishna, I am Krishna,' he finally cried out, whirling closer to me. 'Radha, you are Radha,' he groaned, as if in a rapturous ecstasy, yet his fervor missed depth. I received his attentions icily.

'I am Radha, you are Krishna, but now I am meditating,' I responded, waving in front of me Shankar Baba's gold-colored Shiva cloth. *'Om Namah Shivaya,'* I pronounced, as if holding out a cross before fang-toothed Count Dracula.

Mention of the ascetic god Shiva destroyed Krishna's devotional passion. Broken, he retreated into the ashram, allowing me to enjoy anew my peaceful oasis. The tree's shade provided a perfect place for watching the colorful sadhus passing by.

Most wore the yellow robes of Krishna worshippers while some were naked, except for loincloths covering their genitals. On their face, body, arms and legs they had painted, with yellow, white and red pastes, certain words or symbols associated with devotion to Krishna. Many of them had bare feet, following the tradition that sacred sites, in their case the whole earth, are visited without shoes.

A leaf floated down, into my lap, causing me to look up to see whence it came. Through spaces in the leafy boughs, I caught a glimpse of the sun. A breeze moved the branches slightly, and the sun seemed to wink at me.

In Pondicherry and also in Benares I had become aware that, as impossible as it sounds, the sun is a living being. In addition, it had offered me contact. Hari had referred to Indian mythology to suggest that the sun, behind its appearance, is a living, spiritual entity. To me it represented the ultimate guru, symbolizing the light of creation which sparks all other light. Sitting here at leisure, I contemplated the sun's magnificence and generosity, material as well as transcendental.

Infinite, never ending, it radiates out the energies essential for all life on this planet. It is because of the sun that everything on earth, gross and subtle, continues its existence. Even the very movement of our earth depends on the sun. Light, life, love: they are all one and the same.

Absorbed by these thoughts, my affection for the shining deity turned into a fiery devotion.

'O Surya,' I exclaimed, addressing the sun by the name Hari had used for it. 'Dear Surya, I love you!'

'Come to me,' I heard.

'O Surya,' I continued, 'You are so much greater than us, we minuscule human beings on this tiny planet. You take such good care of us. What advice do you have for me?'

'Be who you are.'

'O Surya, your bountiful love lights up my life.'

A tinkling sound caressed my ears, bringing me back to Vrindavan reality. 'Krishna' danced anew, olé, ringing a small copper bell as he approached.

'Maharaji leaving,' he told, urgency in his voice. 'Back tomorrow. Now take guesthouse you.'

Just then a car raced out of the compound. The person sitting next to the driver, an old man, stared intently at me. That face burned its impression into my mind. Even from afar, I was struck by Maharaji's very powerful presence. I recognized him immediately from pictures in the book of Baba Ram Dass.

The expression in Maharaji's eyes gave me the feeling I was not a stranger to him. He knew, better than I perhaps, what I was doing here and I felt a strong current of inspirational energy coming from him to me.

Then the car, with screeching wheels, turned onto the road and sped off. I could not help but laugh. What a cosmic comedy!

'What funny?' asked Krishna, with a confused look. 'Maharaji leaving, not till tomorrow back.' At my continued amusement Krishna shrugged his shoulders and returned to the ashram.

With the unexpected departure of Neem Karoli Baba, I supposed that whatever had to happen for me in Vrindavan had perhaps already occurred.

Nonetheless, something prevented my getting up. Again I clearly felt the life-force of the tree. My mind knew very well that everything which exists is alive, interconnected, and part of a huge whole. I still had to experience this with my heart, totally, and myself become one with what is omnipresent and omniscient. An irresistible longing for communion with the divine surged up in me.

While I sat looking through the opening in the tree's leafy boughs, watching with delight the sun's flirtatious winks, the same face appeared as at the Bay of Bengal. My countenance had never been more luminous.

'O great one, you are a mirror,' I said. 'Again you show me my own reflection.'

Suddenly understanding dawned on me.

'O Surya!'

And swiftly His golden rays turned into arms which stretched to the furthest ends of the sky before reaching down and lifting me into a blazing embrace. Taking me up, He gave all of Himself. I moaned and melted.

When I was back again, in the tree's shade, I had no doubt that Surya and I were the same. Only my ignorance could separate us.

Looking around, I noticed Krishna, who observed me in silence. This time he approached respectfully.

'Arranged room guesthouse,' he said in a soft voice. 'Maharaji tomorrow back.'

Thanking him, I replied I would leave immediately. Obviously the purpose of my visit to Vrindavan had been accomplished.

'Maharaji come back,' he stressed.

'We already had darshan,' I insisted.

For one reason or another I took out one of my visiting cards and wrote a word in front of the 'Norma Green' printed there.

'Please give this card to Maharaji,' I requested, handing it to Krishna, who read it.

'What?' he exclaimed. 'You have Indian name?'

'Yes,' I declared, mustering up the courage to pronounce my new name aloud for the first time. As I said 'Surya', all kinds of positive associations with the sun vibrated inside me. In an instant I realized that the last syllable of Surya sounded like the Dutch word for 'yes'. My 'no' name started to fade and a process of consciously releasing negativity began.

I was grateful to my friend Simon Vinkenoog, Dutch writer and poet of cosmic joy, who in Amsterdam had advised me to read *Be Here Now* and to visit Neem Karoli Baba when in India.

From Vrindavan I traveled back to Mathura, to catch there a train for Delhi. In true Indian style the station overflowed with people, cows and luggage. When my train arrived, its second-class passengers could hardly get off because of the elbowing and pushing on the platform by those who wanted to board.

I stood back, perplexed, wondering what to do. At that instant appeared before my eyes, as a vision, a luminous white horse. Instinctively, I touched the talisman. The cotton cord broke and the amulet fell into my hands.

He had been right, the earlobe-man. At a certain time the talisman would no longer be needed and I would know when that was. For seven days he would chant for my protection. I counted back. Indeed, today was the seventh and last day of his prayers.

'Come on, there are still places in first class,' I heard a man's voice next to me. It was the train conductor.

'I don't have a first-class ticket,' I told him.

He smiled very kindly. 'The way you look, you don't need any ticket at all,' he said. 'In India, *sadhus* travel for free.'

Purpose Fulfilled

Back in the capital I phoned Sinha. Sounding surprised to hear my voice, he commented: 'Things went faster with you than I anticipated.'

I did not mention my new name until we met at the Press Club.

Sinha nodded casually and advised me to use 'Norma Surya' in my byline until the old name dropped off by itself. This led into an account from my side about the sun, Kalki, the talisman, the white horse. Without censoring anything I related my recent experiences. Then I confided some of the visions I had had of the future, my own as well as the planet's.

'Am I crazy?' I blurted out.

'No,' he said, unruffled.

'What?' I jumped up. 'But all this is impossible!'

'Sit down, don't make a scene,' he ordered, calmly leafing through a newspaper.

After I regained my poise, he cautioned me not to speak of these matters except to certain persons whom I would recognize at the right moment. In Amsterdam I would need much strength to withstand the disbelief of others. He reminded me of the difficult period between March and May, when I would be wrongly interpreted and misjudged. At that time I had to exercise tolerance, understanding and compassion as well as subdue my obstinacy. But we would continue this subject later. He was expected at a press conference.

At seven he rang me up and announced I must leave India immediately, be on my plane within seven days, at the latest. My stay was over, the purpose of the trip fulfilled. Writing called. I was to put full energies into my work. He told that he worked hard, slept little and had much self-control. He described me as the opposite, in fact I had no discipline at all. He accused me of not writing enough.

'I've been writing in my notebooks daily,' I objected, 'and since Pondicherry I've been getting up every morning between three and six.'

'Maybe here,' he answered, 'but back in Amsterdam you'll return to your routine of late going to bed, late getting up. In the West, with your hard capitalist currencies, you don't have to work as hard as we in the poor countries.'

'You earn your money from the capitalists,' I retorted. Then, catching myself, I added: 'Why are you attacking me? Have you been drinking?'

'No, I have not been drinking,' he replied. 'Get up early tomorrow, have a good protein breakfast, and do some writing,' he said. He hung up.

Ten minutes later he phoned back, saying: 'You have been very disrespectful to your guru. You do not treat me well, very rude.'

'What do you mean?'

'Your remark about drinking. Are you so sensitive that I cannot criticize you?'

'I'm very sensitive, yes. You haven't been drinking?'

'You are very disrespectful and also obstinate. The earlobe-man told me this. "She is very obstinate," he said.'

'And you are very mysterious,' I declared. Ever since meeting the earlobe-man I had been interested to hear the details of Sinha's vision, the basis of his guru claims, but he always postponed this topic. Now, when I asked again about his revelation 13 years ago, Sinha declared his mission to be finished, saying I had been awakened in India, my life had changed, I had to carry on by myself. After repeating some of the earlobe-man's predictions, and even adding that at some time I would start a spiritual movement, he stated we would not meet again for many years, other helpers would be sent.

'Really? I thought you were my guru,' I said with a sarcastic undertone. Sinha replied that my behavior angered him.

'Isn't a guru above such emotions?' I asked.

'Once you are perfect yourself, then maybe you can indicate what's wrong with me,' he countered. He advised me to get on with my work, repeating that everything would happen automatically. But, 'You must do exactly what someone from New Delhi will tell you, mainly by mental communication.'

Our relationship had to set an example, he said. 'There should be no emotional or physical attachment between a guru and a disciple.'

After we hung up, I regretted that the role Sinha played in my life remained veiled. From the outset of our association, I had known only confusion regarding him. Yet his suggestions about where to go and whom to meet had been good ones, and he had given satisfying answers to my many questions. But then, I was only a naive beginner.

Sinha's directive to leave India confirmed the timing of my inner clock. On the other hand, I had the desire to remain in these supportive surroundings which allowed me to be myself in my changed identity. Because of this ambiguous state of mind, I made no flight booking.

To my distress, each passing day brought increased disharmony. My room phone broke down, appointments did not work out, promised informational material never arrived. In short, what previously had been a harmonious flow, became an obstacle course. I got impatient and irritable.

When I saw Sinha, he had an explanation for my plight: 'You have been receiving negative vibrations from me, because I want you to leave.'

Around this time I recognized that my stubborn insistence on staying longer was contrary to the itinerary arranged for me from on high. Without delay I fixed my departure for the first possible date, three days later, which happened to be the twelfth.

Buckminster Fuller, Planetary Citizen

My last non-vegetarian breakfast was taken with R. Buckminster Fuller, on my final day in India. Bucky, as everybody called him, had agreed to squeeze an interview into his program by getting up one hour earlier to answer my questions over his morning meal at New Delhi's Ashoka Hotel.

By then I knew he was Research Professor of Design Science at Southern Illinois University, an author of many books, and a consultant to governmental and private agencies in his various functions as architect, engineer and forecaster of trends in science and technology. Decades before anybody thought about the fragile ecosystem and the need to preserve the earth's resources, he was patenting environment-friendly inventions in the field of low-cost housing and transport.

I had been introduced to him the previous evening, at the home of Robey Lal, the director of planning for the International Airports Authority. Bucky had eagerly presented his wholistic views on the harmonization of technology with nature to an attentive group of Indian teenagers. The young people were especially interested in his famous creation, the geodesic dome, a free standing structure constructed of triangles which uses only a small percentage of the material and weight required by conventional buildings.

In the hotel dining room I apologized that our appointment obliged him to start the day so early. He smiled. 'Over 45 years ago, when I was in my early thirties, I said I'd never again ask anyone to listen to me, and I never talk to anyone unless they ask me.' For those interested in his discoveries, he would always make time.

After this brief exchange, Bucky began expounding his ideas at such a rapid pace that I had to listen very intently to follow the development of his thoughts. He envisioned 'humanity being accommodated in an integrated world community realized by competent environmental design, where one got the most advantage for the least effort'. People 'should not do what machines can do better'. According to him, we should be freed to work at what we like and can do best, work which 'shows our ingenuity on behalf of our fellow man'. He advocated 'clean technology' and disliked 'myopic specialization'.

My pen dashed furiously over the paper to keep up with the supersonic velocity of Bucky's discourse. Suddenly he pulled the brake and pointed to my neglected food.

'You better eat your eggs before they get cold,' he said with fatherly concern.

To pick up the fork would have meant to put down the pen, and Bucky's words were the nourishment I preferred at that moment. Anyway, eggs were already on my black list. Could I be consistent on this, came the fleeting thought, were I one of the world's 'have nots' to whom he now referred?

'In the "have not" countries they like me,' he told, offering a buttered toast. 'They know what I'm talking about, for instance, when I say "Do more with less".'

What magic phrases Bucky composed from few words! Several of his slogans, reflecting his comprehensive vision of global oneness, became rallying cries for the ecology movement.

Speeding on, he compelled me to cling tightly to each word as the flow of his agile mind took me over rapids of forceful ideas and around bends of unconventional thinking. His words evoked inspiring images of a new future for our 'Spaceship Earth', another phrase Bucky introduced into the American language.

'The only reason why I use the concept Spaceship Earth is to get human beings to understand Isaac Newton's law of motion,' he elaborated. 'We are on a planet so superbly designed, it makes absolutely no noise while we are traveling 67,000 miles an hour around the sun, doing it so well that you and I are unaware of it.'

Then he asked rhetorically: 'How does it feel to be on this spaceship? Try to think of planet earth as a ship, deal with it in a totality, think of the total inventory of resources, capacities, problems. Consider how we can use the principles of the universe to make our spaceship work.'

A question arose in me but he was racing forward: 'We are little human beings on a minuscule planet. It couldn't be smaller compared to the sun, yet with our minds we've been given access to universal principles. Man has a monitoring function. What is common to all history and all lives is problems. The purpose of us on this planet is problem solving.'

He mentioned having flown over 3 million miles and lecturing several times each week to large audiences, consisting of 75 percent of people under 30. His visits to countless universities had brought him in contact with thousands of students, many of whom were becoming 'strong citizens' in their respective countries. This confirmed for him the validity of 'whatever communicable wisdom' he had to share.

'Young people are coming out and becoming earth people,' he commented. 'Nationality grew up because people were living near their roots. Now we move around more.'

He himself traveled so much he wore three watches 'set for time here, time where I'll be tomorrow, time at my Illinois office.'

To Bucky, work was joy. 'I would work 18 to 20 hours a day if I could.' When he said, 'We must stop the division between life and work,' I knew definitely that tourism writing did not serve my development.

His halting for breath gave me the chance to ask: 'What do you mean by "life"?'

'What I mean by "life" is to be aware of others,' he answered, pouring some tea into my half-filled cup to warm it. Looking at me intently through his thick spectacles, he declared: 'Life begins with otherness. Unity is plural and, at the minimum, two.'

'I believe this also,' I affirmed.

'Belief is blind,' he replied. 'I don't believe in anything, never accept the explanations of others. I proceed from personal evidence, based on experiences.'

'What do you mean by "belief"?'

'Accepting explanations without having experiential proof. You must only go by your own experience.'

'If I may ask you,' I said, 'have you had personal experiences of what we call "God"?'

Bucky paused as if debating how to make his next point clear.

'I find that word very inadequate,' he then answered, 'but we need something to designate an integrity operating in the universe which is greater than our human intellect. We are finding out that none of the general principles contradict, any other. They are all interaccommodative, eternally operative.'

Checking to see that I followed, he continued: 'When you have a complex of interaccommodative principles, it is a design. So the human mind is gradually discovering a little bit of the great design, and I assume *a priori* that there is an intellectual integrity in operation.'

'On what do you base this assumption?'

'I pay attention to all the information we have and that's what it seems to be saying. I'm overwhelmed by it. But the word "God" is fundamentally inadequate.'

After relating that long ago he had developed a self-discipline to explore scientific, technological, philosophic and economic frontiers, he went on to analyze the state of our planet. He discussed plenty and scarcity, selfishness and its opposite, individual initiative and intellectual continuity. This led to his conclusion: 'We are coming into a period where mind will take ascendancy over matter.' By 'mind' he meant 'the whole mind, which includes intuition as well as reason'.

When I uttered my high regard for his vision, calling him an exceptional man, he said there was nothing even mildly extraordinary about him except that he was 'durable and inquisitive in a comprehensive pattern'.

Bucky finished by saying he valued 'universal people, who don't accept the obvious, are less reflex-conditioned, and have integrity along with an awareness of others all around the world'. They gave him hope. He thought I fitted into this category, and even asked me to keep in touch with him.

An extra awaited me outside the hotel. During the photo session a picture was taken of us together. What a contrast – Bucky, the 'global citizen' as he termed himself, smartly dressed in dark suit and tie, and me next to him in my orange Benares outfit complete with *sadhwi* sandals.

I was flattered to be photographed in the company of a man who had such a tireless zeal for encouraging people to extend their limits. Bucky's revolutionary approach had evidently grown out of a deep concern for humanity. Being with him stimulated my childhood desire to work for the betterment of the world.

Dadaji, Servant of God

My plane was to leave about midnight. I was all packed and ready to go, but part of my heart would undoubtedly stay behind. Like many travelers to this singular land, I had come under its mysterious, captivating influence which can be felt by anyone willing to see more than merely India's chaotic exterior.

Although resigned to my departure, I found it clouded by the obscurity around Sinha's guru role. Any mention of it to Elizabeth was taboo, by his emphatic request, and there was no one else in whom to confide.

But my stars must have been aligned favorably on that final day in New Delhi. Some light on the issue troubling me was still to be given. As I had promised Elizabeth, I accompanied her to Dr. Mehta, a spiritual teacher she visited occasionally, and he was the person to provide the wise counsel I needed.

Dr. Dinshah K. Mehta, called 'Dadaji' (Elder Brother), headed the Society of Servants of God. A non-profit organization founded in 1954 after Dadaji received guidance in meditation, the Society aimed 'to help people realize the divine Self within and to introduce and propagate spiritual values in all walks of material life'. Further, recognizing that all of the world's religions are based on the same spiritual truths, it worked to bring a unity in this diversity.

Dadaji was also one of India's most respected naturopaths. For over three decades he had been bringing successful innovations into the field of naturopathy, also called nature cure, a system for the cure of disease that employs no surgery or synthetic medicines. The body's inherent healing processes are encouraged through natural methods and treatments, such as detoxifying the body, diet therapy, and a corrective regime based upon what Dadaji termed the 'five fundamental laws of health'.

As Mahatma Gandhi's nature cure physician from 1932 to 1948, he supervised two of Gandhiji's three 21-day fasts and many other shorter ones. His own 50-day fast, at the age of 33, brought him experiences of inner hearing, seeing and awareness.

After our taxi had brought us to a well-to-do neighborhood, an immense 'Society of Servants of God' banner stretched across a modern apartment building told me we had reached our destination.

'Quite an unexpected location for an ashram,' I remarked to Elizabeth, who commented that this Chanakyapuri section of New Delhi housed many embassies and diplomatic residences.

Although she had phoned for an appointment, we had to wait some time before Dadaji appeared. His assistant, Dr. Sundri Vaswani, took the opportunity to present reading material about the Society as well as cups of a tasty grain beverage composed by Dadaji himself.

When I expressed my surprise to encounter in India something else than the usual *chai*, coffee or cola, Dr. Vaswani explained that wholesome foods and drinks belonged to Dadaji's nature cure program. His ideas on healthy diet had also been introduced to Indian parliamentarians as part of his Needs of Life movement. Dadaji tried to influence governmental policies aimed at minimizing the nutritional deficiencies of the masses. Under his guidance the first health food store in India was eventually opened, in Calcutta.

The picture I had of Dr. Dinshah, after hearing about his medical accomplishments, certainly differed from the man who entered the room. Long hair, white beard and bright saffron-colored robes gave the 69-year-old Dadaji the classical appearance of an Indian guru.

Yet the air of a doctor still hung around him. A very self-assured, even authoritative bearing conveyed the message that Dadaji knew how to relieve people of their suffering. According to the information I had just read, patients given up by other doctors as lost cases had been successfully treated by him. He must be equally adept as a doctor of souls, I sensed.

His bedside manner, however, was anything but gentle. In fact, during our get-acquainted talk I found myself becoming increasingly uncomfortable by the slightly sharp edge to his searching probes about who I was and what I had done in India. His powers of perception were piercing through me like an investigative x-ray.

When the diagnostic examination disclosed that I was on the verge of leaving India, Dadaji asked quite unmercifully, as if insinuating I had been wasting my time, why I waited until the last moment to visit him. His attitude made me think of someone who saw the glass of water as half empty rather than half full. With memories of parental reproaches ringing in my ears, I stammered out my respectful excuses.

Although the matter ended there, a guilty feeling accompanied me as I followed him into a small chamber filled with photos, statues and symbols from many religions and spiritual paths. Incense perfumed the air and a candle glowed on the altar.

'What can I do for you?' inquired Dadaji in his no-nonsense tone.

I chose not to distract him with any details but simply posed the question burning inside since my first contact with Sinha: 'What is a guru?'

Dadaji began by tracing back the word to its Sanskrit origin: *gu*, darkness, and *ru*, light; someone who guides from darkness to light. In India any person who teaches a subject or a skill is called a *guru* because he or she takes away darkness by giving knowledge.

More rare than the teacher-guru is the *sat guru* who can lead the disciple to know *sat*, truth. Such a guide, one's own highest Self manifested through another person, is venerated as the true teacher. His or her job is to take students to the light of that truth, knowledge and freedom which liberates one from the bondages of body and mind. If the *sat guru* appears and is not recognized, we might not be granted such an opportunity again in the same life.

Then Dadaji quoted the Indian mystic Paramahansa Yogananda, author of *Autobiography of a Yogi*, a book Shankar Baba had advised me to read.

Yogananda wrote: 'The guru is the awakened God awakening the sleeping God in the disciple.' The guru points the way and the student follows, but not blindly, emphasized Dadaji. Through discipline and right action the student progresses to self-understanding and self-mastery. True teachers neither impose their will nor use coercion.

'Someone who drinks alcohol, smokes cigarettes, eats meat, or is obsessed by position, power and money – can he be a guru?' I asked.

Every disciple has the right to observe the teacher's actions, was the reply. If it seems that the teacher does not live according to the standard of morals and norms of discipline he himself proposes, then the student might decide to leave, without ill thoughts, although we can also learn from negative example. At a certain stage, however, a guru is above all rules.

The spiritual path, not unlike other areas of life, requires caution. At the beginning we have to be extra careful not to let our openness and trust be manipulated. Unfortunately, there are persons who would abuse our innocence and naivety for their own ends. With time we develop *viveka*, discrimination, the ability to distinguish reality from illusion, the true from the false.

In those days *viveka* certainly was not mine. I simply was unable to see through the games people like Sinha played with me. That was the price I had to pay for wanting to be open under all circumstances. Since my belief in the goodness of others never brought me to harm, I have no regrets.

Finally Dadaji wanted to know if anything in particular made me raise this subject, and I mentioned that in my newly-opened state I had come under the influence of a questionable person. His advice was very clarifying: 'Until you can raise your mind to the level where you directly and continually get God-guidance,' he said, 'and if you do not have a guru who can help you interpret the teachings which come spontaneously, then let your conscience and the force of circumstances guide you.'

I thanked Dadaji profusely and took it as a great privilege when he invited me to visit whenever I came back to India. In him I recognized a man of uncompromising values, sincerely dedicated to assist people become God-centered. His qualities of integrity and honesty were easily discernible, as was his original approach. Nevertheless I was not quite sure whether my free-spirited attitude would be acceptable to his world.

Before leaving, I signed up for a subscription to the Society's monthly publication, *The Discourse*, not in the last place because it contained 'scripts'. These were truths revealed to Dadaji in higher meditative states, particularly after he completed a 118-day liquid fast in 1959.

Through the issues of *The Discourse* sent to me, I maintained a tie with the Society and gained a perspective of Dadaji's extensive knowledge of the transcendental. Like Sri Aurobindo, he too taught that the basis for further human evolution is the descent of the higher spiritual force into matter, and it was upon this very theory that the Society was founded.

Over the years I read how Dadaji, interested in all aspects of human development, was able to manifest his ideals and principles in concrete projects designed to aid people meet the material needs of life as well as the higher goals.

The extreme contrast Dadaji presented to Sinha answered my question about gurus just as much as his useful counsel.

In the evening Sinha was to come to my hotel, to bring me to the airport. As I had anticipated after his elusiveness during our last conversation, I waited in vain. This did not disturb me. His behavior and, last but not least, my meeting with Dadaji, had made it clear that my connection with the jet age guru was no issue of importance. I was free to leave India.

Flying to the West

Living sun, everlasting union, Shiva-Vishnu-Krishna-Buddha-Kalki, guru India, Spaceship Earth, global consciousness, spiritual oneness, personal task, individual responsibility . . . . So many thoughts raced through my mind during the flight back to Amsterdam.

Gazing out of the window at the clouds floating below me, I imagined my new shining future as Surya, attuned with the sun. I was Surya, we are all Surya, Surya is but a symbol. What we really are cannot be named, it is nameless. I realized that my Self and the Divine were one.

I heard whisperings of a knowledge which, until this journey, had simply lain dormant. Whatever I would seek from now on, I was already that. There was nothing to attain, all was already known, but had been forgotten. I was beginning to remember.

Having become aware of what could be retrieved within myself, I clearly recognized my goal: nothing less than to reach the highest spiritual development possible. Any activity not geared to this end would be wasted time. In my eagerness, I was ready to go to the extreme.

By the way, I was sure that the grace revealing to me some of life's many mysteries was not destined for my own benefit alone. What I had encountered could perhaps be written down one day for others to read. Spiritual experiences are real! And they can happen to anyone! This was part of the joyous message I wished to convey.

Of the pictures rushing by, one kept repeating. It was my vision in Mathura of the luminous white horse, flying through eternal skies. With it I had very personal ties which implied a task for me in the future, but whether these associations belonged to the realm of illusion, I did not know. My reasoning mind, always on the alert to exercise dominion, cautioned me not to speak about this topic. It had to remain concealed safely in a far corner of my heart. Talking about Surya would already be difficult enough.

What awaited me in Amsterdam? What ramifications would my Indian experiences bring forth?

No need to worry. Had not the earlobe-man predicted: 'All will happen automatically, naturally, spontaneously.'

The landing signal flashed. Time to fasten my seat belt. Our 747 was approaching Schiphol Airport in down-to-earth Holland.

PART II

The Transformation

Back But Not Back

Distressingly grey weather, so typical for these damp lowlands by the North Sea, welcomed me back. A chill wind greeted me, the day moist with tears. Was I deserted? Where hid my sun?

The taxi brought me to my apartment on the Lauriergracht, in the center of old Amsterdam. The steep Dutch gable of my house and the water of the *gracht*, the canal, had the same dark colour.

So began a transitional period in which negativity replaced the uplifting atmosphere which had surrounded me in India, just as the earlobe-man had forecast. Most of my friends and acquaintances, unfamiliar with the spiritual, listened to me sceptically, often with annoyance.

A journalist colleague stopped by for a visit. When I asked him to remove his shoes before entering the apartment, my temple to the divine, he became irritated.

'Naked feet feel so much freer,' I tried to joke, wiggling my bare toes. 'And everything stays much cleaner,' I added smiling, 'with no street dirt being dragged through the house.'

'I only hope my feet don't smell,' he replied, with the finest Dutch humor. Resigned, he lowered himself onto the mat on the floor, my reception area. Studying the posters of Shiva, Krishna, the Buddha and Lord Surya decorating the room, he asked, 'What are your plans?'

'I want to stop all commercial work and spiritualize my writing,' I answered. 'The flow of life guides me, no longer my mind.' I did not hear how pompous this sounded, though meant sincerely. 'Even if my experiences in India come from an overactive imagination,' I declared, expressing one of my doubts aloud, 'commercial writing no longer interests me.

Nothing interests me any more, except permanent union with the divine.'

'Don't you think you may be trying to escape reality?' he asked.

'I didn't say I don't want to work,' I continued. 'But in India I discovered that my tourism writing has no correspondence with my true work, which has to attune with my path of inner fulfillment. There should be no division.'

Edvard, a talented novelist engaged in news reporting for the steady income it brought, impatiently changed the subject.

'And why have you stopped drinking alcohol?' he demanded to know. 'Even Jesus drank wine.'

Then Edvard told he had also visited India, more than once in fact. The longest stay lasted six days. What most impressed him?

'The material poverty of the country.'

'Poverty of the spirit is more depressing,' I commented. After having talked in India with a number of so-called poor people as well as with religious renunciates vowed to voluntary poverty, I had reconsidered my understanding of the words 'poor' and 'rich.'

'Spirituality is a means to keep the poor people down,' he countered.

'Spirituality is something else than religion and church,' I began – but he would not let me continue.

'Why India?' he asked. 'Couldn't you have had the same experiences here in the West?'

'Certain countries are economic leaders, others predominate in beauty, culture, law. India ranks first in spiritual matters.'

Our conversation ended when Edvard abruptly announced his departure. I was relieved. Putting on his shoes, he wished me good luck and expressed his hope that my changed lifestyle would bring me happiness. It was not his goblet of wine, however. Good old-fashioned financial security, nothing could beat it on a rainy day. He offered to keep his fingers crossed that I would not have to sit around too long waiting for work acceptable to my new view of reality. In the meantime, if I needed a good meal, with plenty of good healthy protein, he would be delighted to take me out for some wickedly delicious *coq au vin*.

Reactions of this kind, frequently complemented by an unpleasant interrogation, kept assailing me. With my heart I trusted that the forces in action were guiding me well, but in my mind doubts arose, making me insecure. What precisely had happened to me in India? Had my experiences been real, or had I simply been swept into space on a magical flying carpet? The few friends who had some understanding for my situation were not able to give the explanations I needed.

The upset and pain generated by Edvard's visit took a while to subside. I went into my workroom and moved my chair to the small altar newly installed there, next to the desk. My eyes wandered over each object I had carefully placed on the polished marble top.

The white soapstone Shiva lingam brought back from resplendent Kashi, whose ancient winding streets had been so familiar, reminded me of the universal energy it represented. Then a picture of Lord Krishna called my attention. 'Hare Krishna,' I chanted. Growing sentiment for the beloved Hindu god of cosmic ecstasy further supported my desire to connect uninterruptedly with the transcendental. Contagious peace and serenity was radiated by a small photo of a Gautama Buddha statue, offered to me in Sarnath by Hari.

The luminous face of the Mother shone at me from her picture on the blessing packet she herself had placed in my hand. It contained dried flower petals charged with spiritual force. 'Purity' they said, as did the white rose close by, preserved carefully since the day Mother presented it to me.

In her book *Flowers and Their Messages*, she interpreted the specific energies transmitted by each different flower. The white rose expresses a love for the divine which is pure, complete and irrevocable, a love which gives itself forever. White, the perfect blending of the spectrum's seven colors, represents positiveness. The rose itself is the Western counterpart of the East's lotus as a sacred cosmic symbol.

All these objects comforted me. They fortified my faith in the workings of the divine and in the path I wanted to follow.

I got up and went to the window with its expansive view over the tranquil canal. The North European winter sun, gentle compared to the blazing Surya I had experienced in India, tapped softly with its afternoon rays on the glass pane.

Encouraged, I picked up my pen. Words rushed out announcing: 'I'm back from India, but I'm not back.'

A rather lengthy, impulsive kind of poem followed, expressing what I wished others to know about my present state. The most significant lines were:

Do I look the same? . . .
Do I sound the same? . . .
Becoming becomes became. . . .
Are you ready for 'Surya'?
I didn't pick it, had no choice,
*   didn't find it, wasn't seeking.*
No one gave it, but it was given.
It just happened. . . .
It lit on me.
Things don't just happen – or do they?
Back, not back, yet here.

A photocopy of the poem went to my friends and acquaintances, many of whom I would neither hear from nor see again.

Claude Vausson, editor of the French travel trade magazine *Le Répertoire des Voyages*, countered by sending a poem written for the occasion. He started every new line with a letter of the Yiddish word *meshuga*, meaning 'insane'. When in her postal response my Yugoslav friend Tamara called me crazy, 'or a little bit more than that', at least she added, 'but I like crazy people.'

Reactions covered the full gamut. Aunt Sheila Gottfried sent me a letter on orange-colored stationery which began: 'Dear Norma, It was wonderful to hear from you though I can't exactly say I got the message.' My mother, Florence Silberberg Eisner, wrote from the 'Sunshine State' of Florida: 'Your new name is very pretty, sounds Hebraic.' As I later found out, there is a name 'Seraya' in the Old Testament.

I was grateful to both of my parents that, as incomprehensible as my changed outlook was to them, they were willing to adopt my new Indian name without much objection.

Less flexible was Will Hoogstraate, owner of the D'Eendt art gallery in Amsterdam. Perhaps he was showing his affection when he adamantly refused to call me Surya, saying: 'You will always be Norma to me.' My hairdresser, Loek Limburg, his services no longer required, took a similar stance.

'Just tell people that Surya is your artist's name,' advised Diana Vandenberg, painter of mystical themes. 'This they will accept.'

The most delightful response came from my Australian photographer friend Erik Buttars. 'Dear Surya,' he wrote, 'Welcome back, even though you're not back. Do you look the same? Hell, I don't know, I have not seen you! You may sound the same, but jeez, you sure have changed your style of writing, baby. Sounds like you had no choice. You got it whether you wanted it or not. I hope it isn't catching.

'What's in a name? A meaning, a purpose, a destiny? Who knows. Things happen, so while you're still on the earth planet, skreww and make merry, for you never know how long you'll really be with us. Enjoy whichever life you have. Surya? Surya-ki? Christ, it's all Japanese to me! Friend for life, Erik.'

At this time I commenced living as a self-styled nun, married to God and dedicated to the spiritual in all its simplicity. My clothing fashion and looks changed too. I wanted to be natural, rely on my own inherent beauty, without exterior adornment. It goes without saying that my make up and perfumes were discarded and my jewelery was packed up.

Months passed by in this way. My parents wrote with alarm about my total reliance on vegetarian food, and said they would regularly send vitamin supplements. My mother ended her admonition with the perceptive remark that I had a tendency to do things to extreme. As true as this was, I sensed that a non-flesh diet had to be observed strictly by me. I felt impure for having eaten dead animals. In fact, I decided that I needed a total inner cleansing.

Even more important, what could be done to wash out from my mind my accumulated doubts, worries and fears? Surely the mental pollutants built up during 33 years of ordinary, self-centered life could not be expected to disappear in only a few months. I had been awakened, the rest was yet to be.

One afternoon, while heading for the Paul Année whole-grain bakery, I met my journalistic colleague Jules Farber. His public relations firm was located on the picturesque Keizersgracht, a few blocks from my apartment.

'Norma!' he cried out, not having seen me since my fateful Indian journey. Seizing me in a vast embrace, he said warmly: 'What's happened to you? Barbara and I received your poem.'

'I fell in love with God!' I bubbled out.

'Is that any kind of suitor for a smart big city girl?' he teased, adding: 'What do your parents think?'

I grinned and Jules nodded knowingly, coming from a background similar to mine.

'Why don't you go to press conferences any more?' he asked.

Admitting I did not understand the whole situation myself, I told him that since India a strange modesty had overcome me. Jules looked puzzled, as if wondering what this statement had to do with his question, but he heard me sympathetically. I rambled on about the love I had for the Lord, my beloved, and how the sight of my arms or legs were intended for no one's eyes but His.

'I just can't wear any other clothes but these,' I summed up, indicating my long-sleeved orange kurta and long orange skirt. 'How could I show up at a press conference or interview like this?'

Jules listened in silence, without a comment. The sun danced lightly on the canal waters, a marvelous inner exuberance liberated my tongue, and I rattled on.

'I once was an actress,' I reminded Jules, who knew some of my biography. 'Now there is a new play, a divine one, in which I take part.'

He said I had never looked more radiant, had never been as vibrant, and I could always call on him and Barbara if in need. As we waved goodbye, I was glad we had not spoken longer. That had prevented me from gushing out my new concepts of right livelihood and service-for-humanity, which might have sounded like criticism of the business way of life he followed.

Besides, how could I talk about higher values when still producing a monthly column for the French travel trade magazine edited by Claude? Although I would rather write exclusively on spirituality, any other work now being off my path, common sense obliged me to retain a steady source of income, at least for a while.

From the bakery, I strolled to the Vondel Park. This large oasis of green in the inner city was enjoying its heyday as popular meeting center for flower children from all over the world, who considered Amsterdam the 'Do Your Thing' capital. I was always cheered by the festival atmosphere created by the large numbers of young globetrotters settled into the park with their sleeping bags, guitars and communal spirit.

It was May and all around fresh life delighted in spring's celebration. Seeing the newborn flowers affirmed my own reinterpretation of myself. By mid-month I would be counting my first birthday not as Norma's thirty-fourth, but as Surya's first.

Confusions and Confirmations

Getting accustomed to my new secluded lifestyle, I kept turning down social invitations. Alone at home I could bathe in my bliss-filled meditations. All I needed was the divine.

Nonetheless, when Albert and his wife Mies phoned me several times to attend a trendy soirée, I finally relented. They promised an evening in true uninhibited Amsterdam style, enlivened by many local and foreign writers, artists and other colorful personalities. I warned Albert I was quite different from the worldly Norma they had met at their weekend extravaganza a year ago, but his friendly persistence succeeded over my endeavors to avoid the frivolous gathering.

Beautiful people, fashionable and free-spirited, were gaily chatting, drinking, laughing and smoking when I stepped into Albert's party at his palace like canal house. The open-minded 'anything goes' atmosphere helped me be at ease in my orange outfit. I had even worn my Benares Shiva beads for the occasion. The host was playing energetically on the piano as I entered the grand living room, and his wife offered large amounts of luscious delicacies from the buffet.

'Ah, you must be Miss Saintly,' I heard.

The speaker was an attractive man with a full head of bushy brown curls. His offbeat good looks were highlighted by the simple white background of his clothing.

'Can I get you a scotch?' he continued with a pleasing British accent.

'I –'

'Right, you don't drink,' said the man.

Sorry I had left the protection of my own surroundings, I turned to leave. 'Come on, Miss Puritan,' he said. 'We'll get you some water.'

Noticing the tears in my eyes, he commented that I must be either very sensitive or insecure. To my reply that I might be both, he declared, with a wink: 'Doubt presupposes an option.'

These words stopped my retreat and my acquaintance, who introduced himself as Clifford Smith, painter and writer, apologized. As he did, a huge black dog by his side sauntered over and licked my hand. Clifford was surprised, terming such behavior with strangers to be unusual for Gregory. Observing the animal, which displayed an inexplicably humanlike behavior, I remembered how Elizabeth had described her dog Bingo as the reincarnation of an ancient soul. Clifford, who with Gregory's blessings had become genuinely friendly, led me to a couch where we spent several hours exchanging views on India.

The next day we met for a snack in Clifford's favorite coffee house. After a talk similar to the one of the previous evening, he invited me to his place. A special energy reigned there, as in a temple. On top of a chest, converted into a small altar, stood the photo of a luminescent young yogi.

'Are you familiar with *Autobiography of a Yogi?*' asked Clifford. Again this book! I decided I definitely had to read it.

'Know anything about the Immortal Babaji, the deathless yogi of supernatural powers, who has lived in the Himalayas for thousands of years?' continued Clifford.

I regarded the photo intently.

'Feel anything?' queried Clifford. 'This is the present-day materialization of the Immortal Babaji. He was not born through a woman's body and has no biography before 1970, when he simply appeared, in North India. His name is Herakhan Baba.'

Little did I know that after my return to India I would have unusual experiences in the presence of Herakhan Baba, on various occasions, and would even attend his 'funeral' in 1984.

The encounter with Clifford was another sign to me. I had to devote all my attention to my true goal.

Not long after the difficult period predicted by the earlobe-man, I got an unexpected phone call.

'I'm in Hamburg,' sounded a familiar voice. Sinha! It was our first contact since I had airmailed him the Surya poem and he typed back, in part: 'You are fine and taken the right road. The poem rings the bell, repeat bell. Title it *The Indian Sunshine*. I am sure you would have courage, strength, wisdom, goodness and love.'

On a visit to Europe to confer with his various editors, he asked me to book him into a centrally located Amsterdam hotel for three days. 'I'm coming with a message from the lobe-man,' he told, evoking my curiosity.

Giving his train number and arrival time, he requested me to be on the platform. I was there, holding a welcome bouquet of sun-yellow flowers, but no Sinha was to be spotted among the passengers. By now I should have known his unreliable style.

As soon as I reached my apartment, sure enough, the phone rang. 'Where were you?' he snapped from the other end. Time was precious. There was an allotted period for our seeing each other, 12 hours, counting from now. This evening we would have dinner with Jan van der Pluym, our mutual acquaintance.

The dinner passed uneventfully, with Jan there to share with me Sinha's lengthy accounts of his recent journalistic scoops. I saw the 12-hour deadline ticking away. In the presence of Jan, who had to be kept ignorant of Sinha's guruship, as had Elizabeth, I could not receive the lobe-man's mystical disclosure. Sinha's monologue eventually became an animated discussion with Jan about Indian politics and economics.

At the meal's end we drove to my house for a goodnight drink of herbal tea. It was not exactly what they preferred, but all I could offer. After removing his shoes, Sinha commented that my rooms breathed the spirit of India. Jan poked fun at 'Norma's transformation', but took my changes for the best.

Around eleven our small meeting of the press broke up. Sinha signaled me he would call later. At seven in the morning the phone got me out of bed. Sinha was exhausted. The evening had gone on longer than anticipated. Would I meet him for breakfast?

'What about the 12-hour deadline?' I queried.

'How can I talk when totally fatigued?' he replied, ill-humored. In India he could work endlessly, but the heavy materialistic vibrations of the West weighed him down.

At the hotel restaurant Sinha greeted me with the remark: 'You look pale.' When I chose only toast and butter from the breakfast buffet counter, he ladled a large spoonful of bacon and eggs onto my plate.

'Eat that,' he commanded. 'You need protein.'

I pushed the plate aside and he said with approval: 'Good.'

When I started to speak of my love for the Beloved, he cut me off: 'Don't get emotional. Tell me what your thoughts have been. There is little time.'

'What time is it?' I asked, no longer wearing a watch. He responded that one life was not enough for all that needed to be done.

'Please tell me the message from the earlobe-man,' I requested, increasingly anxious because of the deadline. Sinha looked at me mysteriously, as if calculating the effect his words would produce. Giving me a sly glance he said, utterly deadpan: 'Things will get better now.'

'That's it?' I exclaimed.

'Yes.'

I laughed, too loud and too long. Sinha ordered me to behave, we were in public. He had to talk fast, because the permitted time had almost expired. Again he maintained he was my guru, but said he had been too busy with his political work to be able to give guidance. The main reason for stopping in Amsterdam was to see me. Unfortunately, after three tiring weeks in Hamburg, his exhaustion prevented a proper conversation now. I should, however, not worry about changes, they would happen by themselves.

'Do not doubt, have strength,' he advised. Help would be sent.

Then, without warning, Sinha demanded I leave the table. The authority of his tone compelled me to stand.

'The twelve hours are nearly over,' he stated. 'We won't meet again for very long.' It sounded like an afterthought when, quite casually, he added: 'Have you heard from the swami?'

'Swami?'

'One of the rarest of the rare.'

'Please tell me more.'

'Leave now, immediately, the deadline is reached,' he declared. 'Write with any questions.' When I did not move, he got up and walked quickly away.

At the table, I reviewed Sinha's surprise visit. There were always so many complications around him, so much theatre. Why had I not confronted him, insisting he tell me what was going on? Twelve-hour deadline! What exactly was his game? What did he want from me? I definitely needed to have some answers before he left Amsterdam. I decided to go to his room.

When I knocked at his door, a cleaning woman informed me the guest had already checked out.

Afterwards I wondered how to continue. So much remained unclear. But I told myself that the force sending voices, visions and experiences must be good, deserving my trust.

On a certain evening I prayed that I might be able to express my inner discoveries through my pen. Others should know that the grace touching me was available to everyone. Although I wished to write about this, my mind could not find the words.

Absorbed in this ardent supplication, I got up from my desk and, not knowing why, selected one of the books from my collection. It fell open to a page bearing a photo of Sri Aurobindo.

His eyes looked at me. Life entered his features. The face became alive. It was no longer just a piece of paper, Sri Aurobindo was in the room. Immediately I was in tune with him, and received the very clear instruction to go to the altar. There my hand automatically picked up a card, sent from the Sri Aurobindo Ashram and signed by Sri Navajata and Sushila. A printed message from the Mother read: 'We want to show to the world that man can become a true servitor of the Divine. Who will collaborate in all sincerity?'

I closed my eyes and remained in a very peaceful state. Afterwards, the picture of Sri Aurobindo was once more just a picture.

Reality or fantasy, who could give a definite reply? Be that as it may, I was more certain than ever that the Great Integrity, to use Buckminster Fuller's words, was taking good care of me.

Spiritual Friendship

Although I found pleasure in my solitude, I regretted I was not able to communicate my experiences in some way. I wanted to share my discovery that life is not what I had thought it to be, and point out our usual inability to see the divine workings.

Of course there were still so many question marks about what had happened to me in India. I needed to speak with someone who would take me seriously, someone in whom I could confide that the sun was a living being, that I talked with the sun, that I was the sun!

Restlessness visited me, as it would in an unwanted confinement. Yet I had chosen this path – or had I? 'Those who choose the Divine, have been chosen by the Divine,' said the Mother of Pondicherry.

Diana Vandenberg phoned. 'Hello sun, here's the moon.' She called us relatives because her name, Diana, represents the Roman goddess personifying the moon.

I had met Diana three years earlier, at a pop festival held in Rotterdam's Kralingen Woods. Out of 80,000 people who squeezed together on the grass before a large outdoor stage, we happened to sit next to each other.

During the long hours of rock music we occasionally exchanged remarks and, at the concert's end, she introduced herself. I recognized her name immediately. She was the well-known painter of transcendental subjects, and only a few days before a Dutch magazine had assigned me to interview her. From my purse I produced a piece of paper on which was written her name and phone number.

After my return from India, Diana was one of the few friends who accepted my transformation as a very positive occurrence, and her moral support always encouraged me. Because of Diana, I attended the coming weekend's Spring Fair at the De Kosmos Meditation Center in Amsterdam.

What perfect timing. I was ready to go out and meet like-minded souls.

At this pioneering festival, organized by the Dutch alternative scene, I spent much of the day and evening helping Diana sell books and postcards of her paintings. She had her own display table in a busy room where unconventional folk offered rainbow-colored candles, self-made clothes, astrology consultations, hand-crafted paper and tarot readings.

When my turn came to look around in the building, I was like a child exploring a gingerbread house of tempting rare treats. Sounds of Indian sitar, classical piano and of Sail, the local rock favourite, filled the premises, an old patrician mansion of which the walls and ceilings were adorned with symbols and paintings rendering the intangible by means of the visual.

Over the weekend I absorbed diverse bits of information on everything from macrobiotic food to Tai Chi Ch'uan and non-polluting battery-operated cars for public transport. Films, theatre, video tapes, discussion groups, speaker's corners. . . . I tasted all.

In these environs I noted with relief that I could become part of the crowd. What a delightful surprise to see that many of the women wore long skirts and, with their Eastern styles, looked similar to me. One of them fascinated me with her wild locks coiled atop her head, similar to Lord Shiva's hairdo. She too was a self-styled *sadhwi*. Many men as well were gaily attired in clothes of Oriental fashion. I felt quite at home in this Kosmos.

In the basement tea house, misty with flowery incense which elicited a poignant nostalgia for my India, a soft voice behind me called 'Surya'. There stood Denis, whom I had met briefly a year before through a mutual acquaintance. Interest in my name change had prompted him to phone me during the winter, but in that non-social phase of my adjustment period I had declined his invitation to meet.

Providing amicable company, he escorted me upstairs to the room where Diana awaited me. She and Denis knew each other by sight, from having attended various Kosmos events.

For awhile the three of us looked through the book called *The Hermetic Painting of Diana Vandenberg*. It was a scholarly investigation of her work and philosophy by Dr. Johan Stellingwerff of Amsterdam's Vrije University.

'*Hermetic* here does not mean "airtight",' Diana explained. The word referred to the ancient Egyptian author Hermes Trismegistus, whose writings embraced mystical, theosophical, astrological and alchemical doctrines. His ideas influenced her canvases.

'I try to paint universal themes of life and death,' she said. Like Elizabeth Brunner in New Delhi, she stimulated my aspirations to find my own form of creative spiritual expression. Our talk ended because it was Diana's turn to wander through the Kosmos. Before setting off she whispered to me, 'Denis would be a good friend for you: he's serious.'

When Denis, shyly and hesitantly, asked what had happened to me in India, nothing seemed more appropriate than to relate my odyssey and its aftermath. He listened with interest. Repeatedly he set me pondering by such questions as: 'How do you feel about that?' and 'What does that mean to you?' An air of gentleness exuded from him.

Telling my story brought relief. For months I had been obliged to give explanations and defend myself. Suddenly there was someone who simply accepted me for what I was.

Denis, born in Jakarta of mixed Indonesian-European background, was a student working towards his master's degree in the psychology of religion. Then 25, he had already been practicing yoga for six years. For reasons of inner cleanliness he was a pure vegetarian, and neither drank alcohol nor smoked.

Before we parted, he took a book from his shoulder bag and handed it to me, for reading at home. It was *How to Know God*, a commentary by Swami Prabhavananda and Christopher Isherwood on the yoga aphorisms of Patanjali, a great Indian sage who lived 1,500 years ago. Thumbing later through the pages, I found precious sentences which, like wise friends, helped me better understand my current thoughts.

Pen markings applied by Denis introduced me to a significant section:

When an aspirant enters upon the spiritual life, he naturally does so with great enthusiasm. The first steps he takes are almost always accompanied by feelings of peace and delight. Everything seems so easy, so inspiring. It is therefore very important that he should realize, right from the start, that this mood will not continue uninterrupted throughout the rest of his course. Religion is not simply a state of euphoria. There will be relapses; phases of struggle, dryness and doubt. But these ought not to distress him unduly. Conscious feelings, however exalted, are not the only indications of spiritual progress. We may be growing most strongly at a time when our minds seem dark and dull.[6]

The paragraph's last sentence was underlined: 'There is no failure as long as we continue to make an effort.'[7]

A few days after the Kosmos turning point, Denis invited me for a walk. We strolled along Amsterdam's charming brick-paved streets, heading for the Vondel Park. There, under a tree, my new friend gave me insights into his past and his general outlook on life.

His ultimate goal? 'To attain enlightenment, nothing less will do.' For more rapid progress, he meditated daily, morning and evening, and frequently in between as well. He also practiced *hatha yoga*, bodily postures, and *pranayama*, yogic breathing exercises.

From his shoulder bag emerged another book, checked out of the library for me, a volume describing the lives of women saints.

The story of Saint Teresa of Avila particularly impressed me. Her experiences suggested I was not insane. On the contrary, I might be blessed.

In Teresa I found soul attunement. After having seen the Lord's beauty, she had written, no one else seemed handsome to her in comparison. I knew exactly what she meant, also when she complained that, in the early stages of her mystic life, she had no one with whom to discuss her joys and tribulations in loving God.

Denis and I began meeting weekly, to exchange ideas on different aspects of spirituality. He diagnosed the strange pains I was now experiencing in my body, and which my doctor dismissed as 'nothing', to be caused by the arousal of *kundalini*, the primordial cosmic energy often pictured as a sleeping serpent rolled up at the base of the spine.

The kundalini is considered an ultra potent force that underlies the higher functions of consciousness. If kundalini awakens and rises upwards along the spine, the man or woman evolves in wisdom. When the energy activates, either naturally or as a result of specific exercises, pains can appear in parts of the body unprepared to receive the force or blocking its way. Purifying our system enables it to become an unobstructed channel.

Denis encouraged my spiritual aspirations, giving support at a moment when I needed it. His gift for understanding helped me greatly. Co-travelers, we exchanged what we individually had found so far. He passed on his knowledge, whereas I inspired him to make a tangible contribution to the world and its betterment. But both of us wanted to come into touch with someone who had already reached advanced states. Only such a person would be able to explain the deeper significance of my experiences in India.

Then one beautiful summer day, after I had just been watching an elegant family of swans glide by my canalside window, the postman delivered a letter from Germany. Even before I could read the sender's name, I felt this was the sign I had been awaiting. With anxious hands I carefully opened the envelope and found a typed note: 'Dear Miss Green, I have the honor to inform you that H. H. Swamiji arrived last month in Germany from New Delhi. Kindly contact him as soon as possible.' A Bonn postbox was given.

The same day I wrote back and the reply came unusually fast. Under the penned-in signature of 'Swamiji', I saw the name 'Swami Purna' together with a Bonn phone number. Without delay I rang up. As I dialed, my heart started to pound with anticipation. The phone was instantly answered, as if the person had been expecting my call.

'Hello,' came a sweet voice. I knew it was the swami. Excited beyond measure, I recognized the importance of the moment.

'This is Surya,' I burst out enthusiastically.

'I know,' he replied with familiarity. 'I must see you in Amsterdam before returning to Delhi.'

'When is that?'

'Next February.'

'Oh, now is only July,' I said gaily. 'There is plenty of time.'

We discussed his possible arrival date and I explained I had just finished the research for my master's thesis on Dutch broadcasting. The manuscript had to be written and sent to my California university by the end of October. Probably I would need all my time to meet the deadline. And then in November I would go to Africa for journalistic work. Afterwards I might want to stay and travel on my own, as I had in India.

'Everything has its own timing,' responded Swami Purna. He as well had commitments. During the December and January holiday period he had to be in England, but he could arrange to fly back to India via Amsterdam, permitting a visit sometime in early February.

February? That was seven months away! I would have preferred to see the swami much sooner but definitely knew I had to finish certain things before meeting him. My old life had to be properly completed; only then could I give myself totally to the next stage. Swami Purna, I intuited, would usher it in.

In India there is a saying: when the student is ready, the teacher appears.

The Dalai Lama

Just as I was tackling the last sections of my thesis, Denis brought news that His Holiness Tenzin Gyatso, the fourteenth Dalai Lama, would arrive in Amsterdam in October, as part of his first visit to the West. This was the very beginning of the Dalai Lama's worldwide travels and talks to the international community on the need for trust, kindness and love among people.

In these early days, long before his winning of the Nobel Peace Prize in 1989 made the Dalai Lama a figure familiar to the general public everywhere, information about him was not so easily available. Nevertheless I learned, among other details, that this greatly esteemed representative of Tibetan Buddhism was considered an emanation of Avalokiteshvara, the Bodhisattva of Compassion.

A *bodhisattva* is someone who, after reaching enlightenment, stays active in the world. Such a being voluntarily and repeatedly takes rebirth in order to help others be delivered from life's sufferings.

Born in 1935 in northeastern Tibet, Tenzin Gyatso was recognized at the age of two as the reincarnation of the thirteenth Dalai Lama, who died in 1933. According to a traditional Tibetan process he passed certain tests which confirmed his identity as the *Dalai* (ocean) *Lama* (superior one). In 1640 the ruling Mongol prince had bestowed temporal and spiritual control of all Tibet upon the Dalai Lama. Each Dalai Lama is accepted in turn as the direct reincarnation of the previous one.

In Tibetan Buddhism there are four main schools. Despite differences between them based on separate lines of transmission and the emphasis given to certain elements of the teaching, all share the same goal: the attainment of buddhahood.

The oldest of the four schools, Nyingma, whose name itself means 'ancient', traces its origins to Guru Padma Sambhava, an Indian prince who was the first to bring the Buddhist teachings to Tibet in the 8th century. The second oldest, the Kagyu, or 'oral transmission', received its characteristics from Marpa and Milarepa, two 11th-century yogis. It combines both the first and the second influx of Buddhism into Tibet. The Sakya line was founded by an 11th-century saint, the Indian sage Atisha, who spent his last years in Tibet. The Dalai Lama was mainly trained inside the Gelug, or 'virtuous' school, established in the 15th century.

As is well known, the present Dalai Lama left his homeland in 1959. His official residence became Dharamsala, a small village in the northwest of India dominated by the snow-capped Himalayan peaks of the mighty Dhauladhar mountain range.

The day of the Dalai Lama's public program in Amsterdam, Denis and I arrived at the lecture hall to find an immense crowd already assembled in the street. With so many people ahead of us, we doubted whether we would gain entrance.

Yet patience and faith were rewarded, and as by a miracle we found ourselves at last inside the building. Our relief was of short duration because very soon we heard that no more places remained. Then another wonder occurred. We could hardly believe our good fortune when one of the organizers signaled us to follow her, led us all the way through the packed hall and ushered us to the space directly in front of the stage, where she said we could sit on the floor. We were only a few meters from the dais of His Holiness! As we installed ourselves, the First Secretary of the Indian Embassy, Sri Tripathi, greeted me from his seat right behind us.

By now the general excitement had reached the higher altitudes, and it was certainly no anticlimax when the Dalai Lama and his entourage appeared, colorful and all smiles. He addressed the public in a delightfully fractured English which the translator rendered more understandable, and told us he had been asked to speak about the message of the Lord Buddha.

In Tibet the Buddha's teachings are referred to by the traditional term *Dharma*, derived from the Sanskrit root *dhr*, upholding. Dharma supports our efforts when we practise in accordance with it. It is also the law of truth which governs the eternal arising, existing and passing away of all physical and psychic phenomena.

In a style quite light-hearted considering the weighty subject, the Dalai Lama said that although human beings had made much progress over the centuries, many basic problems that we had thousands of years ago still remained and had even become worse.

'So it is clear', he summed up, 'that material progress and modern science alone are not sufficient. With them we have achieved physical comfort, but no mental peace. For that, the great spiritual teachings continue to be very important.'

Discussing several basic Buddhist ideas, he started with the law of karma. To live happily, he explained, we must accept that everything in life, both the pleasant and the unsatisfactory, is due to our own actions.

'From this point of view,' he said, 'the main responsibility lies in yourself and not in others. This enables you to bear a difficulty or problem better, and it also reduces your feelings of hatred towards others.'

As long as we are in the grip of *sansara*, the circle of recurring birth and rebirth, there is always suffering.

'This concept helps you face problems. When you realize suffering is the very nature of life itself, it is easier for you to accept all difficulties. You say to yourself, "Oh, this is not something unnatural, it is something which happens."'

But, he hastened to add, this outlook should not make us pessimistic or passive. 'These karmas, these actions, have been accumulated by you. If you have gathered good karma, the result will be good. This clearly indicates that the control over karmic forces lies in yourself. That is why the Buddha said you are your own master. When confronted by problems, we should bear them. At the same time we should make efforts to avoid them in the future. You have the power to do this.'

Looking at the Dalai Lama, considered by Tibetans as most holy, he was very human, natural and real. How else could an enlightened individual be?

At the end, when questions were posed, someone wanted to know if meditation could be properly practiced by Western people. The Dalai Lama looked surprised and answered with a radiant smile: 'Why not?' The audience laughed appreciatively.

Without the translator's aid, he went on: 'If you look Westerner, superficially, then of course there are many differences. Even, you see, face is difference. His face, my face, quite different. But in the deeper, this is human being, I am human being.'

His words were so simple but so true. They confirmed that an evolved person experiences unity and becomes one with others. The message that we are all brothers and sisters we cannot hear often enough. The Dalai Lama never tires of repeating it, wherever he goes.

'I mean,' he continued, 'due to the environment and traditional and social systems, on superficial level we have different way of life, different way of thinking, and of course, different language.' Here the crowd laughed warmly again.

'Many different things. Important is the real nature of human being. On that basis, all same. So no reason why meditation cannot be practiced by Western people.'

What struck me about the Dalai Lama more than his words, was the atmosphere of gentleness and kindness he created. In his presence I felt a truly expansive love, and I understood why Tibetans believe that the compassionate Bodhisattva Avalokiteshvara incarnates in the succession of Dalai Lamas.

My heart unguardedly opened to this unusual person in front of me, an eminent spiritual leader and at the same time an unpresumptuous, warm and sensitive human being. As he looked into the audience, his eyes caught mine. 'Your soul, my soul, same source,' I thought to myself. But indeed, quite a different level of development.

His evolution had already taken the Dalai Lama to completeness, how else to explain the constant radiance of peace and joy emanating from him? A smile almost continually heightened his pleasant countenance and a spontaneous laugh was his usual response to any matter.

The Dalai Lama seemed to fulfill his many responsibilities with serenity. His mission was to convey the Buddha's message of love, understanding and peace for all. To the Dalai Lama these were not merely words. He practiced what he preached. His living example did not fail to impress me and I determined to try and see the positive side of everything.

Green in the Field

My trip to the Ivory Coast in November, to cover an international conference for the French travel magazine, turned out to be my swan song in that domain. Too many elements of this work were incompatible with my altered viewpoints. I decided that undistracted focus on my new aim was a necessity.

Back in Amsterdam, I resigned from the Foreign Press Association and wrote farewell letters to the magazines I represented as Holland correspondent, stating literally that I had to 'spiritualize' my work.

It goes without saying that I was thankful to tourism for still having brought me to Africa. Extending my stay to visit the neighboring countries of Ghana, Togo, Benin and Upper Volta, I had enjoyed meeting beautiful African people who opened their homes and hearts to me as had Ahalya Narayanan in Madras.

The stimulating African vitality had stirred my physical energies to an unexpected degree, enticing me to socialize and dance as I had not since my teenage years. At a certain moment I felt like an African myself.

By February, the month marked for the arrival of Swami Purna, Denis had moved into my small apartment which we termed our ashram of two. We were living as monks thoroughly engrossed in other-worldly studies. In those early years my zeal knew no limits.

My daily life was organized around a systematic discipline. Rising early, before the sun's arrival, I took an invigorating cold shower and then began with yogic breathing at the open window. Whether clouds filled the sky or not, I did sun and light practices followed by yoga postures and other exercises.

Then I covered my head and shoulders with the white woolen shawl brought back from Benares, and went into meditation.

Daily meditation, Denis affirmed, calmed the mind and opened doors to higher rungs of existence. Awakening, which had occurred to me spontaneously, had been effected in him through disciplined endeavor. We meditated in the morning and in the evening, and sometimes in between.

Denis showed me the classic concentration technique of India. Eyes closed, I fixed the inner sight on the third eye between the eyebrows. When the mind wandered, I silently repeated the word *Om*.

Om is the most sacred syllable in the Hindu tradition. *Om*, or *aum* as it should be pronounced, represents not only the totality of sound but of existence itself. When *Om* is used in the proper way in spiritual exercises, the power of *Om* can awaken our consciousness to an intuitive understanding of eternal truths impossible to convey in words.

My day was spent partly at the desk, reading what I thought to be of spiritual benefit, and writing in my notebook. No acceptable work had yet made its appearance. I sought a right livelihood which would give me more insight into the greater reality of life but also go beyond mere personal gain by allowing me, in some way, to share my findings with others. My bank savings on the wane, concern about meeting my expenses started to engage me. With good timing Diana introduced me to J. P. Klautz, the founder of *Bres*, a bi-monthly Dutch journal devoted to the esoteric. When he and his co-editor Alexandra Gabrielli, heard I had met the Mother of Pondicherry, they requested an article.

Writing for spiritually-oriented magazines! I had not even known such publications existed. I was still so green in the field.

Swami Purna, the Spiritual Prince Charming

Early in February Swami Purna phoned to say he would arrive in Amsterdam the next weekend.

'Would you like me to arrange any talks or meetings for you?' I asked.

'Do whatever you think appropriate,' he answered.

A flurry of activities filled the following days. Cleaning and sprucing up the house, food shopping, fitting the swami into the Kosmos agenda.

Saturday arrived and with it the anxiously awaited weekend so pregnant with promise to me. I was hardly back from the market when the doorbell rang. The swami was early.

A quick brushing of my hair, a speedy fluffing up of the seat cushions, and I stepped out of my second floor apartment onto the small landing, together with Denis. Pulling the handle which springs open the street door, a device in many Amsterdam houses, I called down for confirmation: 'Who's there?'

'It's me,' a voice announced in a familiar tone.

We waited eagerly as the sound of footsteps ascended the steep wooden stairs. A good-looking man attired in white Indian cotton robes, a woolen shawl casually draped over his shoulders, came into view. Very long pitch-black hair contrasted with a fair complexion. A small beard, a moustache and a big smile completed his pleasant appearance.

After my faltering welcome, I simply stared at this spiritual Prince Charming, unable to remove my gaze from the dark eyes. The attraction was as mutual as it was instantaneous.

Swami Purna said that downstairs in the car were two women who drove him here from Germany. Could I suggest a hotel? Of course they could stay with us, I offered. First of all he wanted to come in, and removed his sandals. He wore no socks and was altogether very lightly clad for the cold North European winter climate.

In my unpretentious two-room apartment, he strolled around like a person of high rank on a benevolent inspection tour. At my desk he looked out of the window, admiring the old Dutch houses on the opposite side of the canal.

'Anno 1658,' I read out from the Roman characters on the gable directly facing.

Then he proceeded with noble bearing to the living room and commented, 'This will be fine.'

When I informed him there was also an attic room, he wanted to see it and up two more flights we wound. At the upstairs door, obviously pleased with the sun image I had taped there, he mentioned that Lord Surya was the main deity and symbol of his monastic order, at least of the branch to which he belonged.

'Really?' I exclaimed, and his next remark astonished me even more: 'We are the only sun order of monks in India.' This information caressed my ears like a precious whispering from wondrous sources.

The swami entered the tiny slant-roofed room where I had prepared a mattress for him on the ground and a small table topped with candles, incense and fresh flowers.

'It's like a Himalayan cave,' he observed with a delighted expression, and we both laughed. Everything seemed to meet his approval and he went down to the car, to return a few minutes later with two well-dressed German women approximately in their forties.

'Is it really all right for us to stay?' asked one of them, introduced as Annelies Felix.

'You didn't expect us. We don't want to inconvenience you,' joined in the other woman, named Mia Bauer.

Embracing them both, I said we were glad about their visit and certainly appreciated that they had brought Swami Purna to Amsterdam. While they installed themselves, the swami examined my music collection. The Indian classical records interested him particularly and he wanted to hear my favorite.

Sounds of Pandit Ram Narayan's divine sarangi created a peaceful, meditative atmosphere as Denis improvised a simple dinner and I prepared the table, a cloth spread on the ground. Before the meal we sat together in prayerful silence. Retreating into myself, I sent a big 'thank you' upwards. A picture came of the swami and me looking like Radha and Krishna in an affectionate pose. When I opened my eyes, the swami was regarding me thoughtfully. Could he read my mind?

Whereas the rest of us ate heartily, the swami sipped a few spoonfuls of the lentil soup, nibbled at a half slice of bread and popped a few almonds into his mouth.

'Swamiji doesn't eat much,' Annelies informed us with the worried tone of a concerned mother depositing her son at summer camp. When she tried to place a leaf of lettuce on the swami's plate, he laughed, saying he was not used to stuffing himself. He partook of meals, he said, only to please people. In the Himalayas he goes completely without food.

'When people came to know I could go without eating,' recalled Swamiji with amusement, 'some of them sat before me day and night in rotation to check whether I ate anything or not.' He laughed again.

'What does the word *swami* mean?' I asked.

'*Swami* means "one who has mastered himself",' he replied in a serious voice. 'One who has such control is given the title *swami* by a guru or a high being or by the circle of high beings in the Himalayas. This occurs at the end of the *sannyas*, the period of renunciation and spiritual training. In the ancient monastic system of India, *sannyas* usually lasts 12 years.

'*Sannyas* means total withdrawal from all sides and unattachment to all material things, persons, places and even thoughts,' he further explained. 'The sannyasi who becomes a real *swami* is a living knowledge, just like the sun and the fire: pure, bright and available to all. The usual drives influencing a person's behavior no longer affect him or her. You are not controlled by desires, your senses, the environment . . . by nothing. No forces can dominate you. You are the one who is master – over your food, sleep, whatever.'

'Nowadays people easily call themselves sannyasi and swami and master,' I commented.

'Anyone can have the names, but I have told you the true meanings,' answered Swamiji. 'Like much in today's world, yogic titles and terms suffer degradation when they are incorrectly used.'

'And the title *ji?*'

'Others attach it to your name to imply affection, love and respect.' By his tone I could taste the sweetness of this suffix.

'May I also ask you what *Purna* means?' I next inquired.

'It comes from the Sanskrit and signifies "complete", "whole".'

During dinner, Annelies remarked how much Swamiji and I looked alike. 'Except for the beard!' he squealed in childlike glee.

More than any exterior resemblance, the swami and I shared a similar vision. He now described an ideal society, where human life and institutions would reflect the great spiritual laws and principles existing behind manifestation. His thoughts were not unlike Sri Aurobindo's or the Mother's. Higher consciousness would be directly experienced by each individual. He stressed how urgent it was for people to become aware, and I could not agree more. As Swami Purna talked, I felt increasingly attuned with him.

In an animated discussion the two of us exchanged ideas, stimulating each other more and more, until I realized we were the only ones speaking. Annelies and Mia did not say a word, and Denis assumed his usual silent reserve when in public. Taking into account I still had a whole week to sit in conclave with the swami before his scheduled departure for India, I directed my attention to the women who would both leave the next evening to be at their jobs on Monday.

Eventually Swami Purna declared: 'It's been a long day. Time to dissolve ourselves.' We all giggled.

I escorted the swami up to his cave. When I switched on the electric radiator to combat the cold, he said I could 'off it'. When he is in the Himalayas, he never has heating. Subjected to the rigors of nature at high altitudes, at times wandering naked amidst the snow and ice, he survives by *rasayana*, the yogic alchemical process, and generates his own internal energy.

'Is that why you can dress so lightly?' I inquired.

'Year-round I wear the same, wherever I am,' he responded. I had brought up an extra blanket, but he would not use it.

Dismissing myself, I returned downstairs where the women started asking questions about my background.

'I can hardly believe this is the first time you and Swamiji are meeting,' Annelies exclaimed. She and Mia had supposed that we knew each other very long 'because Swamiji so insisted to visit Amsterdam to see Surya'.

Later on, when I asked details about him, I heard to my surprise that our Prince Charming indeed was a prince. From an ancient kingdom in the north of India, he had renounced wealth and position for the spiritual life. The women did not know his exact age, but he looked much younger than he was.

After wishing them goodnight, I sat in contemplation. 'Thank you, Lord, for all you are giving me,' I prayed. With closed eyes, I concentrated on the spot between the brows.

Swami Purna appeared, inside a cave, in meditation posture. Next to him there was somebody else. Looking closely, I discovered it was me.

The scene shifted. I was still absorbed in meditation, but now under the bodhi tree, like a buddha. A moment later I was sitting under the tree in Vrindavan, and at the same time I was the sun, shining down on myself. What presumption! Who was I really?

By two o'clock, all the others asleep, I prepared my mattress, thinking of my guest in the attic.

Arising very early as usual, I quietly went through my morning preparations and was already in the kitchen when the swami entered. Greeting me with a smile, he asked: 'Did you get any sleep?'

'Some,' I replied. Why did he mention this? Indeed I had not slept very much. He seemed to know it already.

'Who is your favorite spiritual entity?' he asked out of the blue. Perhaps because of the image in last night's meditation, I answered 'the Buddha'. Without doubt I would be able to tell Swami Purna about the sun, but not yet.

Just as unexpectedly came his next question: 'Do you have the desire for a child?'

'No,' I said surprised. 'I have always considered the books I would eventually write as my children. Family life never really attracted me.'

The swami made no comments, except for nodding thoughtfully. As if wanting to test my ability to concentrate while preparing our breakfast, he began a dissertation on the ancient monastic system of Dasnami Sannyas. I successfully continued my culinary tasks while ingesting that, in 8th-century India, the great saint-philosopher Adi Shankaracharya organized the renunciates on the path of Shiva into ten divisions. One of Swami Purna's titles, Giri ('mountain'), implying the Himalayas, he received from the specific Dasnami Sannyas division to which he belonged.

Denis came into the kitchen and gave me assistance while the lecture continued.

Each of the ten divisions of Shaivite renunciates is associated with one of the four *maths*, holy seats, established by Adi Shankaracharya in the four cardinal points of India: north, south, west, east. Over each math presides a Shankaracharya, a spiritual leader of exceptional prestige.

Unlike Roman Catholicism, which is headed by a single person, the Pope, Hinduism has a collective directorate. This is composed of spiritual leaders such as the four Shankaracharyas and, under them, Mahamandaleshvaras, 'Lords of the Great Circle', as well as other high beings. Swami Purna added that he came from the Dasnami Sannyas center in Benares.

'Benares?'

'And our symbol is the sun, because we are of the lineage of Surya,' he said as the women joined us.

We spent that day mainly outdoors, sightseeing. Quite naturally we began in my neighborhood, one of Amsterdam's most colorful areas, the Jordaan. I noted his interest when I remarked that all the streets here were called after flowers, trees and animals, my own canal after the laurel tree.

'*Jordaan* is first of all thought to be a corruption of *jardin*, French for "garden",' I explained. In the 17th century, when this part of town took shape, French was the main international language. 'It is nice, though, to imagine that the name has something to do with the River Jordan, in which St. John baptized Jesus.'

'There are high beings, alive today, who have known Jesus,' remarked Swami Purna, hinting that he was one of them.

'Just how old are you?' I asked incredulously, but he turned away to speak with Denis.

After dinner, Annelies and Mia made their tearful farewells. We accompanied them downstairs and waved goodbye until the car turned the corner.

Back in the living room, Swami Purna enthroned himself on a cushion, looking like an eminent ruler of some unknown mystical kingdom. Here then was the longed-for person of higher spiritual attainment who could give me an authoritative explanation about my Indian experiences. No one more suitable could have been sent. How would he evaluate my story with all its improbable elements? My hour of truth had come.

'Um, would you like some tea?' I commenced.

To the swami's positive reply, Denis immediately left for the kitchen, giving me a sign of encouragement to approach the subject obsessing my mind.

'What are your questions?' Swami Purna inquired as if he knew my thoughts. His tone implied that nothing was beyond his ken.

Out of habit I set up the tape recorder but he told me to turn it off, suggesting to rely more on my own built-in recording mechanism. The most pertinent statements of our ensuing conversation he repeated into my microphone shortly before his departure from Amsterdam.

Abandoning the equipment, I searched for a way to come to the point. How difficult it often is to find the right words for something important.

'It's all light,' he said, causing me to smile. Of course he meant 'It's all right,' but what is right is indeed the light.

'Where to start,' I sighed. 'Well, I guess I should go back to the beginning.' And then, gradually, the story flowed as I lost all prudence: the official trip, Pondicherry, the sun. Tears rolled down my cheeks when I said, 'The Mother died the day I flew to Africa for the travel conference.'

'Yes, it was a sign to you,' the swami commented. I explained that to me the Mother was not dead, and I still felt her presence. He nodded gently, motioning me to continue.

The rest of my account rushed out: Sinha, the earlobe-man, Benares, Shiva, Vrindavan. With trepidation, I even told about the vision of the white horse in Mathura and my associations with it. The word 'Kalki' slipped from my lips.

'No, you are not crazy,' declared Swami Purna, answering the forthcoming question before I could pose it. His simple statement dissolved my uncertainty. I could have thrown myself at his feet, in gratitude. Instead I murmured a 'thank you' intended not only for him. He nodded again, and Denis sent me a glance of support.

'So many signs confirm my Indian experiences,' I told Swami Purna. 'Your coming into my life seems part of the big master plan as well.'

Then doubts arose in me. 'How can all this be true?' I burst out.

Understanding me perfectly, the swami presented his interpretation: 'You went to India and found yourself very near to the high beings and God, especially the Sun God. You felt you were getting energy from the sun, you were tuned with the sun, you experienced oneness with the sun. You saw that your mission was quite different from what you were doing.'

Outside, the carillon of the majestic *Westerkerk* (West Church) chimed the late hour, providing a melodious accompaniment to the assuring words of Swami Purna.

'That you were exposed to the sun entity was not accidental,' he continued. 'It has a great meaning and purpose, later to be fully realized by you. According to the experience, you came to the conclusion that you are a reflection of the sun. To express yourself, to symbolize that you want to free yourself and be who you are and what you are, tuned with the source, a name has been revealed to you. Surya means sun, the bright appearance. It means the giver who gives everything, who inspires the light, where there is no dark, no ignorance, no untruth, no negative, where everything is sparkling.

'This name was revealed to you in India. It was not given, but it happened. Nobody chose it, but it was chosen.'

I was quite right in my poem announcing the name change.

During our tea pause, Denis and I served Indian sweets especially purchased for the visit. Taking only a few crumbs, the swami passed the rest on.

'Now this is *prasad*, food blessed by the guru,' he said.

Guru? This possibility had of course already crossed my mind. Swami Purna seemed to possess the higher knowledge I sought and, moreover, an immediate attunement existed between us.

He poured some of the steaming tea into his saucer, then sipped it up noisily, in the popular Indian way. Denis and I exchanged wondering looks, unaccustomed as we were to the company of a prince.

'Swamiji,' I asked him, 'what is my main task in the future?'

'Eventually you will not have to do anything, only be yourself,' he replied. When I looked puzzled, he said: 'This is the duty of the sun, isn't it?'

Though getting used to Swami Purna's indirect manner of answering certain questions, I could not say that this style satisfied me. It did not give me the assurance that I understood him correctly. Often enough I was left with new mysterious messages to decipher. Was he testing me, or trying to stretch my imagination?

More than a Guru

A period of great intensity followed, giving me scant possibility to write in my notebook. We spent all our time together, our tiny ashram energized by the dynamic force of Swami Purna's presence.

In one of our discussions he spoke of Guru Maharaj Ji, the 16-year-old Indian teacher. Guru Maharaj Ji started delivering spiritual discourses at the age of eight, when he took over the guruship from his father, Shri Hans Ji Maharaj, who died in 1966. Shri Hans was a monk who had married. As Swamiji related this detail, his eyes and mine met and remained fixed on each other for a long moment.

One evening I suggested to Denis that we invite Swamiji to sleep downstairs, because I thought the attic room too chilly and uncomfortable, even for a yogi. Maybe my charity was founded rather on my own not quite defined needs, but in any case the protests of Denis had no chance to succeed over my resolve. Swamiji accepted.

We slept in our clothes, Indian style. A small night lamp stayed burning at Swamiji's request. After our 'good-nights', he recommended we close our eyes and survey the last 12 hours: 'Ask your consciousness, ask your own God who is within, what you have done. Think: will that thought or act help me to improve my consciousness and develop my life? If not, drop it. If you are careful, much can be corrected.'

When my eyes opened again, the new day already flooded the room. We all seemed to have awakened simultaneously.

'Did you sleep well?' Swamiji asked us.

'I don't know if I slept at all!' I exclaimed. Chuckling, he went into the bathroom and I confided to Denis that I lay awake much of the night, listening to the whistling sounds which came from Swamiji's lips.

'It was more like blowing,' corrected Denis, who also was not sure whether he had slept much. Curiously enough, neither of us felt tired.

Denis proposed that Swamiji should return to the Himalayan room, but I disagreed. If we were to do that, Swamiji might feel rejected. He was above such low-level emotions, Denis reminded me, adding that Swamiji could leave in a second and never see us again, it would not trouble him at all.

Did I not remember the story of how he had broken all ties with his family of philosophers and rulers? How he had left home one night, climbing over the palace walls to escape detection by the guards? Buddha-style, that is to say. Because on the one hand he did not want to live in the narrow confines of power, politics and pomp, and on the other wished to avoid the marriage arranged for him?

It was a great opportunity to sleep in the same room with a high being, I said. 'Some vibration will come to us, as spiritual food. The chance may not come again.' Denis had to admit the truth of my words. Seized by his own eagerness for inner growth, he nodded in acquiescence.

My affinity with Swami Purna had been evident since our first phone conversation. I expressed my delight about this during one of our letter-writing sessions, at the desk. He was going through his correspondence, dictating responses that I had to prepare in his high-standard style and then type. No easy task, for he gave nothing but thoughts.

'Swamiji,' I said as I clipped a new sheet onto my writing-board, 'it is as if I have known you for a very long time, as if we were associated before, in other lives. I was aware of it immediately. When Sinha mentioned you, the moment your letter arrived, the first phone call . . . .'

'Of course you feel closeness with me,' he responded, 'because I am more than a guru to you.'

'What do you mean?' I asked.

'Don't you know?'

Yes, I thought I knew. Of course I knew. He too tuned with my beloved Surya. His was the only order of monks in India with the sun as main deity. Typically, Swamiji would say no more. Instead he questioned: 'What do you think of my watch?'

Denis and I had already noticed it. Gold, grand design, obviously very expensive.

'Did you wear that in the Himalayas?' I tried to joke, but a slight tone of disapproval colored my words.

'Very costly,' he went on, ignoring my judgmental attitude. Unsnapping the gold band and turning the watch over, he read out: 'Made in Switzerland'. Then he showed the brand name. 'Top quality,' he concluded proudly, in the manner of a *nouveau riche*. How could someone with his background make so much fuss about a mere watch? Besides, was he not an ascetic, vowed to simplicity?

The watch had been a gift from a wealthy devotee. Swamiji had not wanted to accept it but the man insisted, arguing that for the work in the West he would need a timepiece.

'But why such an extremely costly one?' I inquired. 'Doesn't it contradict your professed plain lifestyle?'

His devotee wanted him to have the best, he explained. 'Nothing is too good for the guru,' declared Swamiji, quoting the man's words. I took this as a direct hint. Several times already he had remarked that Westerners do not know how to treat a spiritual teacher.

Even if I too might have wanted to buy him the best of everything, I simply was not able to do so. I was skimming by financially, and the other member of the ashram, Denis, was still studying. Besides, it was probably beyond anyone's means to recompense at their true value the teachings Swami Purna could give.

Then Swamiji told that he was different from other people in his total detachment from anything material. He used the things which came his way, they did not use him. He had lived in a palace as well as in a cave, had eaten his food from plates of gold as well as from the palm of his own hand. In both circumstances he had maintained the same equilibrium, neither feeling superior in the royal abode nor inferior in the state of extreme simplicity. He did not judge his worth by outer trappings.

And, even if he had nothing, not even food to eat or water to drink, he could manage. I believed this. Had Annelies not informed us that Swamiji hardly ate? Very soon had food become of minor importance to me too. In Swamiji's company I was never hungry, at least my body did not require food.

Yet I certainly hungered for the solution of the guru question he had several times raised.

'Swamiji,' I dared to ask him one morning, 'if you are more than a guru to me, does that make you my Beloved?'

'I am also more than the Beloved to you,' he stated.

I was confounded. What can be more than a guru . . . and more than the Beloved . . . my other half?

This I had not expected. No, certainly not. Could it be true? Certainly I was fascinated by him. Denis had more than once shown his irritation at my not very nunlike glances in Swami Purna's direction.

A moment later he said, 'I can give you a great spiritual fruit, but I cannot be bound at the worldly level.'

'But aren't you above all restrictions?' I asked.

'For the mission, I cannot be around all the time,' he answered. He let me know that another of his titles is Parivrajakacharya, meaning 'the preceptor who is always on the move'.

One day, just after Swamiji had been for some time in the attic room, there came a slight tap on the front door.

Opening it, I saw Oma (Grandma) Mimi, my 80-year-old upstairs neighbor.

'Ooooh Surya!' she sang out. Her eyes looked much wider than usual and were glowing. '*De Heer, Onze Lieve Heer!*' ('The Lord, our Lovely Lord!'), she exclaimed, rapturous. 'I just saw Him!' Ecstasy possessed her.

I smiled, accustomed to Oma's visions of the Christ. Her husband, also in his eighties, had warned me, when I moved to the Lauriergracht a few years before, not to take Oma's religious ravings seriously. 'She is senile,' he confided, dismissing her occasional visitations as 'crazy'.

Today Oma, quivering with excitement, described that she just saw Jesus! She was hanging up the wash in the attic passage when, lo and behold, appeared a man with long hair and beard, dressed in white robes like an angel. Light shone all around him, a halo encircled his head. Before she could say anything, he had disappeared.

I hugged Oma affectionately and invited her in. Entering the apartment, she spotted Swamiji who was standing in the front room, the sun streaming in through the window and bouncing luminously off his white garment.

'Aaaaah!' Oma cried out, clasping her hands in delighted wonderment. Rushing to him, she threw herself at his feet. With a swift movement she removed the cross from her neck and handed it to him. Swamiji, showing good-hearted amusement, blew on it in blessing and gave it back. Oma kissed the cross fervently. All happened very quickly, with contagious joy.

'*Bidden, geven, helpen,*' she proclaimed jubilantly to Swamiji, now herself the teacher. 'Pray, give, help,' I translated for him from the Dutch. '*Alles gaat zoals God het wil.*' ('Everything happens according to God's will.')

'*Dag, lieve schat*' ('Goodbye, dear treasure'), she crooned, embracing me. '*Twee harten, een gedachte*' ('Two hearts, one thought').

In the rarefied atmosphere left behind by Oma Mimi, Swamiji said warmly that she was a very pure soul, with a child's innocence.

'And ye be as a little child and ye shall enter into the kingdom of God,' I quoted, upon which Swamiji commented she could have benefited greatly from having had a spiritual guide. I told that Oma suffered much mental abuse from her nonbelieving husband, who bossed her around unmercifully. She meekly did everything he ordered.

Swamiji pointed out that Oma's submission had in fact served her, because surrender is a necessary requirement for any *bhakta*, any faithful devotee. Concerning obedience, I could learn a lot from Oma. When he made such an issue of unremitting compliance to a guru's will, I wondered if my inborn independence would ever allow me to meet this requisite.

I was therefore anxious to deliver myself from this dangerous subject and redirected the conversation by asking him, 'Why exactly have you come to the West?'

'The life is a play,' answered Swami Purna in his characteristic style. 'Many things happen by themselves. You do one thing and out of it many things grow. There are reasons why I cannot define for you, at this stage, my purpose for being in Europe or America. You will come to know later on.

'But', he continued, 'much knowledge from our ancient India would help Westerners understand more about life.'

We were looking out of the window. On the other side of the canal sat an old man fishing. As casually as possible, I asked Swami Purna: 'When did you take sannyas?'

'Before India's independence,' he replied.

That meant prior to 1947? And before that he had studied in Europe, he told. Judging by his appearance, I would not have thought him more than 30. Where Ponce de Leon failed, had Swami Purna discovered the Fountain of Youth? When I expressed my surprise and asked again his age, he left the room.

Just then, as if for my solace, the sun peeped out from behind a cloud and winked at me. I was reminded. When I already had a guru who was truly ageless, why consider another? Compared to my dear sun, all other lights paled.

Enjoying What is Higher

A few evenings later, at the Kosmos Meditation Center, a small group assembled to hear Swami Purna. After I had introduced him as a 'high guy from the Himalayas', he chanted '*Om*', followed by a song in Sanskrit. His sweet devotional music tuned us all to the same chord.

Once more I saw we spoke a common language when he began: 'In fact, there is nothing that has to be learned. Everyone is a source, everything is complete. But we must be able to receive that message, or energy, from the source – which is within us.'

Quoting the 15th-century Indian mystic-poet Kabir, he recited: 'My Beloved was sitting just beside me, but I could not see him, because there was a veil.'

Explained Swamiji: 'The veil is ignorance and the things that take you down, which lower your mind and body. The Beloved is sitting there, but you do not see. Another saint said he himself was the veil, but he did not realize.'

After a short pause, Swamiji continued: 'The spiritual life, the life divine, is a development and progress until a completion or perfection is reached. This is described in various ways: realization of the Self or Self-realization, realization of God, *nirvana*, *mukti*, *moksha*. Our job is to know what we have to do, where we have to go and what we have to follow in order to complete our journey, to attain the mission which is already there.

'Spirituality, the highest development in life, is not a monopoly of any person, group, society, country. It is available like the sun, who does not prevent anyone to come but is for all. Spirituality is total advancement,' he emphasized. 'Total love, total peace, total perfection. Totality in love, in attitude, in behavior, in manner, in doing, in living. The totality of everything. Whether you achieve it or not, is a different question.'

Some of his sentences stayed very clearly in my mind.

'When a person does not understand the true meaning of *sukha*, happiness, he runs after *duhkha*, suffering. The body and the senses are not the final source of pleasure. Many people think that the body and senses are able to enjoy the fruits of life, but fruits decay.

'The only thing that never dies is *Atman*, the individual soul. It is part of the divine force powering the universe. Because the veil of ignorance covers truth, we think we are separate from the divine both within us and without. As we evolve from life to life, we come to the point where the veil is removed, and we experience our full Self.

'How to be with Atman – that is the main problem,' he continued. 'Sometimes when you are very calm, concentrated, peaceful and happy, you don't feel you are in your body. You feel you are somewhere else, and that you are something which cannot be harmed or destroyed. Such feelings help you understand you are near to Atman, getting the reflection of Atman.

'Atman, the immortal soul, is that which the sword cannot cut, the air cannot blow, the fire cannot burn. Death cannot reach Atman, it cannot be killed. If the human body is operated on, we find flesh, bones, blood and nothing else. It means that Atman has no form and no name, but it does exist, within and around the body. When the experiences of immortality begin, you understand you are near to or under the protection of Atman.'

I confess that I did not grasp all that Swamiji said, but he confirmed a knowledge inside me.

'True happiness belongs only to the immortal soul,' he went on. 'Pleasures enjoyed through the senses are but a tiny reflection of the bliss experienced in the highest spiritual state.'

Then he started to speak about *tantra yoga*, the use of the body to go beyond the body, a yogic path employing the sexual energy to intensify and raise consciousness. Tantra was a 'big subject', he declared.

'When there is physical union between a man and a woman, it creates pleasure,' he said. 'This sensation does not stay. Tantra is practiced for lasting happiness. The man and the woman do all physical things, but the motivation behind it is different. Tantra gives direction to the Shiv–Shakti energy present within each one of us. This is the energy of activating, creating and accelerating, which leads to total fulfillment of body, mind and spirit.

'Tantra is a way to fulfill all desire while being the complete witness,' he stated. 'In Sanskrit we call it *vadi sukh*, the sexual pleasure with awareness, where there is no falling off from where you are. Sex is transformed. As Lord Shiva told his wife Parvati: "The highest creation of this body is life, and it is very near the Atman." The highest pleasures of spiritually transformed sex in tantra can be compared to the pleasure of the immortal soul.'

Tantra, as a medium for spiritual growth, had a great tradition in India. It was a legitimate path. One could reach ultimate communion through *trigunatit*, confluence of body, mind and spirit. But unless the prerequisites and conditions of tantra were met, it could result in suffering.

'Tantra has always remained underground, to prevent its misuse for the fulfillment of lower desires,' Swami Purna explained. 'Because tantra deals with the highest energy, it must be practiced only under the guidance of a competent teacher.'

We also heard that in ancient India, about 2500 B.C. every baby was planned and conceived consciously. Conception had to take place on a certain date, at the right time, with much preparation, purification and prayers. People today do not understand the life, he said, and therefore produce children out of ignorance, even when there is love. The more conscious the man and the woman are when they come together to conceive a new life, the more evolved can be the incarnating soul they attract.

My heart flowed over with admiration for this exceptional man, who possessed the wisdom others still sought. With every passing day I was more and more looking up to Swami Purna, there on his elevated heights. I believed I was entering hallowed domains. I had risen, rather than fallen, in love – or so I imagined. Still I wondered, would my sentiments be the same were he a shriveled up elderly guru with thinning hair? That question, however, was hypothetical, because Swamiji corresponded quite agreeably to my aesthetic values.

The discourse ended, he invited our questions. Silence ensued until someone declared: 'It's so hard to find a question!'

'Yes,' agreed Swamiji. 'If we listen carefully, so many answers are given. In my life, especially during sojourns in the Himalayas, Tibet and other parts of the world, I encountered many high beings. I lived with them, listened to them, observed them. They could take questions into their mind and give an answer indirectly, as part of their discourse. When they had something to tell, they rarely did it in words. Things just developed. So many answers were given by their actions.'

Was this a clue for me about his method of teaching?

He looked around. 'So, no questions?' he asked, grinning.

'How's the tea?' inquired a young man.

'All right,' replied Swamiji. 'I am drinking, yet I do not know whether it is hot or cold, salty or sweet. My consciousness is elsewhere, I am so much tuned with you. There is no desire in my mind for this tea. That is detachment. I just hold the cup and drink.'

'If you do not realize and do not enjoy, why do you drink?' persisted the questioner.

'This tea will work in my body, it will have an effect even if I do not consciously enjoy it,' answered Swamiji. 'I am enjoying something which is higher, more important than this.'

Someone asked how to solve the problems of life.

'There are actually no problems except those we create,' responded Swamiji. 'If you think there are so many problems in life, they will happen. I do not have problems. Whatever people around me are doing, I do not suffer. I behave in such a way that, from my side, there is nothing wrong. I am always mindful, always careful about my own acts and thoughts.'

Then he requested us to meditate on the thing we liked most.

'Suppose you like something,' he began. 'Eventually the idea will come that you don't give so much value to it, there is something more essential. Then you are bound to think of that, and after it of what you like even better, until you come to the next. In your thoughts you circle until at last you zoom in on your real entity.

'Now concentrate on the most valuable thing in your life, on what you like most. Please close your eyes and between your eyebrows try to see your lover, your husband, some person you respect highly, a flower, a tree, Himalaya, Krishna, Christ, Muhammad, whoever or whatever. As soon as you have the habit to concentrate, you will easily do so on your entity. It is a process.'

A short period of silence was followed by our saying aloud with Swamiji: '*Sri Ram Sri Ram Sri Ram Sri Ram, Jai Ram Jai Ram Jai Ram Jai Ram.*'

The repetition of sacred syllables creates an environment able to assist people to attune more easily to higher vibrations, he said. Sound has effect; so does the chanting of mantras. He explained that *Jai* is Sanskrit for 'victory', whereas the *Ram* keeps the mind focused on Rama, the seventh incarnation of Vishnu.

Swamiji mentioned that Rama's life and exploits are related in the ancient Sanskrit epic *Ramayana*, 'The Career of Rama'. In the 16th-century Hindi-language adaptation by Tulsi Das, the *Ramacharitamanas*, 'The Sacred Lake of Rama's Deeds', emphasis is laid on duty to one's neighbors and on the doctrine of universal friendship.

Rama is also a personification of the highest evolved self. Rama, said Swamiji, means 'one who is always present, within you and without'.

As the evening progressed, the group converted into a small congregation.

'It's a spiritual law,' said Swamiji. 'What you think, you create. So instead of making problems for yourself, you can create a super or supra environment by repeating a mantra, preferably in silence, without moving the lips, as often as you can remember it, no matter what you are doing at that moment.

'When I think of something, the content comes to me,' he went on. 'Suppose I think of light, then light comes to me.'

He was addressing this to me, I knew. In an indirect manner he let me understand why it was important for me to continue contemplating the sun.

'Suppose I think of the sun, then the light of the spiritual sun behind the physical one will come to me,' he said. 'Even the spiritual sun is only a symbol for Atman, the immortal soul, which has no name and no form.'

Swami Purna's next statement confirmed again that our spiritual task is multifold.

'It is the duty of our time to prove that everyone has the divine seed as well as the possibility to bring it to bloom,' he asserted. 'Provided people are ready to open up, they can discover the treasure of the divinity within.'

The Mysterious Departure

It was Swami Purna's last evening in Amsterdam. Moving from subject to subject in our usual attempt to straitjacket God into the limitation of words and ideas, we could once more not find an end to our talks. Stimulated by the impending departure, so many questions arose that we finally stayed up the entire night. Swamiji, who never betrayed tiredness, patiently answered all we could ask on philosophical lines while sweeping aside our enquiries of personal nature. During intermissions, Denis prepared tea and I typed up Swamiji's last-minute letters.

With my minimum of sleep and little food for almost one week, the pain of Swamiji's leave-taking began to affect my reason. Denis observed my demonstrative fluttering about Swami Purna with resentment, irritated by my intoxication. Taking me aside for a moment, he reprimanded me severely. From the beginning he had not liked the closeness that naturally existed between Swamiji and me, and he lost no opportunity to try and keep me away from him. Nevertheless, he had to admit that, in Swamiji's presence, he also felt high.

There was not much time left for reforming, as several instructions still had to be passed on and certain explanations repeated for the tape recorder.

'This is Surya,' I announced gaily into the microphone when we had once more gathered in the living room, 'and I am looking at... what is your name, Sir?'

'Swaniji,' he said, giggling at the pet name I had made from his title Srimat Paramahansa, 'the divine swan, who is ever discriminating, who sees clearly the right thing'. When he had told that this was another meaning for *swami*, the sobriquet 'Swaniji' had spontaneously sailed from my lips. Sometimes I called him as well 'Rama', a name he had invited me to use in private.

Soon my Rama repeated, as an aid for my memory, the explanations about my Indian experiences which he had given me the first evening.

A moment later he picked up an orange marking pen and began writing on my white living room wall.

'This is *Om*', he said.

'What does *Om* really mean?' I asked.

'Three things: the sky, the earth, the other planets. *Om* means the creation, preservation and destruction which leads to re-creation. It is the symbol of the Almighty or the Source, the complete cosmos or the source of the cosmos. Everything is inside *Om*. It is the most universally accepted symbol of Hinduism and even other Eastern philosophies have adopted it.'

He went on writing, in Sanskrit.

'Now this is *Om Suryah Namah*, the praising of the sun. I bow down to Surya, that is *Suryah Namah*. I bow down, I praise, I call on Surya who is equal to *Om* and is the center of power and light.'

At my request, he affixed his signature, 'Swami Purna', as well in Indian script.

'What do you want now?' he asked, checking the hour on his gold watch. That object of our contention, by the way, was eventually given by Swamiji to one of his devotees. In fact it struck me that, unlike other leaders, Swami Purna never used ornaments on his body, not even spiritual symbols or rosaries. Neither did he wear any cloth except simple, unstitched cotton and plain woolen shawls.

I reminded Swamiji that he had not yet told the sequence of the hatha yoga exercises he advised me to do every morning.

'Lie on the carpet,' he said, 'and relax comfortably. Loosen all the joints–' The phone rang.

'Annelies, calling from Bonn,' Denis informed us from the other room. Swamiji excused himself.

When he returned, a good 15 minutes later, I was amazed that he resumed exactly the same sentence he had been pronouncing before we were interrupted. He executed several *asanas*, postures patterned and named after certain animals and plants for the forms and qualities they represented, and promised me photographs of himself demonstrating them, as a boost for my practice.

Denis reminded us of the time and I hurried to ask my last questions.

'What is the purpose of *Om Suryah Namah*?'

'With it,' he replied, 'you evoke a whole picture and remembrance of the sun and *Om*, and are affected by all their positive qualities. The mantra reminds you, concentrates you on that. Whether you concentrate on the physical sun or on the sun which is formless, pure light, it helps you in so many ways.'

'How, for instance?'

He acted annoyed, perhaps only to show me his displeasure at my wanting an example for something so evident. Nevertheless, he gave an answer: 'As I said at the Kosmos, when I think of something, the content comes to me. Suppose I think of light, then light comes to me. If you think of any person, his or her vibration will come to you, you receive something from that person. This is a science.

'So anyone interested in spiritual development is advised to concentrate on the higher things, whether it is Krishna, Moses, Buddha, Christ, Muhammad or whichever high being or guru most appeals to him.'

'What will happen then?'

'The influence of that being will come to him, of course!' snapped Swamiji. 'Suppose a high being stays with you,' he specified in a gentler tone, 'something comes to you of how he talks, moves, his vibration, his whole mixture. So you are influenced, perhaps impressed, and try to follow what he does so he'll be pleased with you, and when he's away, you do the same.'

Was he telling me to think of him after he left Amsterdam? How could I not?

Here ended the final session in our week-long seminar and we prepared to leave. I alone was to escort His Holiness to the airport because Denis had to attend university.

As our bus speeded towards Swamiji's plane, the quaint historic streets of Amsterdam were quickly replaced by endless stretches of highway. He sat next to the window, engrossed in thought, glancing only occasionally at the flat Dutch landscape.

I, too, found words futile, though inside me the repetition of '*Om Suryah Namah, Om Suryah Namah*' built to a crescendo, supporting my prayers that Swami Purna might stay longer in Amsterdam. To follow the Mother's teaching of 'no preferences' was no easy task. I just had never met anyone like Swami Purna.

For all his perplexing ways, he was a master who offered prospects of new spiritual heights and could guide my journey to God. But Swami Purna had made it clear I could not always be around him.

Why not, O God, why not? As much as I understood, my heart had difficulties in accepting the facts.

'O Surya,' I besought, 'why can't I be with him all of the time?'

'Non-attachment,' came the answer.

I remembered that whatever was happening in the present had its antecedents in the past. There was nothing to do but to accept, gracefully, the workings of karma. What a hard lesson!

At the airport, Swamiji checked in and went through customs. In those days, before terrorism made flying a nerve-racking round of security procedures, I was allowed to accompany him beyond passport control.

Many passengers were already boarding the plane. Because of the crowd, we decided to wait until the line dwindled. I just wanted to remain in his presence as long as possible. By the time we were sitting together in the departure lounge of his flight OO6Y for New Delhi via Bombay, I had totally resigned myself to our separation.

'Well, have to go now,' he said as the last persons disappeared through the departure door. Free and unbound as Swamiji was, he surprised me with the statement: 'Don't think that this situation does not bring me pain. That is always one result of attachment. To have the *sukh*, the pleasure, one must also accept the *duhkh*, the sorrow.'

'I know.'

'But I am always with you.'

'And I am with you,' I responded.

'That is the duty of the sun,' he said kindly.

I smiled and brought my clasped palms, in prayerlike position, to my chest. This traditional Hindu greeting of *namaskar*, used at both meeting and parting, silently expresses: 'I honor the light within you.' He returned my salutation with a blessing and walked away. I lingered, retaining the last glimpses of him. He was like no one I had ever known.

At the gate, a hostess motioned Swamiji to stand aside. What was going on? Unperturbed, he shrugged his shoulders as I rejoined him. His manner told me to remain quiet. Strangely enough, I felt like a co-conspirator in some unwinding plot.

Passengers rushed by, heading towards the plane. The door closed with irrevocable finality.

Another hostess checking ticket carbons declared: 'There is no seat left for him,' and asked for Swamiji's baggage tags.

Meanwhile, Swamiji and I did not say a word. Life is a play, was this not what he professed?

A woman stepped over to us apologizing, 'It's all very regrettable, but nothing can be done.'

'But what happened?' I queried.

Sighing, she answered: 'I don't know. When we saw Mr. Swami Purna was not present in the departure lounge, we issued a call for him over the loudspeaker. When he did not respond, and we saw no other person in the lounge except you,' and she nodded in my direction, 'we gave the seat to someone who urgently had to go to India.'

'Swamiji needed urgently to go to India too,' I protested, repeating Swamiji's words that on Sunday he was to open a conference in Bombay.

'Bombay? Then why did he have his bags tagged for Delhi?' she asked.

I turned to Swamiji. 'I don't have to account for my actions,' he said curtly, not looking at the woman and addressing himself only to me. 'I have a confirmed reservation, my luggage was taken, a boarding pass was issued.'

With curiosity I asked the woman: 'Why do you say that you saw only me in the departure lounge? Didn't you notice Swami Purna sitting next to me?'

'No,' she replied, and before she could say anything else, the controller called her away.

Swamiji laughed mischievously, like a playful Krishna.

'You see, I have used my yogic powers to make myself invisible,' he said with a chuckle, 'because I must stay in Amsterdam with you some time longer.'

'What about the conference?' I asked, mystified.

'It can be held next week too,' he answered, making me wonder even more what was going on, though from his behavior I had an inkling of the cause.

An attendant brought the luggage, telling us that Mr. Purna could not be put on another plane until next Wednesday, all flights being fully booked.

Not for a moment had I imagined that, on my bus ride back to the city, Swami Purna would be at my side, engaging me in happy conversation. During the journey he mentioned he had a special air ticket. He had to fly today or the ticket would have lost its validity, except if the airlines rescheduled the flight, as actually happened.

At my house, I rang the front bell. 'Swamiji back!' I shouted out joyfully. Denis, who had returned from the university, rushed down and took the baggage out of our hands.

'It's all right,' giggled Swamiji.

Upstairs, we told the whole story and Swamiji instructed me to draft a letter of complaint to the airlines.

'Why?' I asked.

'A matter of justice,' he replied. 'They should know that passengers are treated this way. What sort of beginning is this for someone's trip? Do you realize I was not offered any accommodation or expense costs for the extra days I must stay in Amsterdam because of their mistake? Suppose I was a low-budget traveler?'

'Swamiji, we would be busy writing letter after letter if we want to amend all the injustices in the world.'

'What do you think we should do?' Swamiji asked, turning to Denis.

'What about the woman not seeing you, and your comment to Surya about having used yogic powers to make yourself invisible?' he responded. 'Well, I understand. The ticket could be extended only when there was a fault on their side.'

On the evening of our reprieve, reassembled in our small, cosy study circle, a heightened affectionate familiarity connected the three of us.

When Swamiji started to speak, he compared God's creation to a big machine and all of us to instruments who have to fit into God's master plan, 'the Plan which is actually already planned'. This concept had become commonplace enough to me, but Swamiji knew, when he wanted, how to bring the abstract into understandable, concrete reality.

'So we should not make plans,' he said. 'Five-year plans, ten-year plans . . . .' We laughed.

'It is not a plan, something final that we make,' he went on, 'but a program, which is necessary for life.'

Checking to see that we followed, he explained further: 'On Wednesday we will go to the airport, where I will fly off for India.

But do not get attached to this plan, to what we have thought to do. Keep it a program. Otherwise it becomes a plan and you will suffer again and again when things don't work out in this exact way.'

As long as we have desire, he reminded us, we are subject to birth, death and rebirth. Nothing can break this cycle, unless we know the clue, the formula. And that, he pronounced seriously, 'is to fit into The Plan'.

Fitting into The Plan

The rest of Swamiji's visit affected me as strongly as had the first part. Going far beyond the limits of usual conversation, we continued staying up very late, analyzing the human condition with the aid of Indian philosophy, and discussing and devising utopias.

Swamiji took a keen interest in my writing. The article in progress on Sri Aurobindo and the Mother received his complimentary remarks as well as perceptive insights which improved the text while encouraging my beginner's attempts at treating spiritual subjects. His willingness to look at future manuscripts signaled to me that, most likely, I would do more in this field. In fact, he suggested that I now concentrate only on spiritual writings, and on meeting spiritual teachers of all kinds.

'This will help train you in spiritual matters and give you the skill to recognize who is who and what is what in the spiritual realm,' he said, adding: 'Then you will know me better.'

Into our crowded program a top priority was assigned to Swamiji's correspondence. He had a seemingly bottomless briefcase which, similar to a magician's top hat, always produced new letters for answering. It became my duty to compose and type his messages and mail them to addresses all over the world.

One evening he sat before the gas heater in the living room, gazing into its flames. 'A body without arms and legs cannot do the required work,' he declared cryptically.

Again he stated that he and I were bound together by a special tie. I had a certain number of years to finish my mission, and he would assist me. At its completion he would take *mahasamadhi*: end his life voluntarily in a deep yogic trance. Before consciously leaving his body by his own will, we would travel together to the

Himalayas where he would transmit all his knowledge to me. By then I would be better prepared to receive than in the case of my Indian experiences, which had overwhelmed and unbalanced me.

'Keep contemplating the sun,' he instructed. When I thought of or talked with the sun, I had to be aware of the Supreme Transcendence behind the veil of material existence.

During these days Swamiji gave me an actual glimpse of the subtle dimensions.

One afternoon he wanted to join Denis' food shopping expedition while I had to stay behind and work on the correspondence. As I sat at the desk typing away, my thoughts traveled for a moment from Swamiji's letter to the natural foods store in the nearby Berenstraat. I imagined Swamiji looking at all the goods on sale and Denis purchasing fresh vegetables for our dinner, when suddenly the downstairs bell rang.

The marketing could hardly have finished so soon, and no visitor was expected. Raising the window next to my desk, I leaned out and looked into the street below. There stood Swamiji, all alone. Immediately I went to open the door.

After I had advanced no more than a few steps, I saw Swamiji already standing before me, inside the apartment. How had he moved up the stairs so quickly? Had he flown? And how had he opened the downstairs door, not to mention the apartment door?

Quite startled, I heard myself asking: 'Denis gave you the keys?'

'No,' answered Swamiji.

'Then how have you entered?' I queried. 'The door was locked, and so was the one below.'

'Didn't you see?' he asked back.

A big smile crossed my face. 'You mean you really walked through the closed door?'

'Do you have any tea?' came his next question, and then he went to the living room, settling himself into his imperial throne on my floor cushions.

After awhile Denis returned. The keys were still in his possession. Familiar with stories about the *siddhis*, the supernatural powers attained by certain yogis, he accepted the amazing possibility that Swami Purna had indeed passed through the locked door and had materialized himself before me. He reported that Swamiji had left him at the food shop, saying he would find his way to the Lauriergracht on his own. 'Surya can open the door for me,' he had told Denis.

Of course with this miraculous appearance Swami Purna had given us a message, but at that time neither of us had any idea what it was.

Whether the happenings with Swamiji were unusual or mundane, the days passed quickly. By Wednesday I was able to accept being separated from him far more easily than on the original departure date. The additional time together strengthened my conviction that I was indeed to progress in a kind of unofficial, free-styled *sannyas*.

Swamiji would fly to London, changing there for New Delhi. We were early enough for his plane, but what a shock I got when I phoned for a taxi and heard there was a one-hour strike.

Seemingly upset, Swamiji rushed us out of the house. His insinuations that it was all my fault assailed my ears all the way to the bus stop. I could not believe that my wish to have him stay longer had created the taxi strike and, not excluding that once more he was merely acting, I had difficulty in taking his anger seriously. Had I not already witnessed that, to all appearances, nothing discomposed him? Yet if he were acting, for what reason?

As we waited for the bus, I said: 'If everything is the divine will, then there is nothing to get upset about, is there? We simply have to accept. Whatever is, just is.'

'Remember this when a situation comes up that does not please you,' he responded.

At the airport he strode rapidly towards the airlines counter. I followed behind, pushing the baggage trolley. At the check-in counter the attendant informed him: 'Final boarding was ten minutes ago.'

I said nothing, a silent spectator of the latest twist in the fairytale of Prince Swami Swaniji in Amsterdam. His flight once more was re-routed. This time he would travel to India via Paris, leaving the next day, 21 February. The birthday of the Mother! And she was born in Paris!

I counted back. He had arrived in the late afternoon of 9 February and was now to leave in the early afternoon of 21 February. This made twelve days – of course, the number of the sun. Tomorrow he would definitely depart, of that I was sure.

Back at the Lauriergracht, Denis again rushed down for the baggage, this time expressing no surprise. We exchanged knowing glances, and I was curious what the additional hours would bring.

True to his unpredictable style, Swamiji spent the day in

complete withdrawal, hardly speaking. He ate none of the food we placed before him, he only sipped tea. His sulky behavior caused me to see him in another light.

Why did he drop mysterious clues about his age and supposed noble background, for example, and then evade giving specific details? Why did I sometimes mistrust his words? Doubts outbalanced my positive thoughts about him.

The next morning I asked Swamiji's pardon for not accompanying him to the airport. He made no comment and behaved totally undisturbed while I arranged for a taxi, which arrived promptly. Giving the driver the fare for the ride and full instructions on where to bring Swamiji, I saw him off. As the car pulled away, an exalting wave of freedom came over me.

Soon afterwards I questioned myself, whether my recent thoughts of Swami Purna had not been too negative, and whether he had purposely instigated them in me to enable an easier parting on my side. Urgently I had to hear his voice.

Desperately I placed a call to the airport in Paris and entreated the airlines personnel to page him. He had to be there still, waiting for his connection to New Delhi. 'Please give him the message to contact Amsterdam,' I implored.

Eventually, to my relief, the telephone rang.

'It's me,' said Swami Purna.

'I need you,' I told him.

Aftereffects

Rather than signifying the end of our story, the departure of Swami Purna initiated a new series of unusual occurrences related to his visit.

In the next weeks I found myself moving my arms and hands as he had done. From time to time I tied my hair into a knot at the crown of my head, Shiva style, following Swamiji's occasional fashion. Frequently some of his expressions appeared on my face and I heard his voice in my mind. Was this Swamiji, communing with me from afar?

At the same time, I would see him. Not outside me. It was rather a feeling, inside. At those moments his face merged with mine. Had I become one with him? I remembered he had said that when we think of someone, the person's vibrations could come. Or did his continued influence result simply from our close association during 12 days?

Denis also was talking like Swamiji, and using the same gestures. We both guessed that Swami Purna must have an energy able to influence and change people around him, but Denis questioned whether this energy was beneficial or not. Having received a decidedly negative judgment from a clairvoyant woman to whom he had shown Swamiji's photo, he urged me to dissociate myself from him.

When the intensity of my 12 days with Swami Purna had lessened, I saw him primarily as another intermediary. My relation with the sun was greater and longer-lasting. I recognized anew that the living sun of light, knowledge and consciousness was my main teacher.

As I gained more and more distance from the involvement with Swami Purna, I began reconsidering some of his statements, especially about my having a certain planetary mission. I had tried to look into Swamiji's mind, to uncover his thoughts and motives, but without success. Could all his assertions be true?

Whatever confusion he left behind, Swami Purna's visit had confirmed that my experiences in India had been real and part of a master plan outlined for me. The name Surya belonged to it.

Swami Purna's stay had other results as well. As after my return from India, I had a deep need for solitude, and Denis went to live for some time at his mother's house.

To my surprise, in that period I hardly ever felt hunger. My food was uncooked and comprised minute portions of fruit, nuts, cheese, yogurt and milk. I completely stopped drinking coffee, black tea and other stimulating beverages because they clearly upset my system. Having become so sensitive that the touch of any cloth on my skin caused discomfort, I began walking around the apartment naked, like a yogini in a cave. Although the cold Dutch winter still exercised its power, I turned off my room heater, having no need for it.

I also experienced that all objects had their own vibration, some positive, causing a pleasant sensation in me, others not. Certain vibrations pricked me like needles, producing pain. Wishing for an absolutely clear and undisturbed environment, I packed away all decorative and non-functional items and covered the bookshelves with bedsheets.

My records remained unturned and the TV set stayed neglected in its corner. Neither music nor any sounds of nature could compete with the flapping birds' wings, buzzing bees and other low- and high-pitched tones playing within me.

After my evening meditation I lay down to sleep, but every morning I had the impression I had been awake all night. Curiously enough, I was never sleepy nor tired. A limitless energy activated me.

Diana phoned and expressed concern with my latest news. The Dutch winter climate was too damp and cold for an uncooked diet, she said. I was not in the Himalayas, I had to come down to earth and return to this reality.

One afternoon when Denis visited me, he proposed we go out and sit under a tree in the Vondel Park. On the way I soon experienced that I was floating above the ground, literally walking on air.

As we crossed the busy Leidseplein, one of Amsterdam's main

squares, a host of noises battered me, as if I was standing in front of the blasting loudspeakers at a rock concert. When I doubled up in agony, Denis hailed a taxi and took me back home.

A few days later he informed me that the Sufi mystic Pir Vilayat Inayat Khan would be coming to Amsterdam to speak at the Kosmos. He was known to be able to 'see' people with his inner eye. Denis suggested I try to meet Pir Vilayat since he might be able to answer my questions and help me pass more easily through my present state.

I phoned Noor McGuigan, Pir's disciple who was helping to organize his Holland visit, and requested a *darshan*.

In this period Swami Purna wrote from Delhi, advising: 'You should continue to do whatever you are doing at present and should not get disappointed . . . . You have to develop till perfection and know your true identity. Once you know yourself, your suffering will be over. You should concentrate and meditate between six and seven in the morning and receive messages. I will be sending these messages.'

Consulting the Sufi Mystic
Pir Vilayat Inayat Khan

The prospect of meeting Pir Vilayat Inayat Khan became my bridge back into the world. My inquiring mind wanted to know what Sufism was, and in search of understanding I visited the Kosmos library. There I could borrow books on esoteric subjects unavailable at most shops or public libraries in those days.

My reading told me that although the word *Sufism* was first used in 8th-century Arabia, the mystical phenomenon of Sufism traced back much further, to the mystery schools of ancient Egypt and Persia. Over the years its chain of transmission moved through esoteric orders like the Essenes, in the time of Jesus, and the White Brotherhoods in which the Prophet Muhammad found his teacher. As it evolved, Sufi thought integrated ideas from Jewish and Christian mysticism, Indian philosophy and Buddhism.

Lacking dogmas, scriptures, an ecclesiastical hierarchy or a holy city, Sufism is neither a religion nor a cult but a path of illumination, usually said to be the mystical side of Islam.

The term *Sufi* refused to be neatly pinned down. Perhaps it derived from the Arabic word for 'wool', signifying the coarse material used by early Muslim ascetics for their robes, or else it stemmed from the Arabic word for 'purity'. It could as well have originated from the same root as the Greek *sophia*, meaning 'divine wisdom'.

To me the latter definition seemed most appropriate as my mini-study indicated Sufism to be a knowledge about life gained mainly from within, transmitting the same truths as those upon which all religions are based. Although aware that mystical revelation can never be put into words, the *murshid*, the Sufi master, tries to pass along something of his experience and understanding to the *mureed*, the student, with an aim to uplift and enlighten him or her. Devotional singing, the chanting of God's names, controlled breathing exercises and whirling dance are some of the methods used to induce higher states of consciousness.

Sufism remained an esoteric stream in the Islamic world until this century when a contemporary, expanded form of it was introduced to the West by Hazrat Inayat Khan, the father of Pir Vilayat. Born in India in 1882, Hazrat Inayat Khan gave up a promising career as a performer of Indian classical music and song when he discovered the true purpose of his life in the spiritual path of Sufism.

> *To serve God, one must sacrifice the dearest thing, and I sacrificed my music, the dearest thing to me . . . . I played the vina until my heart turned into this same instrument; then I offered this instrument to the Divine Musician, the only Musician existing. Since then I have become His flute and when He chooses He plays His Music.*[8]

The Sufism that Hazrat Inayat Khan eventually started to teach, bore the distinctive touch of his own inspiration and originality. 'Now if I do anything,' he wrote, 'it is to tune souls instead of instruments, to harmonize people instead of notes. . . . One must put oneself in harmony with oneself and with others. I have found in every word a certain musical value, a melody in every thought, harmony in every feeling, and I have tried to interpret the same thing with clear and simple words to those who used to listen to my music.'[9]

At the request of his murshid, Hazrat Inayat Khan brought Sufism to the United States in 1910 and later to Europe. For the next 17 years he traveled widely, teaching the 'Sufi Message of Spiritual Liberty', as he called it.

'The Sufi message is a reminder,' he said, '. . . . of the truth taught by all the great teachers of humanity: that God, truth, religion are one, and that duality is only a delusion.'[10] Human evolution was approaching a new phase of consciousness, he declared. If not by religion then by science, the human race would be led to recognize the unity behind all things and all beings.

'The solution to the problem of the day', he asserted, 'is the awakening of the consciousness of humanity to the divinity in man.'[11]

To assist in this process, Hazrat Inayat Khan founded the Sufi

Order in London in 1916. That same year he and his American wife welcomed the birth of their first son, Vilayat. Their daughter Noorunnissa (known as Noor) had been born two years earlier, and in 1917 arrived their second son, Hidayat, followed later on by a fourth child named Khairunnissa.

In 1920 Hazrat Inayat Khan established the International Sufi Movement in Geneva, incorporating the Sufi Order of London into it. At about that time he moved with his family to the Paris suburb of Suresnes, which then became a main center of Sufi activity.

'Sufism means to know one's true being, to know the purpose of one's life, and to know how to accomplish that purpose,' summed up Hazrat Inayat Khan.[12] 'The teaching of Sufism is to transform everyday life into a religion, so that every action may bear some spiritual fruit.'[13]

The Sufi, he stated, has only one desire:

> *The seeker after truth goes out into the world and he finds innumerable different sects and religions. He does not know where to start. Then he desires to find out what is hidden under these sects, these different religions, and he begins to seek the object which he wishes to gain through wisdom. Wisdom is a veil over truth, and even wisdom cannot be called truth. God alone is truth, and it is truth that is God. And truth can neither be studied nor taught nor learned; it is to be touched, it is to be realized; and it can be realized by the unfoldment of the heart.*[14]

Steeped as he was in the universalism of the mystic, Hazrat Inayat Khan regarded as unfortunate the sectarian stance of most religions and declared that the main objective of his movement was to work for unity. Wishing to bring people closer together in a deeper understanding of life, fostering respect for all beliefs, scriptures and teachers, he created the Universal Worship. During this devotional service, candles are lit for each of the world's major faiths and selections are read from their sacred books. This reminds us that while the externals of every religion may differ, the light at their inner core is identical.

Hazrat Inayat Khan died at the age of 44 but his teachings continue to live. His mission has been carried on by two esoteric schools directly inspired by his message: the Sufi Movement International nowadays led by Murshid Hidayat Inayat Khan, and the Sufi Order International guided by Pir Vilayat Inayat Khan.

Another offshoot is the Sufi Islamia Ruhaniat Society founded by Murshid Samuel Lewis (1896–1971), an American-born Sufi who was initiated by Hazrat Inayat Khan in 1926. Murshid Lewis created a dynamic and joyful form of group meditation called 'Dances of Universal Peace', wherein participants perform sacred dances, in a moving circle, while reciting the different names of God.

In 1990 the two sons of Hazrat Inayat Khan participated in an inauguration ceremony at Suresnes marking the completion of the Universel, the Temple of All Religions, for which their father had laid the foundation stone in 1926. A temple of light, silent contemplation and worship for all, the Universel is dedicated to the memory of Noor Inayat Khan. Hazrat Inayat Khan's elder daughter gave her life for her ideal in 1944, when she was executed at Dachau for her work in the British resistance.

The essence of the Sufism taught by Hazrat Inayat Khan is that love is God and the highest heaven is none other than our own loving heart. To Hazrat Inayat Khan, and his successors, Sufism is basically an attainment rather than a philosophy, an inspiration more than a study. As Hazrat Inayat Khan wrote:

> The Sufi's God is his divine ideal to whom he attributes all that is good and beautiful in its perfection; and he himself stands before Him in humility realizing his imperfection, being a soul, free to roam the heavens, now captive on earth in the physical body. His aim in life is to release the captive soul from the bondage of limitations, which he accomplishes by the repetition of the sacred names of God, and by constant thought of his divine ideal, and an ever-increasing love for the divine Beloved until the beloved God with His perfection becomes manifest to his vision, and his imperfect self vanishes from his sight.[15]

Over the years the message of Hazrat Inayat Khan has been transmitted by various Western Sufis including his two sons, each in their own unique way. Murshid Hidayat Inayat Khan, a classical violinist and composer by profession, puts his emphasis on passing along the exact Sufi practices and ceremonies which had initially been given by his father. He considers them an important key for unlocking the spiritual storehouse within. 'There is no such thing as becoming spiritual,' he says. 'All of us are born spiritual, but we do not know it. Spirituality is not developed, it is discovered.'[16]

Vilayat Inayat Khan, while following the path indicated by his father, has become a teacher in his own right, having an own philosophy and original teaching style. From childhood trained in Sufism, he also studied at the Sorbonne and at Oxford before serving as an officer in the British Royal Air Force during the Second World War. After the war he broadened his spiritual understanding by orienting himself in diverse esoteric traditions and by making intensive retreats amongst ascetics in India and the Middle East. At the completion of a 40-day fast the title Pir, 'spiritual teacher', was conferred upon him by the same Chistia Sufi Order of India to which his father had belonged.

As a teacher Pir Vilayat has always tried to help people attune their consciousness to that higher level where they can touch upon the origin of all. He expressed this clearly in his book *Towards the One*: 'Let us bear in mind that our purpose is not the curiosity of experience, but the resultant transformation of ourselves.'[17]

On the evening of his discourse the Kosmos overflowed with an enthusiastic crowd. Most of us were in our thirties and, in the style of those days, colorfully dressed. Denis and I greeted Noor McGuigan.

'The gods are smiling on you,' she said to me warmly. 'Pir will give you *darshan* tonight, after the meeting.'

During the ensuing conversation she also mentioned that *Noor* is Arabic for 'light'. She received this name from Pir Vilayat upon her initiation into the Sufi Order.

When Pir Vilayat entered the assembly room, many people rose in respect and greeted him with the traditional Indian *namaskar*. A few persons saluted him in the Islamic way.

Dressed in flowing brown robes, with his white beard and long grey hair brushed back, Pir made a striking appearance.

As he spoke, in a halting style ornamented with many long words revealing his gift for language, I was amazed to hear repeated references to the sun and the Buddha. Several times he looked in my direction. He intimated so many of my present preoccupations that I felt he was speaking especially for me.

After his introduction Pir guided us in a meditation aimed to 'take us beyond our body and mind, to our eternal Self'. He spoke about our 'getting free to be the person we were born to become, and having the courage to be it'. We had to see our life as an evolution of our eternal Self. What he said touched directly on what was still puzzling me about my higher identity.

The public part of the evening concluded, Neeltje de Haan,

another of Pir's students, led me upstairs to a small attic room. Her sweetness helped ease my tension. While igniting the gas heater she commented that I was very lucky, several people had been denied a *darshan* because of limited time.

Neeltje left, and I arranged a rug and two cushions to create a cosy effect. Near the cushion intended for Pir I placed a rose I had brought, along with a packet of incense. Giving incense to spiritual teachers, I had learned from Swami Purna, symbolizes the spreading of their message.

Minutes ticked by, allowing my uninterrupted repetition of the Surya mantra, which never failed to calm me. The attunement with Pir Vilayat during his lecture gave me the hope that his mystical background and knowledge would lead me out of my dilemma towards clarity.

At long last he arrived, smiling and bowing his head to me. Then he brought his palms together in *namaskar*. I smiled as well and returned the greeting, moved by his humble demeanor and openness. Would I be granted, through the venerable Pir as a messenger, a further unveiling of the unseen?

As he sat down, closed his eyes and withdrew inwardly, I shut my eyes too.

After some time he requested me to open my eyes again and asked: 'Do you speak English?' I nodded.

When he began telling me I had been through a lot which I did not understand, I knew he could see into me. He continued: 'You try to understand with the mind, but there are things we cannot comprehend like this. You have always tried to see the meaning in all that happens, but now you can't see it, and it has almost tested your faith. At times you have doubted.'

Pir went on, slowly and kindly, as I set into motion my internal tape recorder. How ironic that I had to go to another person to see more clearly the central truths of the enigma called 'myself'.

'You must have courage,' he said. 'You will need a lot of courage, but you have it. You have so much you don't even let yourself feel pain and suffering. Because of your courage you don't know how much pain you have experienced.'

We were looking directly into each other's eyes.

'You are getting ready to leave the worldly path,' Pir told me. 'For you, the time of the sannyasin is coming. And, in detaching yourself from everything, you will find your real freedom.'

His remarks thrilled me because they confirmed certain

conclusions I had come to by myself.

'This freedom will let you really express yourself,' Pir elaborated, 'especially in a creative way. Express your ideal creatively. That is important for you. You still think about the past; better don't. It's getting time to start the path of the sannyasin, the great spiritual way you are nearing. But the questions and the confusions sometimes affect your self-confidence. Some things will happen in a way completely different from what you imagine.

'Try to do exercises with light, not only seeing or being the light, but feeling the light. Do what you can to get rid of opaqueness and become freer and freer. Don't look for the meaning of everything and don't strive to understand it all. As I said, there are things not to be grasped with the mind. Just become free and you will leave all the suffering behind.'

Then he pronounced Arabic-sounding words and put his hands over my head, in blessing.

'Do you want to say anything?' he asked.

'Yes,' I answered. 'In India I felt tuned with the sun, and my name was revealed as Surya. Now I have a human body but I think I am a reflection of the sun, the sunlit one.'

'Who you are is not important,' he continued.

I agreed immediately, saying I had to be careful not to let my ego get inflated.

'Yes, it is difficult,' he confirmed. 'This does happen at a certain stage. But we go beyond it, as long as we remain aware that the personality is not important.'

'I feel so ignorant.'

He smiled kindly and said that it was therefore difficult for him to use certain words. 'But', he stated with authority, 'your path is one of sainthood and you should not worry about it. All will happen by itself.'

The talk with Pir Vilayat Inayat Khan, a respected teacher who viewed me objectively, showed me a clearer image of myself. As a result of the darshan my mind became more relaxed, some disturbing thoughts had been removed. From then on I lived less in the remembrance of my Indian experiences and the nagging question of what they meant. My preoccupation with an imagined spiritual future and my unreadiness for it diminished. I concentrated on the present and on ripening myself for whatever task lay ahead.

PART III

The Task

The Process Continues

From the day of my darshan with Pir Vilayat Inayat Khan, I noticed a pain to the right of my heart. My head started hurting too, as did the area around my solar plexus. Denis suggested that Pir's presence had affected my *chakras*, those seven invisible centers of concentrated subtle energy in the human system which exist to absorb, transform and distribute the universal life force of *prana*.

When the kundalini energy uncoils from the root chakra at the base of the spine, in accordance with one's evolutionary growth, it rises up through the chakras to the crown center at the top of the head where it brings illumination. Denis again interpreted my pains as caused by the kundalini current on its way through the various chakras, meeting blockages in my system. Whatever the explanation, I became accustomed to states which included dizziness, floating, reeling and nausea.

Although convinced the symptoms resulted from the changes I was experiencing, I decided to go to my doctor, who found nothing organically wrong with me. Then I went to an iriscopist, a health practitioner specialized in detecting disease by examining the irises of the eyes.

His diagnosis similarly revealed no health problems, but he concluded I was going through something inevitable. I was easy to influence, he added, and had to be careful. 'Put your feet back on the ground,' he advised. As an aid he prescribed a tonic containing seven herbs and ginseng, the root used in Asia for thousands of years to promote physical well-being and longer life.

The process initiated in India went on by itself. One day I had the impulse to go through my closet and to discard everything I no longer considered appropriate to my new personality, in particular all clothes not in the color of the rising sun, and all leather items except shoes. In India shoes were available in *ahimsa* (non-injury) leather, made from animals who had died a natural death, but I did not know where to obtain them in the West.

My funds were almost exhausted, despite my low expenditures on rent and other basics. Having decided only to take on work that could affect, in some way, the spiritual upliftment of myself and others, I gladly accepted in exchange for this privilege a lifestyle of 'voluntary simplicity'.

On what to spend money anyway? My focused concentration eliminated most entertainments from my life for I found no nourishment in the violence, eroticism and negativity at the base of most modern art forms. The only creative expressions I now valued were those able to feed the spirit and inspire towards the divine. Few were the films or plays offering that for which I hungered. Once in a while, however, I attended a live concert of traditional music or dance, often finding in them elements of purity and harmony.

Only many years later I discovered mass media artists who were striving to bring the minds and hearts of people in touch with the spiritual. One of the best examples was R. Murray Schaefer. I attended his sunset-to-sunrise performance titled *Ra*, a creative interpretation of 'The Litany of Re', a mortuary text used in Egypt in the period of the New Kingdom (c. 1550–1070 B.C.).

During the all-night theatre happening, I and the 74 other audience-'novices' participated in the spiritual rituals of the sun worshipping religion of ancient Egypt. The living drama, which took place partly outdoors and included our being led blindfold to an unknown location, aimed to reconnect us with 'the open secret of the Great Mystery'. Our thoughts were directed upwards, and we were given insight into the cycle of death and rebirth, light and darkness and, in sum, the whole continuity of life.

I fully agreed when the play's director, R. Murray Schaefer, said to me in our subsequent telephone interview: 'At a time when we want to bring peace in the world, we need art works that help slow us down, teach us to meditate, and bring us together in harmony. . . . It is the artist's job to create models that give an idea of a better reality.'

In my own work, I continued to rely on my resolution to lend my skills only to projects fitting into my new ideals of right livelihood. A few freelance assignments offered me the opportunity to edit texts on spiritual themes, but the work paid poorly. Letters from my mother asked me to be realistic. 'Is God going to pay your bills?' she wrote.

As my health condition had not improved, I returned to the iriscopist who now gave psychic healing, channeling spiritual energies though himself into me in order to correct imbalances in my body chemistry. I cannot say I felt anything when he placed his hands on my back, my solar plexus and the base of my head.

Suggesting I try another bottle of his herbal medicine, which in fact meant a serious onslaught on my meager budgetary allowance for 'incidentals', he declared: 'You are responding well to my treatment.' I had no idea what this treatment exactly was.

Since I had learned that the iriscopist was able to 'read' people through their images, I showed him some photos. About Swami Purna he commented: 'I would never let him into my house, never even drink a cup of coffee with him.'

When I asked why, he would not tell.

'That would be contrary to my professional ethics. Anyway, I have already said too much.'

Some time later I got a call from my contact person at the Government of India Tourist Office in Geneva, concerning the article I had written for the Dutch travel magazine. During our talk I mentioned that his name had come up in a conversation with Swami Purna and added: 'I got the impression you are his follower.'

'What?' exclaimed the man. 'That is not so. I met Swami Purna only once, last June or July. I don't even remember what we talked about.'

I cannot deny that these incidents further harmed my trust in Swami Purna, the more since they corresponded to other unfavorable information received from various sides. Nevertheless, I always knew there existed between us a connection stronger than the negative statements of third persons.

Then on a Sunday evening in May, back from two days spent with the family of Denis, I found a note under my door from Annelies. It relayed that she and Swamiji had just returned from India and that he had wanted to see me very much. They were disappointed I was not home and she asked me to phone him in Bonn. What a surprise. Swamiji had not only arrived unannounced, but Annelies had been together with him in India!

Two days later he was on the line, asking why I had not been in touch. Was I cross? I said I was confused about what he really represented. Everything would be all right, Swamiji responded. He would write me a letter. I asked him to clarify his role in my life and his intentions.

He was in Bonn to work on a film made by the German ZDF TV under his guidance at the last Kumbha Mela. Dating back thousands of years, the Kumbha Mela is a vast spiritual gathering celebrated on one of four sacred sites in India approximately every three years on a 12-year cycle. Could I come and help him? Giving no clear answer, I intimated I wanted first to read his announced letter. Although it never arrived, I eventually did assist Swami Purna in completing the project.

Film was a medium I had always loved. Needless to say, in the years of my extreme austerity I rarely went to the cinema, but once in a while the Kosmos Meditation Center screened a documentary which met my elevated standards. An experimental film about an American spiritual community drew Denis and me there one evening.

Arriving early, we browsed the shelves of the basement bookshop filled with the latest New Age acquisitions. A friendly older man came over to greet Denis, who introduced him as Bruno Mertens, teacher of Vipassana, the Buddhist insight meditation. The instant warmth between us gave me the feeling that I had once more met someone I already knew.

When my new friend heard my name, he told me that he analyzed words, breaking them up into their letters to find the original meaning. The essence of S-U-R-Y-A was, letter for letter: transcendental, cosmic powers, repeating, fertilizing, earth.

'So it all adds up to a very good definition of the sun,' I responded, enjoying his novel approach to language.

Then it occurred to me to ask for an explanation of my old name, Norma. 'The NO comes from Norse, north, no place to live,' said Bruno. 'And R is repeating. MA stands for our Mother Earth, but the NOR is very negative and completely negates the MA.'

These words confirmed that the Sanskrit name I had intuitively adopted in India was positive, for both my personality and quest of self.

The encounter with Bruno Mertens had further consequences. Some years later, after having met through him the renowned Burmese meditation master Mahasi Sayadaw, who invited us to

Burma, Denis and I spent seven months in Vipassana meditation retreat in Rangoon.

Making the acquaintance of Bruno brightened up a dull and cloudy Dutch July, so unusually cold that at the height of summer I was wearing a woolen sweater every day. In this period a restless yearning, like the desire to return to a beloved person or place, often accompanied me. It gnawed at my heart like homesickness and repeatedly I wept, unable to explain why. Thoughts of my parents, relatives and friends on the other side of the ocean brought back many memories, and a great loneliness welled up in me. It was not my distant past in America for which I grieved, nor did I pine for my beloved India. I felt separated from the divine.

'Dear Lord, what do you want of me?' I asked fervently in my bedtime prayers. 'What is your will?'

When, a few days later, I very unexpectedly heard the voice of Sri Navajata on the phone, I took it as a sign. In the several letters we had exchanged since my departure from Pondicherry, he had never mentioned travel plans which included Holland. Just arrived from India, he invited me to meet him at the home of Carolus Verhulst, the Dutch publisher for books by Sri Aurobindo and the Mother.

That very afternoon I was walking in Wassenaar, a stately suburban area on the outskirts of The Hague, accompanied by Denis. In my unstable physical condition I could suddenly be incapacitated with agonizing pains and cramps, and he insisted on escorting me whenever possible.

Because of a mistake or misunderstanding in the coordination of Sri Navajata's tight schedule, there was little time for our meeting. As soon as Sri Navajata returned from an earlier appointment elsewhere, Carolus informed him they had to leave for lunch within minutes.

Without further ado Sri Navajata guided me into a living room crowded with books where an intense conversation ensued in an affectionate atmosphere. The involvement with Swami Purna still occupied me very much and I opened my heart to Sri Navajata.

Sri Navajata gave a very clear counsel: 'For you to have a guru in human form would mean going several steps backwards. You have skipped this stage.

'You are lucky,' he said. 'You were contacted directly. You did not do it yourself. You were the one who was called. The consciousness which made the contact with you,' he continued, 'gave you the name Surya. You must meditate on the sun consciousness. Not the sun in the sky, but the one beyond.'

Without disclosing details, I brought up Sinha's prediction that I would begin a spiritual movement. Sri Navajata responded: 'Starting a spiritual movement is old-fashioned. Do what the guidance is telling you.'

His counsel contained the very same message I had already received from others: I was being guided, all would become clearer, there was no choice.

'Are you thinking too much?' he asked, advising me to imagine light inside and outside my head. He also suggested: 'Bring the light down from your head, and up from your toes. Join the light at your heart chakra.'

When I confessed some of the grandiose thoughts related to my higher identity, he said with emphasis: 'In the spiritual life, one does not foretell the future.'

A knock on the door reminded us of his luncheon appointment. After some last advice, Sri Navajata said: 'I care about you as if you were my own child.'

Tears came to my eyes. I too cherished a great affection for him as a close relative of mine in our universal family, where all of us are children of the Supreme Mother and Father.

Our parting left me with an increased confidence in the path ahead. Sri Navajata had stated unequivocally that I had skipped the stage in which I required a guru in human form, but I felt I still needed spiritual counsel from qualified persons. Denis could no longer answer my questions and besides was going through a lackadaisical period reflecting the grey Dutch weather. Swami Purna still had not sent me the promised letter to clarify our special connection.

He phoned, however, a month later when I was just out. Denis spoke with him. 'Why hasn't Surya answered my letter?' Swamiji wanted to know. I had never received it, of course. Nonetheless I had written to him in Bonn, reminding him of my questions. No mail from me had arrived, Swamiji told Denis.

When I came home and heard what had been said, I was jolted. Was this another spiritual game? Or a lesson to see my patience? Or my depth?

1 Ms. Norma Green, professional journalist and international traveler,
a woman of the world – life looked sunny to me

2 Interviewing Dr. Karan Singh, Minister of Tourism – in India I realized that
we are all on a spiritual journey

3 With Ahalya Narayanan – life is sacred and part of a spiritual Oneness to
which we all belong

4 The Mother of Pondicherry: 'Knowledge comes when you have no preferences and no desires'

5 Sri Aurobindo – both he and the Mother of Pondicherry radiate the power of spiritual transmission

6 The Sun God has many forms and faces, but there is only one Sun

7 If only more of us were as rich as rickshaw driver Sawat Sakhawat:
'Me very poor man. Not much money, but me like my life'

8 Khai Ratchavong (left) follows the guideline that whatever we think, speak
or do, will have its effect, either in the present or in the future

9 Swami Purna, the Spiritual Prince Charming – helping to wake up the sleeping seekers

10 H. H. Swamiji – one with the Sun

11 Are we ready to receive from the Sun, our spiritual elder, the ageless
Sun-knowledge?

12 Swami Satchidananda: 'Everything in creation simply does its duty for which it was created and expects nothing in return'

13 The 16th Karmapa – *Om Mani Padme Hum*, the jewel of enlightenment is
latently present in the lotus of human consciousness; we have only to be
what we by inner nature are

19 With Swami Purna – this is the time to take up The Task

20 With Sufi mystic Irina Tweedie – the phrase 'continuity of The Work' belongs to a declaration of consciousness many more of us will make

21 Swami Purna, the Himalayan Master of the many names – helping to transform seekers into finders, and even into pathfinders

22 H.P.B., Helena Petrovna Blavatsky, helped pioneer the Himalayan task which still requires completion

23 Swami Purna leading a spiritual ceremony for a disciple
who left her body consciously

24 A growing circle of persons are hearing the call of the Sun

Healthy, Happy, Holy Yogi Bhajan

From time to time Denis and I granted ourselves a small extravagance and had a meal at the Golden Temple restaurant, an Amsterdam oasis for the vegetarian seeking a tasty but reasonably-priced dinner. In serene candle lit surroundings, cassette tapes with names in the line of 'Peace and Tranquility' and 'Bountiful, Blissful and Beautiful' produced mellow sounds, while young men and women dressed all in white served imaginatively prepared food.

The restaurant was an undertaking of the 3HO Foundation, the Healthy, Happy, Holy Organization created in America in 1969 by Harbhajan Singh Khalsa Yogiji, the Sikh teacher commonly known as Yogi Bhajan. He took the original concepts of Sikhism, the religion founded in India by the great saint Guru Nanak (1469–1539), and showed how they could be applied to Western thinking and orientation to enable a more conscious and spiritual lifestyle.

His students adopt a rigorous discipline including meditation before sunrise, kundalini yoga, mantra repetition to remember God, vegetarian food, performance of work in a devotional spirit, and service for the welfare of others. Some commit themselves formally to live according to the principles of Sikhism, also known as the Sikh Dharma. *Sikh* means 'seeker or learner of truth'.

One day when I passed the Golden Temple restaurant I saw a sign announcing that Yogi Bhajan was in town and would give a public lecture at the Guru Ram Das Ashram, the Amsterdam home for a small group of the yogi's disciples. All in their twenties or thirties, they lived together in community and supported themselves by running the restaurant, teaching yoga and conducting other small businesses.

Denis and I decided to attend the meeting at the ashram, named after Guru Ram Das (1534–81), the fourth Sikh guru, who founded the town of Amritsar in the Indian Punjab. Amritsar, from the Sanskrit meaning 'Lake of Nectar', has been the holy capital of Sikh Dharma for nearly 400 years, since the construction within its precincts of the Golden Temple. That revered edifice, also called the Harmandir Sahib or Temple of God, was completed in 1601 as the main focus for Sikh worship.

Friendly students of Yogi Bhajan welcomed us at the ashram. All of them followed their teacher's Sikh-inspired customs of dress. The men had long beards and turbans and wore a steel bracelet to express their bond to the universal guru, or consciousness. The women in the ashram covered their hair with spectacular headdresses.

I respected these Western converts, especially the women, for their courage to walk around in such distinguishable clothing. In those late hippie days all sorts of outfits could be seen in the street and people were used to quite a lot, but an all-white oriental costume still attracted much attention.

A Canadian ashramite, Guru Jagat Singh, whom I knew from the restaurant, had told me: 'My clothes make me stick out, so I have to be more conscious of behaving correctly. With them I show that I stand for what I believe.'

We left our shoes in the entrance hall and climbed one flight of stairs to a room furnished with nothing but cushions arranged on the floor. We were quite early, so I had the time to look through the informational material presented to me. I read that Yogi Bhajan was born as Harbhajan Singh Puri in 1929 in a part of India which is now Pakistan. From a young age he had interest in esoteric studies, healing and yoga. As a teenager he mastered *kundalini yoga*, the path of union that arouses the latent power at the base of the spine.

In 1947, when Pakistan was formed out of the areas of India which were predominantly Muslim, riots and massacres erupted between the different religious groups, Harbhajan Singh led the inhabitants of his village on an 18-day escape to safety. His once wealthy family found itself homeless and without resources, but with the hard work and determination for which Sikhs are known, they built up a new existence in New Delhi. Harbhajan completed his studies by earning a B.A. in economics, became an officer in the Indian civil service and married.

A turning point in his life came in 1960 when he was assigned to the district of Amritsar. Every day in his free time he went to wash the floor of the sacred Harmandir Sahib Temple. By then he had become convinced that only through performance of the most modest *seva*, service for the welfare of others, done with love and humility, could he find the fulfilment he sought. Writing about this experience later he said:

> What I am today didn't just happen right away. It took me four and one half years of washing the marble floors of the Golden Temple through a voluntary effort, through the Grace of God and Guru. It was the act of mopping the floors of the Golden Temple which mopped all of the dirt out of me. It was nothing else. I could not shine without that rub. The cub shall never rise to the maturity of radiance as a full lion without rubbing the marble floors of the Golden Temple. Khalsa [the Sikh brotherhood] is the order of the divinity of the lion. Leo, which is the master of all the beasts, stands for Singh, which means that you have conquered the beast within yourself.
>
> It is my experience and I would like to share it with you. The Harimandir Sahib is the nucleus of a spiritually powerful center where the heavens and Earth meet to bring harmony. Not that it is only in India. The Golden Temple is at two places, not just at one place. One is located in the heart of the seeker, the Sikh, and the other is on the Earth in the City of Amritsar.[18]

Next to his work as a civil servant, Harbhajan Singh taught yoga and gave spiritual counsel. While working as a customs officer at Palim International Airport, outside Delhi, in 1968 he met a Canadian man who had been unsuccessful in finding a yogi for a teaching position at the University of Toronto. After Harbhajan Singh outlined his own training in yoga, the appointment was offered to him. Resigning his post, he flew West. The airlines lost his luggage, never to be returned, and in Canada he learned about the sudden death of the man who had invited him to come. Determined to stay, he found a job as a clerk in a publishing house. At the same time he taught yoga and soon was known to his students as 'Yogi Bhajan'.

A few months later, on a weekend visit to Los Angeles, he recognized that California was the North American center of the new movement towards self-knowledge and discovery of real and meaningful values. He had found his home.

Drawing on his background of Sikh Dharma, yoga and natural

dietary practices, Yogi Bhajan created the 3HO Foundation. The times were right and very quickly there developed a vast network of 3HO centers in the United States and Europe offering community life based on higher values, yoga instruction and social services such as drug rehabilitation and prison yoga programs. Yogi Bhajan also established a formal religious organization, the Sikh Dharma of the Western Hemisphere, representing Sikhs in the West, and since then he has had the title Siri Singh Sahib.

An announcement by one of the ashram members interrupted my reading. We were told that Yogi Bhajan would give a five-day course. The fee was amazingly low, not more than the price of a Golden Temple vegetarian meal. When he asked who would be interested, only two persons besides me raised their hand. The young man looked surprised.

'Who has seen Yogiji before?' he asked. Half of us had not. 'Oh,' he said, 'that explains it.'

With the entrance of Yogi Bhajan, a dynamic energy enlivened the atmosphere. The yogi, not yet 50, was a vital-looking man with full beard and moustache. He did not speak but literally roared, doing justice to his second name of *Singh* meaning 'lion'. His good humor put us all at ease.

Immediately he caught my attention with his definition of the word *spiritual* as 'breathing'. It came from *spiritus*, derived from *spirare*, 'to breathe'.

'To breathe is to be spiritual,' he explained, making me see we all are 'spiritual', whether we realize it or not.

'Yoga is an attitude of gratitude,' he said, and I could only agree when he clarified: 'Gratitude for every breath we take. God kisses us 15 times a minute, every time we breathe in and out. Without the breath of life we have nothing.

'God lives on your nostril,' he continued most descriptively. 'But can you see your nose? Can you see God? God kisses you all the time, breath in and breath out, but you don't realize.'

Rather than making me feel guilty for my lapses, Yogi Bhajan inspired me to be more aware.

'All the practices that you do', he said, 'are only to make you sit down and remember God.

'We have been so brainwashed by the middlemen, the con men of God, the gurus, yogis, swamis, priests, etcetera. But nobody has to tell us we are holy. We are holy, we all have nine holes.'

Everyone laughed.

'But we are ignorant and arrogant concerning God. We have the idea God works for us; we want our wishes fulfilled, otherwise we blame Him.

'We are so God-brainwashed we don't believe we are here because of God. Man has become so religious he has forgotten there is a Creator. People today don't know they have been created by the same Creator. When you look into the mirror, you see someone beautiful, right? Don't you want to see who made you so beautiful? It wasn't the barber or the hairdresser!'

I enjoyed Yogi Bhajan's bombastic style but also his moments of seriousness, for instance when he declared: 'We have lost our innocence. But we arrive innocent and must return innocent.

'Once you believe you are a person of God, then you are a person of God. But if you have to *try* to believe, you are not. God has no department of try-outs!' Again laughter filled the room. 'There are no try-outs in Creation. It is easier to belong than to long to belong.'

His catchy language was clear and pithy, charged with the force of his directness.

'There are not many ways to God,' he emphasized. 'There is only one way, the way of righteousness. And', he went on, 'everyone can follow the path without anything; no teacher needed. Everything is planned for you to choose. God provides the means, you have to make the choice.'

It is a curse to have a kind teacher, he warned us. 'If a teacher is kind to you, you are doomed. But you don't need a teacher at all. You can learn from everything. A tree can teach you how to shake your head from side to side and how to stand erect. A stream can teach you how to flow.

'For how does conception happen? The sperm swims around the egg, infiltrating, fertilizing. Who told the sperm how to do that? Some yogi? Some swami? The seed of the being', he continued, 'knows the entire knowledge of truth.'

In other words, all the answers of the universe are within us.

'Initiate in yourself a desire to be a part of God,' he urged us and I knew what he meant. Exactly this had been my main desire since India.

The way to be a living god he revealed as: 'Sense of duty. A sense of duty makes all sense.'

Yogi Bhajan assured us there was no suffering in the sense of duty which made all sense. Those who were not sure of their sense of duty had only to ask: 'What is my motivation?' With theatrical precision he paused, just long enough to let us grasp this important question, before he boomed with great authority: 'The totality is God.'

Of course, I thought, but how to experience this totality every moment?

'The motivation', continued Yogi Bhajan, 'is to go beyond ego to universal ego. The totality is God,' he repeated, defining God as the supreme energy, the Supreme Soul.

Earlier he had referred to yoga as 'finite gratitude for one's own infinity'. Now he complemented this with: 'Yoga is when you are doing your thing beyond you'.

And consciousness was: 'For every action you do, do you remember there is a Creator?' After an interval he added: 'When you become God, you don't need to remember anymore. When life becomes nothing but life, then life is being lived.'

At the end Yogi Bhajan taught us a *mudra*, a hand gesture which expresses or encourages a certain attitude of mind. This particular one was to be practiced before and after sunrise.

While we sat erect, the tips of our thumbs and little fingers touching, we had to look at our third eye. At the same time we repeated silently: *Sa-Ta-Na-Ma*, coming from *Sat Nam*, the mantra given by Guru Nanak. Meaning 'The True Name', it symbolizes the immanent presence of God. In the 3HO organization this mantra is also used as an alternative for 'hello' and 'goodbye'.

During the exercise I observed a tremendous energy. My fingers started to move by themselves and the whole body swayed gently back and forth. Immediately after the meditation several small hives, looking like mosquito bites, erupted on my hands. Impurities being released, concluded Denis.

I liked Yogi Bhajan and enjoyed his light-heartedness, but his rendering of the profound truths seemed rather superficial. Perhaps his entertaining style attracted many students, but after they were captured, could he take them deeper?

Years later, I visited Amritsar and the Golden Temple complex. Before dawn, together with our friends Parvinder and Kulwant Garkel Singh, Denis and I entered the venerated premises, at this early hour already crowded with worshippers. A tangible atmosphere of piety, and the soul-filled sounds of devotional poetry, greeted us. No one spoke, except a man seated in the center who was reciting from the *Siri Guru Granth Sahib*.

This principal Sikh scripture consists of devotional hymns whose main message is spiritual liberation through the divine name. Since the death in 1708 of Guru Gobind Singh, the last guru in the line of nine human successors to Guru Nanak, Sikhs have regarded the *Siri Guru Granth Sahib* as their 'living guru'. They believe that the divine spirit, which had been passed on through ten enlightened men, went at Guru Gobind Singh's death into the collective community of the Sikhs and at the same time into the sacred book. From then on it was no longer called the *Adi Granth*, the 'First Book', but addressed as *Siri Guru Granth Sahib* and considered the embodiment of the eternal guru.

In the temple was a constant activity of people quietly entering and leaving. When I looked around, I noticed a group of young Westerners sitting directly across from us. They stood out, in this largely Sikh congregation, not only with their all-white apparel, but as well because of the turbans worn by the women. Evidently they were followers of Yogi Bhajan. In their midst sat an older man, an Indian Sikh. Totally immersed in prayer or meditation, he was bent over, his face not visible.

As we left the temple, we happened to walk behind the 3HO group and I saw that the older man was no one else but Yogi Bhajan. He looked very different from the roaring lion I remembered. His serious expression revealed a depth and a softness which surprised me. I was grateful that this unexpected encounter let me see Yogi Bhajan in another light.

A Critical Reunion

Bonn is only a few hours by car or train from Amsterdam, but no less than seven months elapsed between my first meeting with Swami Purna and the second one. After we had exchanged numerous phone calls, I decided to visit him in September, together with Denis.

At Bonn Central Station, I spotted Swamiji first. He looked radiant, dressed in his usual thin white cloth topped now by a woolen shawl of bright sun-gold color. His hair flowed around him longer and blacker than I remembered. Smiling shyly, he asked: 'How are you?'

Our separation evaporated while we walked to his new car, a gift from devotees. He drove very skillfully, I noted, on the way to his residence. There we heard first about Swamiji's activities in Germany.

Then he backtracked to tell about his visit to the Kumbha Mela, the most ancient and largest spiritual event in the world, attracting millions of people over a one-month period and recreating anew the legendary spiritual India of the past. His accounts appealed to my imagination in such a way that years later I myself participated in several of these unique live-in gatherings.

'Do you know why we came to Bonn?' I asked Swamiji, switching on the tape recorder.

'Yes, tell me.'

'You know why.'

He laughed. 'What I know I will tell you in a discourse.'

Silence.

'Shall I start?' inquired Denis, and to Swamiji's nod, he began, with a nervous laugh: 'After you left, we talked to people, some of them with psychic powers, and they told very negative things about you. So our confusion increased. Now we have some questions we wish to be answered. Maybe we did some things wrong, by speaking to people about you, so we decided to come here.' After a short pause he added, 'We were suspicious.'

'What do you want to know?' Swamiji asked.

I broke in: 'We would appreciate knowing what you really are to us, our relation, the mission.'

Swamiji requested me to turn off the recorder and launched into long explanations. Very curiously, neither Denis nor I could recall the details afterwards. Yet somehow Swamiji dissolved our doubts about him and his motivations.

In broad lines, he confirmed that all he had said in Amsterdam was true, but he had tried to tell everything at once, teach too much in a short time, we were not ready for it. Some of his points may have been misinterpreted by me, or us, in a gross instead of a subtle way, and we may have missed the symbolism of some of his statements and acts. Although it might be difficult to understand all this now, in time it would become clear.

Being together with Swami Purna, once more I believed he could see my internal conflicts and my struggling level of consciousness which wanted to reach the heights of evolution at an American pace. My inner voice told me he was steadily providing the necessary guidance, preparing me for what was to come.

Denis was less convinced. Swamiji's conduct kept disturbing him. Thinking back, I now realize that the more we expected Swami Purna to be perfect, the more he exhibited a behavior that could do no less but provoke the disapproval of Denis.

Addressing the criticism, Swamiji invited Denis to observe his, Swamiji's, behavior and to decide afterwards if he could accept him as a guru or not. Swamiji stressed that the most uncommon and precious form of teaching on the spiritual path is through close personal contact between guru and student. Later I came to learn that spiritual teachers sometimes do very ordinary and even negative things in order to examine and weed out the students.

One day we drove with him and several of his German followers to a picnic in the countryside. We managed to stifle our horror at the plastic cups used for the fruit punch, but when Swamiji committed the unpardonable offense of throwing his cup into the stream, severely insulting our environmental concerns, Denis uttered between his teeth 'What a jerk!'

Denis continually looked for flaws in Swami Purna. The negativity of Denis at times influenced me to keep some distance from Swamiji, while at other instances his attitude had the opposite effect, as my mind and senses struggled to become objective and independent.

In Bonn, in private, Denis and I argued about Swami Purna. Denis complained that Swamiji contradicted his own teaching that a spiritual person did not speak ill of others. Swami Purna often disparaged other gurus for their commercialism, for the cults they created, and for locking their followers into prisons.

I, however, saw Swamiji's criticisms of certain teachers as his way to point out those practices which harmed the whole tradition of spiritual transmission, commercialized what was authentic, and could make unawakened people still more distrusting of spirituality than they already might be. Denis, on the contrary, accused Swamiji of mundanely sinking to a worldly level where gurus competed with each other.

Even so, by the time we left Bonn, he agreed that Swami Purna's unusual stay in Amsterdam had conveyed many lessons. As for me, I again felt linked to Swami Purna. Having somewhat regained balance after the impact of my Indian experiences, I could be with him in a more relaxed way, and this was probably a prerequisite for the teachings to follow.

Gyalwa Karmapa and the Black Crown

At Christmas time, the year after having seen the sparkle in the Dalai Lama's eyes, I heard that another emanation of Avalokiteshvara, the Bodhisattva of Compassion, would soon be in Amsterdam.

His Holiness Gyalwa Karmapa was completing a six-month tour of North America and Europe. Traveling with fourteen *lamas*, high-ranking Tibetan monks, he was giving teachings and initiations everywhere. In Amsterdam he would perform the *Vajra Mukut*, the ceremony of the Black Crown.

Gyalwa Karmapa was the sixteenth *tulku*, incarnation, of the Tibetan yogi Dusum Khyenpa (1079–1153), 'knower of past, present and future', who gave structure to the Kagyu school of Tibetan Buddhism and was the first Karmapa. The fifteenth Karmapa, before he died in 1922, had a vision showing his next birth. According to a tradition going back to the first Karmapa, he shaped this prophecy into a poem which he sealed in an envelope and entrusted to a close pupil. The details connected to the birth of the sixteenth Karmapa in 1924 corresponded with the prophecy.

Neither Denis nor I knew what the ritual of the Black Crown implied, but we were not the only ones intrigued. When we arrived at the Kosmos Meditation Center, almost two hours before the scheduled time, a huge number of people had already gathered in front of the building. Great excitement filled the air, similar to the kind that had always thrilled me at rock concerts. Most of the crowd was young here too. The night was dark and cold but we all waited patiently, slowly inching ahead.

Inside, we had a first taste of what was to come. A man's voice, loud and insistent, emerged above the din. Our ears caught phrases such as 'Seeing the crown can end your suffering', and 'This is a very special opportunity; use it'. Moving forward, we distinguished: 'You cannot get a better contact with direct and very deep methods to become enlightened in this lifetime.' Some people burst into laughter.

Finally we saw a young man, to whom the urgent voice belonged. 'There may be no time left to explain upstairs,' he warned. His English contained a Scandinavian lilt. 'So I have to prepare you here. In there, don't think, just try to receive,' he pleaded. 'Be open, be open,' he entreated.

The hall was already completely filled. Only in the back, on an elevation, were we able to find two chairs disregarded by others who preferred to sit closer, cross-legged, on the floor. This raised us above the crowd, placing us in a direct line with the throne obviously set up for the Karmapa.

A Tibetan man, dressed in suit and tie, took the microphone.

'Please,' he said. 'So many persons wait outside, so little room left. If you saw before, please will you get up and give a chance to others?' Some people departed, others squeezed in. The tension was mounting.

Then a monk, with shaved head and maroon robes, started to speak in a musical British accent. It was not a man but a Western woman, the Venerable Gelongma Palmo, the Karmapa's secretary. I switched on the tape recorder.

When the first Karmapa attained enlightenment, she told us, and the knowledge of the past, present and future was bestowed upon him, he received from several heavenly deities an invisible black crown. Woven from the hairs of 100,000 celestial beings, the crown is always present above the head of the incarnate Karmapa.

'When we, who are born in a Christian society, think about angels,' explained Sister Palmo, 'they always have wings. Why? Because at a certain point people began to see angels in dreams or visions and they had wings and flew. Ever since, even people who have never seen angels have represented them in this way.

'Similarly, some disciples and devotees saw the first Karmapa in visions wearing the mysterious supernatural crown. At the time of the fifth Karmapa, Debzing Shegpa, who lived from 1384 to 1415, the Chinese ruler had the same vision. Wanting others to see the crown as well, he made a visible replica of it. This very same crown will be used tonight in the Black Crown ceremony, which only a Karmapa can perform.

'Every time the Karmapa puts on the Black Crown, he goes into *samadhi*, a spiritual trance,' stated Sister Palmo. 'The crown has a miraculous quality consecrated by hundreds of thousands of samadhis. Even the sight of it is something special.'

We all listened intently.

'It is said that when you see the crown, you don't fall again into states of suffering. It is the end of suffering for you,' she told us. 'At the end of this life you will not fall into hell, all fears of death will disappear, and you will assume a happier form. Illnesses can be cured. Mental troubles can cease.

'So I request you,' she implored us fervently, as had the young man from the entrance hall, 'please open yourselves to the beautiful experience. Open up, just receive. Afterwards you can think about it.'

Intensely, sincerely, she went on: 'Remember that His Holiness is not just an earthly form. His Holiness is a symbol. He is the Buddha, not only in the world but through space, through worlds infinite. He is the bodhisattva who saves the gods and the anti-gods, the animals and the ghosts, who goes into hell and takes people from it to heaven. He is, in one form, all this.'

I could hardly believe such an exalted being was here, right before us, descended from the heights of the Himalayas to the lowlands of Holland.

Sister Palmo paused and looked around at the eyes riveted on her. 'I am telling you more than I generally say in public, because I think the younger generation goes deeper into the unseen. I am sure you will feel something of the depth of this experience and I pray that, as the buddhas have promised, you do not fall again into states of suffering.'

Our concerned young man, now identified as Ole Nydahl from the Tibetan Buddhist Centers of Scandinavia, took over the microphone and announced that this evening the Karmapa would also give Refuge in the Three Jewels, the Triple Gem. In Buddhist tradition the first jewel is the Buddha, and the meeting of our potential for enlightenment. The second jewel is the Dharma, the Sacred Doctrine of the liberating teachings. The third is the Sangha, the practitioners on different levels of attainment.

Ole explained the basis of 'taking refuge' is our wish to reach enlightenment in order to help liberate all sentient beings. He advised us, while taking refuge, to think not only of His Holiness the Karmapa, but of the entire guru line he represents.

Then the Tibetan man wearing the suit and tie, introduced as Akong Tulku, leader of the Samye-Ling Tibetan Center at Eskdalemuir in Scotland, added that above the Karmapa's head we should visualize the Buddha. We were to surround the Buddha with books containing the Enlightened One's teaching. If we could see His Holiness the Karmapa in the center of this and have faith, we would receive the Refuge directly from him.

'Repeat after the Karmapa what he chants,' instructed Akong Tulku. 'This is the Milarepa initiation. The whole line of Milarepa, Marpa and the Karmapa will be above the head of His Holiness.'

Ole showed us how to open our body, speech and mind by touching these three centers with our hands. We did this three times, then bowed our head as low as we could. We opened our body, speech and mind and bowed down again, then again. 'And now you are open to His Holiness.'

The rest of Ole's words were drowned in the blaring sound of Tibetan brass instruments. Akong Tulku signaled us to rise and we all scrambled to our feet. A somewhat portly man, dressed in maroon robes with one shoulder bared, entered with an entourage of monks and ascended to the throne. On his head the Karmapa already wore a crown. According to the information sheet, this was the meditation hat of Gampopa, teacher of the first Karmapa.

The monks began reciting a request in Tibetan that His Holiness would take his transcendental form of Avalokiteshvara, the Bodhisattva of Compassion. Calling on the whole line of Karmapas to be present, they offered a round metal plate with rice, symbolizing the universe. To the accompaniment of horns, bells and chanting, other offerings were made, including the bodies, the minds and the speech of the participants. Our imperfections were offered as we surrendered to a higher wisdom.

Karmapa-Avalokiteshvara was asked to turn the Wheel of Dharma and make the sacred teachings visible. A hat box appeared, carried by a monk whose nose and mouth were covered by a white cloth. He opened the box. Out of it the Karmapa took crystal prayer beads while chanting continuously the invocation 'Om Mani Padme Hum' which dissolves all disturbing emotions and is the most used among Tibetan mantras. While chanting, the Karmapa prepared to enter into his manifestation of complete awakening and to beam out the power of compassion.

Finally came what we had all been awaiting. The Karmapa

withdrew from the box the Black Crown and placed it on his head. For a second he reeled backwards, as if a great power unbalanced him. His eyes rolled upwards. Then he looked straight ahead. From my position I was directly in the Karmapa's line of view, and his eyes locked with mine, piercing deeply.

There was a mist, lines softened. The whole scene in front of me suddenly looked like a *thangka*, a sacred Tibetan painting. In the centre of the thangka was not the Buddha, but the Karmapa himself. Then the whole picture floated upwards, off the ground.

I kept looking at the Karmapa, who bound me with his eyes and lifted me with him. There came a rush of visions – heavenly beings, angels, buddhas. Drawn up by the thangka and the Karmapa, I lost all sense of the place and the people around me, and arrived in a space I recognized from earlier transcendental experiences.

When the Karmapa took off the crown, I found myself sitting solidly on my chair again. The scene sharpened in focus and I watched the hat being put away, with ritual and chanting. Another recitation by the monks signaled the end. They dedicated to all living beings the blessing generated by the ceremony and requested long life for the Karmapa.

During the subsequent Refuge ceremony we repeated the gestures to open and surrender and chanted Tibetan words after the Karmapa. Then he blessed us all. Those who wished for his blessing more directly were invited to come to him, one at a time. Most of the many people in the room started lining up.

It took a long time until my turn arrived. With reverence I approached, and the Karmapa touched my head with a ritualistic object which sparkled like gold. With hardly any physical distance between us, his powerful eyes burned themselves into me, leaving indelible impressions never to depart.

Pouring a liquid into my cupped hands, he motioned me to drink. Although it tasted like orange juice, and I knew that monks do not serve intoxicating beverages, I felt suddenly inebriated. Then one of the lamas poured a different, red-colored liquid into my hands and again I drank. Another lama tied a thin red cord around my neck before I returned to my place.

When the last person had received blessings, the Karmapa left. I remained seated, overwhelmed, in need of a transition back to ordinary activity.

Ole Nydahl, who stayed behind, explained: 'The empowerment

you have received to meditate on Milarepa will also give you the force to meditate directly on His Holiness and to get his blessings.' He advised us to join him, on the spot, for an immediate meditation. 'This helps you to experience what you have received here, and better understand the direct methods used to become enlightened in a single lifetime.'

The next day I attended a luncheon given in The Hague by the Ambassador of India, Mr. K. S. Bajpai, and his wife. The couple had become acquainted with the Karmapa during the ambassador's four-year posting in Sikkim, where His Holiness took up residence in 1959. Now 50, he had ordained more than 3,000 monks and nuns.

While we were waiting for the Karmapa, Mrs. Bajpai told anecdotes about his love for animals and birds, with which he had a special understanding. In fact, she and the ambassador had wanted to arrange the gathering one day later, but the Karmapa planned to visit pet shops then.

When the distinguished guest arrived, without crown or ritual, he looked simple and unpretentious, dressed in plain maroon robes with a yellow silk shirt underneath. I was quite impressed when this venerated figure of Tibetan Buddhism walked up to each one of us and enthusiastically shook our hands, in a charming manner.

'Good . . . very good,' he uttered, perhaps the only words in English he knew, for during the afternoon he repeated them continually, accompanied by a broad smile, laughter and much warmth.

Very easily I came into close contact with Sister Palmo, a British woman who was the first Westerner to receive the full Bhikkuni (nun's) ordination of the Kagyu tradition. An Oxford graduate, she told me she had lived in India for 40 years, had been married, raised four children, and had followed Mahatma Gandhi. Besides being the Karmapa's English secretary, I later found out, she was also a scholar and translator. When not on international lecturing and teaching tours, she lived at the Karmapa's Rumtek Monastery in Sikkim.

At one point during our animated conversation Sister Palmo interrupted me to ask: 'Are you a Buddhist?'

When I answered, 'I am . . . everything!' her face lit up with a smile.

'Oh, you're an Aquarian!' she said.

With this term Sister Palmo was of course referring to the eleventh sign of the zodiac, the astrological sign symbolized by a heavenly waterbearer pouring upon humanity a stream of beneficent cosmic influences. According to astrologers, our earth is leaving the rule of Pisces and entering into that of Aquarius, a movement which will take humanity towards a spiritual era marked by higher ideals and collective effort. Sister Palmo's words alluded to a new category of planetary citizens who identify themselves with Aquarian values of unity, cooperation and the sacredness of all.

At the buffet table I noticed the lamas helping themselves to meat and chicken. With apologies for my boldness, I inquired of Sister Palmo: 'How can meat-eating agree with the Buddha's statement about not taking life?' In Tibet vegetables were scarce, she explained, and meat-eating was necessary.

'Yes,' I responded, 'but they are not in Tibet now.'

'True,' she replied, 'but we are monks. We have no preferences. We take what is offered and don't make problems for people.'

'Yes, but couldn't they have skipped the meat and just taken the vegetables, as some other people here did?'

'Oh, you Aquarians are more Catholic than the Pope!' she exclaimed, laughing in a good humor.

For all the light-hearted atmosphere of the lunch, everyone afterwards had the privilege of receiving a private *darshan*. This occurred in a quiet corner away from the dining room. Alone with the Karmapa, in the beginning I was speechless. All I could do was stare into the Karmapa's compelling eyes, and he returned my gaze. I could almost sense clouds of darkness dissipate all around me, burned away by the intense power of his penetrating look.

Then the journalist in me remembered her sense of duty. I had agreed to write an article for *Bres*. 'Would the ceremony of the Black Crown benefit someone who did not understand anything about it, and felt nothing during or after it?' was my first question.

'Whether someone understands or not, it still goes on, the energies are transmitted,' the Karmapa answered in Tibetan, translated by Akong Tulku. 'It is beyond words.'

Sister Palmo joined us at this moment to repeat what she had told the previous evening: 'The hat has miraculous powers.'

'Why did His Holiness come to perform the Black Crown ceremony in the West at this time?'

'His Holiness says it was not his decision,' was the translated answer. 'His Holiness says his disciples have been calling him for years and years, so he finally came. Furthermore, His Holiness thinks the West is at a spiritual turning point. It is time for the light to spread more.'

Having heard that the Karmapa constantly gave personal advice, I asked if he had any message to offer me. 'Do what you are doing, but be cautious,' he replied, adding: 'I'm just a simple man. I don't look into the future or the past.'

I chuckled, appreciating his modesty. The whole afternoon, in everything he did, the Karmapa proved to be an astonishingly unassuming, normal person. A small incident particularly revealed this. When one of the young Tibetan lamas was shown how to photograph the group with a Polaroid camera, the Karmapa exhibited a child's delight in peeling open and inspecting the pictures as soon as they were ready.

What a difference between this playful, laughing man and the piercing-eyed bodhisattva of the Black Crown ceremony!

I was touched as well by the Karmapa's overflowing spiritual generosity, a sign to me of someone with true attainment. He offered his inner inheritance freely, to all equally, just like the sun. In Amsterdam we had only to pay the modest entrance fee to the Kosmos Meditation Center.

The Karmapa's visit affirmed once more that the spiritual world is something real. The higher consciousness of the awakened state transmitted by the Karmapa could not be seen or heard, tasted or touched. It was as invisible as the supernatural crown said to hover always above his head. Nevertheless, it was tangible to me, through my experience at the ceremony. The energy of consciousness can come to us in a diversity of ways, by varied spiritual traditions, as much as it can reach us directly, from the Source itself.

Forty-eight hours after the Karmapa's visit, a colossal light flashed in my head, commencing a new period of extremely uncomfortable sensations in various parts of my body.

'These are not health problems,' reassured Denis. 'The kundalini process goes on!'

For a long time after the Black Crown ceremony and the darshan with the Karmapa, I saw his eyes, looking at me from inside, during my meditation.

Inside, too, one of his remarks kept repeating endlessly, like a mantra of spontaneous origin: 'I'm just a simple man, I'm just a simple man.' I mulled over these unpretentious words as if they were a *koan*, a riddle or paradox put forward by a teacher of Zen Buddhism as a means to open a student's mind.

By most standards, of course, the Karmapa was no simple man at all. He was a *tulku*, the Tibetan term for a person recognized as the present incarnation of an exalted being. To be precise, he was the sixteenth Karmapa Tulku, the latest offspring of the Kagyu line of Tibetan Buddhism, which traces its heritage back through Milarepa, Tibet's great yogi and saint (1052–1135), to his teacher Marpa the Translator (1012–97), who studied in India with the great Buddhist Naropa (1016–1100).

The Kagyu School preserves the oral transmission of esoteric practice and spiritual realization brought to Tibet by Marpa. The teachings passed from his student Milarepa down to Gampopa, who consolidated and organized them. Gampopa's chief disciple, Dusum Khyenpa, the first Karmapa, established the line. All subsequent Karmapas are considered to be reincarnations of him.

When I met the Karmapa, I found that this 'simple man' exemplified the most pure humility. This virtue is connected with the Buddhist aim to reach egolessness, detachment from the desire to perpetuate our own identification as 'I'. All desires, said the Buddha, bind us to suffering. Until we abandon the sense of 'I', we cannot be freed from our repeated births and deaths.

What a mighty challenge! To leave behind the very sense of individuality and personality which seems to give us uniqueness.

Intrigued to know more about a *tulku*, I turned for help to *Born in Tibet*, the autobiography of Chögyam Trungpa, the eleventh Trungpa Tulku:

> *While we remain more or less enmeshed in a selfhood regarded as our own, past and future lives are continually being produced by those forces which still bind us to worldly existence. In the case of a Tulku, however, the forces which produce his existence are of a different order. Something, or someone, that has no 'individuality' or ego in the ordinary sense decides to work on earth for the sake of all beings. He (or 'it') therefore takes birth over a certain period of time, in a series of human individuals, and it is these who are named 'Tulkus'.*[19]

From his earliest years, the sixteenth Karmapa Tulku knew what he was and what his task involved. He had nothing to prove, neither to himself nor to anyone, he had only to be himself. Modesty derives from knowing what you truly are, on the personality level as well as on the subtle.

Although at the time my journey was already moving ahead on a simple and plain pilgrim's path, I did not realize that the irresistible American theme song 'Be Someone in Life' still accompanied my steps. A modified version of the old tune beat in my subconscious, with the result that I was ever so busy to become a great saint, if not the redeemer of the world.

It took me many years to loosen the ties with my childhood conditioning, nevertheless the Karmapa's example of egolessness had a long-lasting influence. In the same way, the spiritual energy he transmitted worked on in me like a rarefied elixir diffusing its benevolent powers endlessly.

Maharishi Mahesh Yogi and the Scientific Effect

My article on the Karmapa had been written and sent off, but the Tibetan leader's remark about being a simple man continued to engage my mind for quite some time. It was still in my thoughts the following month when I arrived at Amsterdam's Vrije University for the First International Symposium of the 'Science of Creative Intelligence'. SCI, as it is abbreviated, is the theory behind Transcendental Meditation, or TM, the mind-tranquilizing technique promoted by the Indian spiritual teacher Maharishi Mahesh Yogi.

A flower-laden stage enlivened the assembly hall, crowded with TM practitioners from Holland and neighboring countries. Young men and women were putting finishing touches to a couch covered with white silk. Behind it hung a large color photo of the late Swami Brahmananda Saraswati, Shankaracharya of Jyotir Math in North India, whom Maharishi called 'Guru Dev', Divine Teacher.

My chair neighbor engaged me in conversation, telling me that he represented a multinational oil company. The firm had assigned him to investigate whether TM could be utilized to help employees increase efficiency by accepting unpleasant aspects of their work.

'Couldn't such acceptance contain inherent seeds of apathy and resignation, inviting the exploitation of those workers?' I asked in all innocence.

The man suddenly had no time any longer for an exchange of views. 'Before the program begins, I have to finish reading these,' he declared with perfect politeness, indicating the glossy TM material handed out to everyone.

I had already noted the main assertion of the captivating

write-ups: TM is a very easy meditation technique capable of producing stupendous results, not only for the individual but also for the world as a whole. Each practitioner personally receives a mantra and instructions in how to use it, the warp and woof of the Maharishi system.

My research had informed me that by the mid-1970s the TM organization claimed enrollments from nearly one million people in 89 countries. Using corporate business devices, such as computerized mailings, high-speed communication technology and professional marketing strategies oriented to the consumer society, the group was already then generating a considerable yearly income, in many millions of dollars in the United States alone.

What a worldly success story for an Indian monk who in 1955 left the Shankaracharya's Himalayan ashram, where he had lived 14 years, for a simple pilgrimage to the South. His natural charisma earned him many invitations to lecture which led to an extended stay. Extolling the benefits of meditation at a birthday gathering for Guru Dev in Madras, he got inspired by the audience's enthusiastic response and inaugurated a world movement 'to spiritually regenerate the whole of mankind'. Thus the nearly 40-year-old Maharishi launched his international career.

His message was that the suffering and misery so common to human existence are unnecessary. Life in its essential nature is bliss, and every person can experience unbounded bliss consciousness and integrate it into daily life through 'Transcendental Meditation', a name he trademarked.

During the early months of 1958, Maharishi established 25 centers of the Spiritual Regeneration Movement, the forerunner of the TM organization, before embarking on his first foreign tour. A remarkable journey began when he left India determined to popularize meditation. In the late 1960s he captured the media as the guru of the Beatles and other celebrities; by the mid-1970s TM was known worldwide.

'He's coming!' cried someone, and we all rose. In walked a tiny, dark-skinned man dressed in traditional Indian robes and carrying flowers. Long greying hair and beard gave him an ancient appearance though his body looked youthful. On the platform he slipped his minuscule feet out of wooden sandals, identical to my simple Benares pair.

Maharishi, whose title translates as 'Great Rishi' or 'Great Sage', sat quietly with closed eyes. Finally he announced, in a voice much stronger than could have been expected from his slight frame: 'I came here to inaugurate the dawn of the Age of Enlightenment. A good time for the world is coming, a time characterized by light and sunshine, no ignorance, no negativity, no suffering, a time of good health, good mind, good behavior, harmony everywhere, love and happiness all around.'

He spoke in excellent, flowing English with authoritative self-assurance.

'Our vision of the New Age is not based on mysticism, on a dream from the mountaintop,' he stressed. 'The dawn of the Age of Enlightenment is not seen from the astral plane. Our inspiration is very down-to-earth and realistic. We inaugurate the dawn during the night-time. When we see the topsy-turvy confusion of the world today, we know we are in darkness, but we have the confidence to proclaim the oncoming dawn. Who will be responsible for ushering in this new time? Individuals, those individuals who spend 15 minutes morning and 15 minutes evening doing Transcendental Meditation.'

The technique includes sitting comfortably in a chair, closing the eyes, and repeating the mantra assigned by the TM teacher.

'TM has the power to allow everyone to develop his full potential of mind and body, thus contributing to improved quality of life in society,' he said. 'We can prove this scientifically.'

Maharishi went on to tell that TM's Switzerland headquarters had the best brain wave measurement equipment in the world: 'EEG measurements show that a 20-minute period of TM brings the experience of a fourth major state of consciousness, as distinct from dreaming, deep sleep or waking. The body experiences a condition of extremely deep physical relaxation while the mind becomes more alert and orderly.'

During the symposium an impressive assortment of Dutch and foreign scientists, the majority of them connected with the TM movement, reported on a host of TM-related experiments conducted in the past five years. In such knowledgeable company, no doubts had a chance.

Tests reportedly showed that, during TM, practitioners experience markedly decreased heart and breathing rates, oxygen consumption and workload on the heart. Laboratory research verified such diverse benefits as faster reaction time, improved attention, increased learning ability, and reduced use of alcohol, tobacco and drugs.

Studies were cited to back the claim that TM brings measurable betterment to such areas as personal relations, education, government, economics and the environment. Maharishi himself announced the movement's latest success: when one per cent of a city population did TM, crime rates dropped.

With messianic fervor, Maharishi elaborated on solving the world's problems. Wanting to produce huge numbers of TM teachers, he had launched the 'World Plan' to open over 3,000 centers, each to train 1,000 people. The fee for such training amounted to no less than 10 per cent of the person's income for the length of the course, with a reduction for students.

At the end of the conference, Denis and I were graciously ushered into the presence of Maharishi for a personal interview. At the beginning we were just the three of us. Later on, when it was time for his meeting with a group of TM teachers, Maharishi invited me to continue my questioning in front of them.

Offstage, there was little of the scientific dryness and professional jargon that characterized the symposium, where he had praised TM's benefits in terms of galvanic skin response, enlarged beta spindles, decreased blood lactate concentration and so forth.

His warmth and good humor touched me, and I could recognize the Maharishi Mahesh Yogi who in 1965 wrote *Love and God*, which I had read before the meeting.

As a fledgling writer on the spiritual, I was especially interested in Maharishi's manner of verbal expression. I therefore asked him, between questions on yoga, meditation and Indian philosophy: 'To bring across your message you have chosen the language of science. Why? Is it the most effective language available right now?'

'It is the most safe!' he exclaimed flamboyantly, in his distinctive voice, and his students laughed at what probably was an inside joke. Among his intimates, Mahesh Yogi came over as a loving father and guru figure.

'"Safe" means we ourselves know we are not wrong,' he clarified. 'If we talk in terms of "will of God", then people want proof. Where is the will of God? We don't have such proof.

'Similarly, we could talk in terms of "grace of God", that is true,' he admitted, and I noticed that some of the students seemed to pay extra attention. 'It is pleasant but so abstract. One can't hang on to it. So instead we talk in terms of synchronicity of the brain waves, the law of thermodynamics, reduced activity of mind, increased orderliness. It's very simple. We want to keep our language scientific so that it can be verified.'

'But is science 100 per cent dependable?' I asked him. 'Even scientists themselves often disagree on experiments and findings.'

'This is the scientific age,' he replied, 'the age which is going to prove the existence of the sublime, the divine. As far as our movement is concerned, the procedures of meditation are very well sorted out so that someone can go from one level of consciousness to the other and eventually to the unbounded consciousness of unity. No one will miss anything.'

'Then why not also speak now about divine values?' I inquired.

'Not until we have at least one per cent of the world population meditating,' he answered.

'Does this mean we can expect something new at that moment?'

'There has been a lot of talk about the divine,' he responded, 'but there has not been an effective and purposeful formula to experience it. This is why "divine" is an ignored word in progressive life today. People who are practical do not want to waste time on the divine. They want what they can really see: a good house, a car, material things. So in our organization we don't talk of the divine.'

'Isn't there the danger that one-sided reliance on scientific language and tangible proofs will get out of hand before you reintroduce the divine?'

'Our policy is realistic,' he replied.

'But how many of your people will know that reality which you cannot see or touch or taste? You do not tell it in those words, because you realize Westerners do not understand, but – '

' – Transcendental. I tell it in one word,' he cut me off.

'Yes, but you are aware people interpret a word depending on their level of consciousness.'

'Correct,' he affirmed.

'And Westerners understand "transcendental" quite differently from what is experienced when we go back to the source of all knowledge.'

'True,' he agreed.

'With all due respect to you, haven't you merely exchanged one mystique for another, modern for ancient?' I asked him. 'Instead of creating a new elitist vocabulary which has to be taught along with the meditative techniques, couldn't you find a middle way? Some meeting point where the expressions of science and those of ordinary life, not to mention the ones of the divine, can come together to form a more natural language for a larger humanity?'

'Beautiful, very beautiful,' declared Maharishi.

When I tried to press onward, he altered his style and answered with funny, irrelevant remarks that set his admiring devotees into uproarious, appreciative laughter and made me look a bit foolish.

After the meeting, however, several of the TM teachers rushed up to 'congratulate' me for having forced Maharishi to comment on the divine. They told me they could not bring up such topics since the movement demanded a non-questioning, non-critical attitude. The emphasis on science confused them. One man even asked me: 'Did Maharishi actually use the word "God" in his book? We're Christians and we've been wondering about this.'

In the 1980s Maharishi introduced different terms for abstract metaphysical concepts, based on the unified-field theory. It says that nothing in the universe, living or non-living, is solid. Everything consists of vibrations of energy minutely connected to each other. Everything has its own individuality, however, even while belonging to this interconnected whole, or unified field. Maharishi says that during meditation it is possible to experience this all-encompassing field, the ultimate reality underlying all nature, and he uses the terms 'the unified field' or 'natural law' to describe it.

After spending the first part of the 1980s traveling around the world, and the second half mainly in seclusion at his ashram in north India, the founder of TM arrived back in the West in the summer of 1990. For his main residence and the 'Maharishi European Continental Capital of the Age of Enlightenment', he chose a place in the southern countryside of the Netherlands. From this base, a TM academy established in the former Roman Catholic monastery of St. Ludwig in Vlodrop, Maharishi received wide newspaper coverage with his offer to solve the Gulf Crisis.

Maharishi asserted that the energy produced by a group of 7,000 TM meditators permanently meditating together in one place would 'create an influence of coherence in world consciousness strong enough to resolve all international tensions, including those in the Middle East'. This so-called 'Maharishi Effect' would 'automatically render all trends in the world positive, peaceful and in the evolutionary direction'. Seven thousand is the square root of one per cent of the Earth's population. The movement claims it arrived at this number through years of experimenting with the collective practice of Maharishi's techniques.

Because no government came forward to foot the costs of supporting a permanent group of meditators, Maharishi announced that his organization itself would fund this action as an aid towards world stability. By the 1990s, Maharishi Mahesh Yogi had built up an empire with assets worth an estimated three billion dollars, according to figures published in the press. Besides marketing meditation, the TM organization expanded further by offering services and products in natural health care, environment-friendly housing, Indian classical music, and entertainment based on themes of enlightenment.

The very next day after my meeting with Maharishi Mahesh Yogi, Swami Purna arrived in Amsterdam. Another intense visit resulted in more outpouring from his reservoir of wisdom.

'Well, how was Transcendental Meditation?' Swamiji inquired.

'Surprisingly down-to-earth,' I replied.

'But their prices not,' he remarked. 'The costs are the only thing transcendental about the movement,' he commented, asking if during the symposium mention had been made of any other system of meditation.

My 'no' caused him to laugh. 'Meditation is just one of eight parts of the traditional Indian path to Self-realization,' he explained. 'Do you think the highest meditative state, *samadhi*, can be reached with merely 15 minutes of TM practice twice a day?'

From what the TM teachers related to me, I told him, it seems they use TM as a kind of natural tranquilizer. The meditation makes them feel better, sleep sounder and be more relaxed. Very few people begin TM because they want to attain God Consciousness.

No more was said on this matter until the following Sunday, when we went to a musical event at Amsterdam's main concert hall, the venerable Concertgebouw. A colorful assortment of young, long-haired and imaginatively dressed people, part of Amsterdam's home-grown Flower Power species, milled in front of the building.

We had all come for the popular group Shakti, led by guitarist

Mahavishnu John McLaughlin, a student of the Indian spiritual teacher Sri Chinmoy. Sri Chinmoy, who grew up in Pondicherry's Sri Aurobindo Ashram, later moved to New York where he still heads a community of his own and leads meditations at the United Nations.

As we settled into our seats, Swamiji resumed the talk about TM. He never seemed to mind where he discussed what.

Above the buzz of excited voices around us, he remarked: 'Mahesh Yogi brings TM as if he has the monopoly on meditation. Yet TM is based on an old technique practiced in India for thousands of years and passed along, without charge, from teacher to student. Moreover, the use of a mantra is an essential feature of many Indian meditation systems.'

'Is there nothing new about TM?' I asked.

'The manner of presentation as well as Mahesh Yogi's touting of meditation as the solution to the world's problems,' replied Swamiji. In a few minutes the concert would begin. 'But meditation alone cannot carry this heavy burden,' he continued. 'The Buddha said suffering will remain as long as the physical world, the physical body and desires exist. One can become free from suffering individually, through intuitive knowledge and efforts in a metaphysical system, but collective freedom from suffering is not possible.'

Further words were overpowered by thunderous applause, as John McLaughlin appeared on the podium. I was pleasantly surprised at how he began. All of us, he announced, were invited to join him that evening for a group meditation at the Mozes and Aäron Church.

'And at no cost,' observed Swamiji, who was glad to hear about another Amsterdam meeting place for spiritual and cultural activities of Eastern origin.

Swamiji found the concert, jazz-rock with elements of Indian classical music, too loud. At the intermission he wanted to leave, but agreed we would first drink a fruit juice. In the coffee lounge a young man perhaps in his early twenties approached our table. Giving our small party careful scrutiny, he exclaimed, 'Wow! Can I sit down?'

Swamiji, quite amused, nodded yes. The young man produced another 'Wow!' and pulled up a chair. 'Wow!' he repeated again, smiling radiantly. Appearing very happy, he declared: 'Everything I do is for God!'

Swamiji nodded and our unexpected visitor asked: 'Do you like the concert?' Then he took out a small bamboo flute and, eyes closed, played a sweet and haunting melody. At its end, looking wistful, he whispered, 'My only home is with God.'

Before we could respond came the announcement: 'I am glad to be with you, but now someone else needs my feeling.' And away he rushed.

'What was that all about?' I asked Swamiji.

'We may not always know why we have to be somewhere, but there is a reason for everything,' he replied. Back we went to our places.

After the performance Swamiji brought up our earlier subject of discussion, and this topic accompanied us all the way home. He made it a point to stress that the entire cause of spirituality is done a disservice when elements from an authentic tradition are taken out of context and gimmicked up to make them unique and saleable in the marketplace.

'One guideline to determine the purity of intention of any spiritual group or self-development training is to note the fees or lack of fees involved,' he emphasized. 'Spiritual practices are not subject to selling and buying. Once you have bought something, you will try to sell it. You are psychologically bound. Spiritual things you give to all who are qualified.

'A spiritual teacher is not a businessman,' he went on. 'We don't sell our spirituality and knowledge, but help those who are ready. I teach people to serve, to be active.'

Before reaching the Lauriergracht, he summed up that when people had to pay high charges and then did not get the promised results, their disappointment could dissuade them from ever approaching an authentic teaching. The experience could even turn them away from spirituality altogether.

'No one can guarantee: "Do this and you will get that",' elaborated Swamiji. 'All one can say is: "Do this, and there is a possibility it may help you." Committing is very bad. If it is said, "Do the meditation and become relaxed, get freed from other worries," all right. But to claim enlightenment is too much.'

'Still, isn't belonging to a group and deriving some benefit from it better than just doing nothing in the spiritual line?'

'Not if it ultimately serves to keep someone away from the real thing.'

Observing the Teacher's Actions

Two years had passed since my return from India. Circumstances had launched me into meeting and interviewing spiritual teachers as well as writing on themes pertinent to the expansion of consciousness taking place in the West. My aspirations and my work had come into harmony. It had needed courage to break with my former mini-career, but most of the time we can make a new start only by leaving the past completely behind.

After the encounter with Maharishi Mahesh Yogi, I had more than enough material for a substantial article. As a writer, I had taken home a concise message from him: speak to people in concrete language. It sounded very obvious, but I knew all too well how difficult it was to apply this guideline to the spiritual.

My early lessons in the transformation of heavenly thoughts into familiar expressions I received at the desk with Swami Purna, assisting him with his interminable correspondence.

Following our Bonn reunion, Swamiji came to Amsterdam rather frequently, especially in conjunction with the project about the 1974 Kumbha Mela held in Hardwar, north of New Delhi. This was the first documentary ever to be made at the auspicious ancient gathering. Filming was permitted only because of Swamiji's influence with the government of India and with the various monastic orders which manage the month-long event.

Although he had led the German TV team into the fair's spiritual inner sancta, they could not grasp the larger message and the edited film reflected this lack of understanding. Swamiji and I nevertheless wrote an English-language commentary which, synchronized with the already-existing visuals, brought the film closer to the meaning he had hoped it would convey.

No matter what else we had scheduled during Swami Purna's

visits, time was always allotted for his writing work. When we sat together for this purpose, sometimes until the wee hours of the morning, I jotted down everything which came from the streaming flow of his inspiration. Then I had to extract, like a gold miner, the precious nuggets of insight buried within his mystical language. It came to my mind that our adventures with my mother tongue were perhaps only a test, just as all the other absurdities continually occurring around him.

During one of his visits he wished to purchase wooden shoes just like mine. In the shop with the largest assortment of clogs in Amsterdam, he tried on endless pairs before finally declaring he did not want any. This encouraged the salesman to begin a lengthy discourse about the unique advantages of wooden-soled shoes in a cold and damp climate. Swamiji, appearing pressured, instructed me: 'Pick out a pair, any pair, it doesn't matter which.'

Annoyed by his capitulation, I whispered to him that he should not submit like a consumer victim. 'I myself may be indecisive when buying shoes,' I admitted, 'but you are highly attained. You should conduct yourself perfectly in any situation.' I could not hear how disrespectfully I spoke to him.

Over my protestations I bought Swamiji a pair of clogs. Afterwards, 'for practice', he insisted on wearing his 'Holland shoes' in my apartment. With quite some enthusiasm he noisily stomped through the house – on my wooden, uncarpeted floors. I only hoped my neighbors were not at home.

While Swamiji continued his tryout out on the wooden, uncarpeted steps of the public hallway, Denis commented that Swami Purna was highly evolved but had evidently not yet reached completion, as he tried to make us believe.

'He must be doing this on purpose,' I responded. 'I mean, even the most unenlightened person would not behave so stupidly. Don't you see it must be feigned?'

I tended to interpret Swamiji's actions as premeditated, or at least as the workings of a greater wisdom using him as an instrument. It could be that his sometimes blatant ways were exactly what I needed to become more aware of my own limitations.

My positive view notwithstanding, I had many doubts about Swami Purna and was simply unable to submit to him as my guru. This was unfortunate, because total surrender to the teacher is required before he or she will impart the higher knowledge.

'Swamiji,' I asked him one day, 'why is it you usually give vague replies to questions, and why is it you never correct me?'

When he was satisfied with me, he answered, he would tell more. He was actually getting more satisfied, but to correct me now would be futile, for I would not listen.

'I would!' I exclaimed impulsively, really meaning it with all my heart, wanting so much to improve myself. He responded that my main guru to teach me the lesson of obedience lived in this very same building: Oma Mimi.

Well aware that I tended to know everything better, I told myself I should perhaps try and follow Swami Purna's lead. Therefore the next day I asked him to suggest how I could speed up my spiritual progress. He told me to take a job, any job, to end my financial problems. Writing for New Age publications was a worthy endeavor, but the meager fees I received for my articles would keep me in eternal poverty.

Of course I refused, forgetting all my good intentions. 'Your proposal is ridiculous!' I said indignantly, stressing that I needed all my time for undivided concentration on the spiritual work.

Swamiji accused me of being extreme and praised the Buddha's doctrine of the Middle Way. We had to stick to our principles, I countered, especially in these money-mad times. Then he termed me a fanatic, and I got really upset that he, of all people, would so completely misunderstand. The counseling session degenerated into a shouting match. It ended when he jumped up in apparent anger and left the apartment with a loud slam of the door.

'What a jerk,' muttered Denis as I ran after Swamiji, calling loudly up to him as he stamped in his wooden shoes up to the Himalayan room: 'I thought you were such a high being! But your behavior is no better than mine!'

Since my young years, when unable to handle a situation, I easily burst into emotional tantrums which I generally excused as examples of my 'hot Hungarian blood', inherited from my father's side. It might have been Swami Purna's point to confront me with my own weaknesses, but such a possibility did not enter my head.

Hours went by without any sign from above. This was not the first time we experienced Swamiji's sudden departure for the Himalayan room. On the other occasions he had left in a rush because, as he put it, he had to 'answer someone's call'. Needless to say, his actions continued to mystify us.

At dinnertime, when I carried a tray up to the attic, Swamiji laughed and said he would join us downstairs.

During the meal he conversed exclusively with Denis and completely ignored me. Finally Denis asked him: 'What about you and Surya?'

'Her link with me has been for many lives,' answered Swamiji. 'What is happening is for a special reason, all to do with the higher teaching, for the divine purpose.' Then to me he said: 'The day you will realize this on deeper levels, then you will know who and what I am to you.'

Peace reestablished, Swamiji and I enjoyed a renewed closeness. What a surprise when he introduced the forbidden subject of his age. I could not believe my ears when he nonchalantly disclosed that, according to some of his documents, he was 25. He further confounded me by telling that some people have been in his contact for over 50 years.

'How old are you altogether?' I could not help but ask.

'A yogi's age and knowledge cannot be measured,' he answered. 'A yogi can be hundreds, even thousands, of years old. He can leave his body and come back into a new and young body, or he can renew his body and look young.'

'Have you done that?' I inquired.

'You will find out in time,' he replied.

While Swami Purna's visit drew to a close, I thought about his frequent remarks that he was someone who neither wanted nor needed anything. Out of love, devotees gave him all kinds of gifts, and love from his side made him accept and redistribute as *prasad* what they offered. He never asked for anything.

I believed this, yet Denis had many questions. Why did Swamiji speak of establishing an ashram in Holland, and in other places too? Why did someone of his level travel around giving talks to beginners? Why had he allowed his photograph to be used on a flyer announcing the Kumbha Mela film? Did Swami Purna desire a following, fame and wealth like so many contemporary holy men and women? According to Denis, Swamiji wanted to become a guru star in the West, similar to other Eastern teachers who had arrived in recent years.

In my heart I knew, of course, that Swami Purna had a much larger mission. My intuition assured me he was a master of planetary significance, as my first sight of him in Amsterdam had instantly revealed. But since that initial encounter many doubts had arisen in me, and once more I was conscious of the fact that in my contact with Swami Purna, I missed the clarity for which I so longed.

Swami Satchidananda and Faith in the Teacher

Every thought and action has a significance, did not Swami Purna himself teach this principle? Then what was the meaning of his mystifying behaviour?

The same state of unsettled mind which had disquieted me regarding the Jet Age Guru, took hold again. Urgently I needed certain answers. My unshakable faith that behind everything there is the divine plan, with its own kind of reasoning, assured me that the help I sought would in some way be made available.

Meanwhile, I focused my energies on my interviewing work. Hearing of the intended visit of Swami Satchidananda, I prepared to meet him. He was none other than the guru who had opened the legendary Woodstock rock music and peace festival in 1969, the beacon event for a whole generation leaving the old order behind. The swami's favorite mantra, 'Om Shanti, Om Peace' had been quite appropriate for the weekend happening, deep in the heart of the Vietnam protest period. Woodstock turned Swami Satchidananda into a cult hero.

Born in 1914 in South India to wealthy landowner parents who were followers of Shiva, he was named Ramaswamy. Throughout his youth he showed interest in spiritual matters. Upon high school graduation he went into the welding trade, pursued a successful business career, married, and had two sons. When after five years his wife died, he entrusted the children to the care of his mother and devoted himself to inner search.

In 1949 he found his guru, the esteemed Swami Sivananda (1887–1963), founder of the Divine Life Society based in the north Indian town of Rishikesh. Giving up family and possessions, Ramaswamy was initiated into *sannyas*. From Swami Sivananda he received the name Satchidananda, 'Truth-Consciousness-Bliss'.

Four years later Swami Satchidananda was assigned to establish a new Divine Life ashram in Ceylon. He formed other Divine Life centers on the island, opened an orphanage and medical dispensary, and joined a movement for the religious rights of low-caste Hindus. To his ashram came a wealthy American filmmaker, Conrad Rooks, who sponsored the swami's first trip West. The year was 1966, Flower Power high times.

Swami Satchidananda visited Divine Life centers in Europe and, before returning home, flew at Conrad's request to New York for a two-day stopover. He arrived when countless young people, awakened to a new vision of reality with the aid of marijuana and LSD, were being carried along by the spirit of the time towards an emerging New Age. There was an almost collective urge to experience naturally and continually the same expanded consciousness which had been brought about by soft drugs.

The swami's two days in New York became several months. Quickly he attracted a large following and an institute was founded, based on a synthesis of various branches of yoga developed by his guru, Swami Sivananda. What Swami Satchidananda called 'Integral Yoga', by the way, had nothing to do with Sri Aurobindo's self-developmental system of the same name.

Upon widespread request for ongoing guidance, in 1968 the swami took up residence in the United States and eventually over forty Integral Yoga Institutes were established.

On America's East Coast the swami built an ashram named Yogaville, after its aspiration to serve as a model community for living by yogic principles. In the 1980s Yogaville was moved to rural Virginia, where it is thriving as an ecumenical village and spiritual center for persons of all backgrounds.

The ashram's slogan 'Truth is One, Paths are Many' refers to the religious universalism Swami Satchidananda teaches. At its community heart stands LOTUS, the Light of Truth Universal Shrine, a lotus-shaped sanctuary for silent worship, contemplation and meditation. Containing symbols of the world's major religions and sayings from each about the light, it reminds us that all faiths have the same source and that, without anyone's individual beliefs being denied, followers of every path can come together under one roof.

My first darshan of the swami took place at a public discourse in The Hague. He arrived late and entered the hall unceremoniously, a tall, solid-looking man with thick curly shoulder-length hair and silvery beard. Without any fuss he mounted the stage, of which the sole decor was a lone vase of flowers. Gathering his saffron-colored robes neatly about him, he settled onto a cushion in the traditional Indian cross-legged position.

Swami Satchidananda spoke in sweet-sounding English delivered in a low-keyed style. His unpretentious and modest approach was refreshing, particularly when compared to the many gurus who were employing the methods of advertising, public relations and show business to market spirituality.

After thanking the 'beloved friends' for giving him this opportunity to be with them, he asked to switch on the auditorium lights. He did not like the spots directed at him while the audience sat in darkness.

'Certainly God is never so partial,' he explained. 'He gives us all equal light. But now I am getting more light. You are lucky to see me, but I can't see you. I want to enjoy all your beautiful faces, so I can get inspired.'

Naturally the audience smiled at the swami's effusive compliment. In the pleasant atmosphere thus created, he gave his formula for happiness: union, liberation from ego. That implied freedom from desires, wants, needs and expectations; from 'I', 'my' and 'mine'. To accomplish this he advocated yoga, explaining that its purpose was to maintain a peaceful, balanced and neutral mind under all circumstances. *Yoga* he translated from the Sanskrit as 'union of the self with the Supreme Being, or Ultimate Principle'.

In case this sounded too esoteric for a general public, the swami presented a modern-day definition as a practical guideline for inner growth: 'Just lead a natural, healthy life,' he counseled. 'Do *hatha* yoga and *pranayama*. Take care of your food. Meditate. Analyze yourself. Eliminate selfishness. Be useful. Let your life be a one-way traffic: giving, giving, giving. Anybody can give if he has the heart. This is yoga.'

Listening to the swami I clearly understood his popularity, the more as he came over as a non-judgmental father.

The next evening Swami Satchidananda addressed a small gathering of his Dutch followers and their invitees. When I, together with Denis and Diana, entered the living room in the home of yoga teacher Tulia van Twist, the swami greeted us with a warm smile. By the time I had set up the tape recorder, he announced he would speak about the practical applications of yoga.

Coming back to a theme he had introduced at the public talk, he told us: 'Perform your duty, the first duty being to remember your true divine nature. Have no expectations of reward. Give what you can, leave the receiving to others. If people find what you have to give has worth to them, they will use it. If not, not. You don't need to worry. You are what you are. Your mind stays peaceful.'

To illustrate how this principle worked in practice, he used the example of the sun. 'If we ask the sun what it is doing, it will answer: "I just am." If we say the sun is giving light, it can respond to us: "Giving light? I just am light." That the sun is giving, is a perception of the one who receives.

'And if we try to thank the sun for driving away darkness,' continued Swami Satchidananda, 'it could reply: "Why praise me? I am no enemy of darkness, I don't drive darkness away. I don't do anything. I just am myself."

'Everything in creation simply does its duty for which it was created and expects nothing in return,' he went on. 'Take a flower. It does its duty just by being. And it remains the same, whether we appreciate it or not. It is neutral, not getting upset if unpraised, because it has no such expectations. If the flower were to get angry, it would heat up and wither. Anger affects the angry one first. Similarly, praise excites.'

From time to time the swami paused and looked around at us.

'Stay neutral, like the flower,' he urged. 'Do your duty. Don't expect anything in return. Don't wait for the fruits of your acts. It is that fruit which is forbidden to man, not a little apple. Peace of mind is lost when we expect results.

'Take my own example,' he said. 'Yoga friends in this town asked me to come and share with you what I have. I agreed. I am performing a certain duty now. If I expect some reward for this act, for instance new disciples, a great appreciation or a beautiful write-up in the newspaper tomorrow, I would be doing the double work of talking and trying to catch fish. Anxiety would disturb my mind: will I get new disciples or not? I'd lose half the ideas I could share with you. Words wouldn't flow. I would get restless within, wondering: will I get the rewards? Later, if I got them, I'd be excited. Another disturbance. Then the fear of losing the disciples, when I am away from them, would create new distress. At what point would I be peaceful?'

Swami Satchidananda's main advice: 'Serve, give your life to humanity.'

Despite his limited time, the swami agreed to let me interview him the next day. Upon my return to Tulia's house, he asked whether I would not mind posing my questions in the presence of about 15 students. 'My answers are always public, I have no private answers.'

Before I could begin, Tulia set before him a cup of hot, steaming coffee. Seeing this prompted me to inquire: 'Swamiji, how can coffee-drinking agree with your advice to follow a healthy diet? Isn't it important for a teacher to be consistent?'

'Well, I am consistent with this,' he answered, laughing. 'I was very strict for a number of years. Now I know coffee is not really going to disturb me any more.'

Consistency of a guru, the very subject I had on my mind since my last meeting with Swami Purna, came up by itself, through the circumstances. I was not really surprised, having noticed that each teacher appeared in my life at exactly the right moment to reply to a specific need.

Swami Satchidananda explained: 'When the plant is small, you put a big fence around it. When it grows into a tree, you don't need a fence. So I am sure I can handle coffee, or even a cup of whisky, without getting affected by it. But I will tell others not to drink it.'

'You mean, one should be guided not by what teachers do, but by what they say?' I asked.

'That's right,' he said.

This unexpected answer helped me to see Swami Purna's actions in a different light and to release some of my doubts about him.

'Of course,' added Swami Satchidananda, 'this should not be an excuse for a teacher to do anything he wants.'

Whatever he himself did, he advised his students to be strict and not to follow his behaviour: 'If a young plant follows the example of the old tree, it will get eaten by the goats.' The swami's words confirmed my intuition that in this early stage of my spiritual growth, I had to keep very firmly to the disciplined lifestyle I wanted to follow. Later on, when my plant would be more securely rooted and more mature, I would need neither protective fences nor other outside aids.

'If I give top priority to my inner development,' I questioned the swami, 'could this be construed as a selfish act?'

'Wanting to be spiritually perfected', he replied, 'is wanting ultimately to be useful to everyone, not just to yourself. Not only is it not a selfish act, it is a selfless one. Something like the candle wanting to get lit. This is not a selfish act. Unless the candle gets lit, it cannot give light.'

'What if someone appears to be your teacher, but does not seem to light your candle?' I asked, still thinking of Swami Purna.

'A teacher speaks at the level where you are,' answered the swami. 'Watch and wait. See if you get anything.'

Denis interjected: 'And if the teacher always asks you to do things for him?'

'Try to discern if it is just for him personally or if that service will ultimately reach others. No true teacher will demand anything for himself. There is no selfish interest behind the wishes of a true teacher. Ask yourself, what the teacher is doing: is it ultimately for the benefit of all?'

'Same with name, fame and creating a movement?' was Denis' subsequent question.

'Yes,' declared the swami. 'Name and fame may come, but the teacher should not strive for it. If he is a true teacher, he cannot escape name and fame. When the flower opens, it does not have to send invitations for the bees to come. The bees come automatically. What can the flower do? It cannot escape. But the teacher should not get caught in name and fame.

'Sometimes teachers get carried away,' Swami Satchidananda went on. 'A good student can also help a teacher. I may not see that my face has a black mark on it. If you don't tell me, you are not helping me. Everyone can learn from everyone. Be gentle and understanding.'

'Like my coffee-drinking,' he said, taking a sip. 'I have no doubt that stimulating drinks are not good for the nerves, but still I take one cup of coffee per day. It's a weakness of mine, a compromise I make. But it's not a big sin. My coffee is actually milk with a dash of Nescafé. This is why I never like to stay more than three days in a place,' he confided, with a wink. 'When you stay too long, people learn your weaknesses.' The disciples laughed.

'Train your mind as if it is a child,' he continued. 'No need to be rude or rough. The interest is not to break, but to train. You train an animal, not break its bones. If you are regular and persistent, completion will come, but not overnight. Practice with all perseverance, without interruption. Nothing is impossible.'

'How to know what is good and bad in a relationship with a teacher?' I asked next.

'Something becomes good or bad according to your approach,' answered the swami. In the absolute sense, what is "good" is anything that will help you maintain peace of mind. Anything disturbing is bad, even if it looks good. When you act just for the joy of doing, with no expectations, it is a good act.

'The intention is always important. See not the action but the motive behind it. There shouldn't be anything selfish behind an act; it should always be for the good of others. If the teacher expects anything back, it is selfishness.'

I commented that it was difficult to know the intentions of someone else, especially of a guru. 'But I believe we can learn from everything,' I added, 'even from the negative actions of others.'

'Well,' said the swami, 'if you can learn from everything, then you can proceed with this teacher who is apparently the cause of your doubts.'

'I try not to expect, but still I have expectations,' I remarked.

'If you are learning something, keep learning. No need to worry about what he is doing. But if you think you are not getting anything, go away. He may have his own good reasons for what he is doing. It is not possible for us to decide.'

'That is the problem,' I said.

'It's not a problem,' responded Swami Satchidananda. 'When you can't understand something, don't worry about it. Are you developing? Don't worry about the ladder. It will always be there. But you must go up. The ladder is there for that purpose. Make use of the teacher, go up.

'Do not concentrate on his faults. If you see benefit, go ahead. It's a big lesson for the student. If you keep on looking at the faults, you don't learn anything.'

'Sometimes it seems the faults are purposely done,' I told him, 'as if the intention is to teach, and that everything is a test.'

'If you are that faithful and loyal,' said the swami, 'if you have that innocence to trust completely, your faith will take care of everything, even if he cannot. Your faith will help you.'

'Will the power of the good overcome all?' I asked.

'Your faith can change his attitude, make him a better person. In the student–teacher relationship it is not the teacher who helps you, but your faith in the teacher. The teacher does not need to be teaching anything consciously. It is just the presence of the teacher and your faith.

'Else why to kneel and prostrate before statues and symbols and pieces of paper? Because one sees a spiritual vibration in them. A piece of wood like a cross cannot teach, but if you have faith you see the sacrifice and the great vibration of the great teacher behind the cross. In this area, faith can move mountains.

'But how many of us have that faith? The luckiest people in the whole world are those who have faith. If we have even one atom of doubt, it will ruin us. Doubt creates missile sites. It's the worst enemy in anyone's life. It is the worst thing assailing the whole world today.'

The interview continued, covering topics on yoga and spirituality, but I already had the main answers I needed at that moment.

Behind the Scenes

One of the visits of Swami Purna to Amsterdam coincided with another stay of Yogi Bhajan at the Guru Ram Das Ashram. Hearing that the Sikh teacher was in town, Swamiji suggested that I should meet him.

'If you want to work for humanity on a big mission, you cannot sit,' told Swamiji. 'You must go to people, to those who are genuine.'

At the 3HO ashram a woman carrying a baby on her arm received us warmly. We were led upstairs to a simple room where Yogi Bhajan reclined expansively upon a large bed. He sat up to greet us. When he asked if we would join him for lunch, Swamiji politely refused.

While enjoying his food, Yogi Bhajan initiated the conversation with Swamiji. He wanted to know about Swamiji's 'set-up' in the West, and how many students he had. He himself had many thousands, both in Europe and in the United States. Numbers were increasing. The centers he had created were self-supporting entities financed through their own small-scale businesses. He believed all his students should work. Quite a few taught yoga, also to prisoners and drug addicts, helping many people become hopeful and healthy. Furthermore, he urged his students to take up family life.

'Why don't you marry?' he asked Swamiji. 'Find yourself an American,' he suggested. 'Then you won't have visa problems in the States.' Yogi Bhajan surprised us by revealing the salary he received for giving courses at the University of California in Los Angeles, his adopted home town. He also lectured all over America. The country was so big, he explained to Swamiji, there was plenty of room for new spiritual teachers, especially young and handsome ones. He assured Swamiji he would attract many followers, and added that having a wife would protect him from difficulties with female students.

Yogi Bhajan asked the disciple who cleared away the luncheon dishes and who served all of us 'Yogi Tea', to bring him a pen.

'This is my phone number in Los Angeles,' he said, handing a sheet of paper to Swamiji. 'When you come to America, call me. I'll help you get started.'

Swamiji smiled, looking quite amused.

Denis and I observed with big eyes the interchange between the two propagators of higher values. Beginning to see behind the scenes of the divine play called 'Spiritual Teachers in the West', we were not sure whether it was a comedy or a tragedy.

After some discussion in Hindi which we could not understand, Yogi Bhajan turned his attention to me. 'What do you do?' he barked in his somewhat rough but friendly manner.

'I live!' I exclaimed vigorously, imitating his style.

Yogi Bhajan laughed heartily. 'That's it!' he burst out.

Then he turned back to Swamiji. 'She's good,' he declared, as if giving us his blessings. 'You should consider what I advise you, about a marriage.'

Swamiji chuckled. 'I have my tradition,' he answered.

'Things are changing,' said Yogi Bhajan, naming several teachers who had married in recent years.

We were ready to leave. Yogi Bhajan very graciously insisted that one of his students would drive us back to my place, and he and Swamiji exchanged final pleasantries in Hindi. I wondered if Swamiji was trying to top Yogi Bhajan by inviting the Sikh guru to phone him when he got to London, Bonn or New Delhi, where Swamiji had informal centers and students.

At my apartment, Swami Purna remarked that Yogi Bhajan had come a long way since his years as a customs inspector in India. He was having a good influence on many young persons, but Swamiji did not appreciate some of the methods used. Putting Westerners into Eastern uniforms, he said, could take away their freedom. It did not have to, if people were developed enough in consciousness. One of the main purposes of a guru, Swami Purna repeatedly told us, was to help others become totally free from the attachments of body and mind.

Yogi Bhajan was earning very well with his good works, Swamiji added. He had really made it in America. The Sikh guru had no idea, as I also had not at that time, that Swami Purna had had a following in the United States already in the 1960s, years before Yogi Bhajan reached there. But the founder of the 3HO Foundation judged Swamiji by his youthful appearance, and considered him a beginner trying to succeed in the West like other teachers.

Amused by the discussion in the guru's bedroom, Swamiji interpreted Yogi Bhajan's offer to assist his branching out to the United States as sincerely meant. More cooperation among teachers was required, he said, telling us that some gurus competed with each other just like people in worldly society.

'I always emphasize there should be unity among spiritual people. Otherwise, how can there ever be mass unity? On the higher level of consciousness there is no division at all, there is unity. When a highly developed person meets another one, there is no quarrel, no difference of opinion. They always come to the point where they can work together, where they can do something everlasting for the people, for society and humanity.'

'What is the basis for unity?' I asked.

'No one has a monopoly of truth,' replied Swamiji. 'Truth is one, and so God is one. When you have one aim to achieve, then why a division? If a division exists, it reveals there is no mutual aim of unity.'

After the visit to Yogi Bhajan, Swamiji joked that now he wanted to see the 'set-up' of some other well-known New Age groups with branches in Amsterdam. To get a true picture, he proposed we go unannounced.

Our investigative journey took us first to the International Society for Krishna Consciousness, ISKCON, founded by A. C. Bhaktivedanta Swami Prabhupada upon his arrival in America in 1965. A monk from Vrindavan, he brought to the West a version of Krishna worship that traces back to 16th-century India. Swami Prabhupada's students read his interpretations of the ancient Vedic texts as well as of the *Bhagavad Gita*. In this celebrated yoga scripture, part of the great epic tale of India, the *Mahabharata*, Lord Krishna sets forth the various paths to salvation.

A large 17th-century mansion on an attractive Amsterdam canal served as ISKCON's Dutch center. At the door a zealous young man with shaved head and dressed in saffron Indian robes asked what we wanted, all the while reciting the *Hare Krishna,*

Hare Rama mantra. I presented Swamiji, giving several of his titles, and expressed our interest in talking with someone about Krishna Consciousness. We were requested to wait.

After some time another young Dutchman came to us, announcing himself as the center's president. I introduced Swami Purna with all respect and mentioned again several of his Sanskrit epithets, but it was like speaking Greek for the president kept addressing Swamiji as if he were a novice arriving at an ashram for elementary instruction.

Invited to sit on the floor, we had hardly a chance to say one word because our host began without delay to teach us the basics of Krishna worship as propagated by His Divine Grace Swami Prabhupada. Only a few moments passed when Swami Purna corrected the young man's pronunciation of Sanskrit and asked how long he had been studying. While Denis and I watched the roles reverse, Swamiji quoted lines from the *Bhagavad Gita* and gave commentaries challenging the interpretation on which Swami Prabhupada based his movement.

An argument ensued. During it the ISKCON representative dutifully defended his guru, steadfastly disallowing any other viewpoint to enter his thought process. Swamiji finally threw up his hands as if in exasperation and signaled our departure. His repetitions of 'close-minded' and 'ignorant' provided an unusual counterpoint to the Hare Krishna chant of the devotee who led us to the door.

'Merely from knowing a few Sanskrit words this boy was trying to tell me the meaning of the *Bhagavad Gita*, insisting that his guru's interpretation is the only one,' said Swamiji as we walked along the canal. 'He knows none of the commentaries by the great men of the past. How can he say Prabhupada's version is right and the only one, and all the great commentators have interpreted wrongly?

'With all the emphasis on the chanting of the Krishna mantra, the bowing down to idols, shaving of the head, and wearing of Indian clothes, this group gives too much attention to the external. But it is not worthless what they are doing,' added Swamiji. 'They obviously get happiness out of it, and peace of mind.'

Not yet having had enough of our New Age fieldwork, Swamiji decided to proceed directly to the Amsterdam center of the Divine Light Mission. Founded in 1960 by the late Shri Hans Ji Maharaj, the DLM grew rapidly in the West after the son and successor of

Shri Hans, Guru Maharaj Ji, visited London in 1971 at the age of 13.

At the DLM center we were welcomed by one of Guru Maharaj Ji's enthusiastic followers who asked us almost immediately: 'Have you taken the Knowledge?' He was referring to the four simple meditation techniques taught aspirants during their initiation.

Swamiji laughed and said, 'What knowledge?' This prelude characterized the ensuing talk at cross-purposes. As at the Hare Krishna ashram, our hopes for a fruitful dialogue proved illusory. Our host was totally immersed in his guru's presentation of truth and to all appearances had no room in his mind for anything else.

We enjoyed, however, the friendly atmosphere which marked the entire research session, and we noted a loving attitude in all the people around us. They did justice to their guru's name for them: 'premies', from the Hindi premi meaning 'lover'. This in turn from the Sanskrit prem: a love whose nature is devotion to the divine and whose character is self-giving. At the DLM the premies restricted their devoted love to their guru, though in the deeper sense a premie is in love with God.

I experienced the same gentle and peaceful mood the following August at a three-day festival of the European premies headed by Guru Maharaj Ji himself, then 18. I was quite impressed by his depth, something I had not expected after all I had heard about the teenage guru and his penchant for costly cars and luxuries.

For several hours each day he held an audience of 8,000 followers totally concentrated on his every word while he spoke about heavenly ideals and living a good and moral life. The guru's smoothly running organization, complete with professional staff and public relations department, presented a varied and entertaining program. A discourse by the young True Master, who sat high above the crowd on a theatrically-decorated stage, constituted the climactic final act in a daily superprogram of spiritually-oriented films, pop music, meditation and vegetarian food in a meeting center on the outskirts of Essen in Germany.

When we had completed our mission at the Amsterdam DLM center, Swamiji remarked: 'In some of these groups people are learning how to be even more separate. The Bible says one should be judged by the fruit. What is their fruit? Denying everything except their own guru, their group, their way of life? Anything that divides people is no good.'

It had been a crowded day, rich in impressions of the Amsterdam spiritual scene, and Swamiji left us little room for contemplation on it. In the evening, my tape recorder turning, he lectured us: 'No group can give you Self-realization. A group can make arrangements, assist people to become familiar with certain information and provide a system, but it cannot give the main thing. To learn a system it is good to have an organization, but if an organization promises to give you everything, don't believe. What is an organization? It is only a group of people whose state of consciousness is of course not as high as the guru's.'

I commented that some groups promised enlightenment to those who followed their system.

'Never!' declared Swamiji, amused. 'In a group you may be able to reach a point where you can understand, and then you can prepare yourself towards Self-realization. For that you will need individual guidance. I always suspect those teachers who form organizations and bind people to them and to their person. This violates the very essence of spiritual development: freedom.'

'Have you yourself made many disciples and followers?' I asked, having wanted to pose this question for quite some time.

'Followers, yes. The principle I generally observe is to make no commitment to anyone, except to a few selected individuals, those who will carry on the work. To the others I just give as much as I can, then part with no attachment or connection whatever. I leave people free, and say that others will come to teach them when they need.'

Swamiji explained the differences between disciples, followers and devotees before he stated: 'There are only a few very special ones worthy to be disciples. Adi Shankaracharya, who had millions of followers in India, chose only a handful of disciples and through them did the work. When I myself make disciples, I don't necessarily initiate them immediately. First they have to be made ready.'

His tone indicated that this was usually a long process.

'A true master says nothing, he simply does his work,' he continued. 'I have seen many saints who had no ashrams, no group. They gave their teachings to those who were qualified, unconditionally. Anyone involved in the service of humanity must be especially careful of the desire for three things, as described in the Indian scriptures: the desire for fame, wealth and followers.

'In the present time organizations may be necessary, but only for legal reasons. Why a sect that makes you different and separate? Why become an Aurovillian? Why not a human being?'

Swami Purna concluded his polemic by declaring we must work for the final goal of Oneness and not get confined in the narrow thinking of most groups. A teacher for the new era, he said, will consider the ideal of unity among people to be possible and will work towards it.

Pir Vilayat Inayat Khan and the New Consciousness

Ever since my soul-comforting darshan with Pir Vilayat Inayat Khan I had hoped to interview the popular New Age teacher. My wish was fulfilled one year later, when he presided over a four-day Sufi gathering in The Hague. After listening to Pir Vilayat discourse in Dutch – he speaks several European languages – I met him privately for a recorded conversation.

'What exactly is the New Age?' was my first question.

'The New Age is the Aquarian consciousness of the spiritual which is rising in humanity,' he replied. 'It is a time to get detached from dogmas and to abandon the belief that material prosperity is the ultimate aim of life. A certain disenchantment with materialism is accompanied by the emergence of expanded dimensions of consciousness.'

What happened to me was apparently occurring, in various ways, to an increasing number of people.

Pir continued: 'The so-called modern life, based on the industrial revolution and on competition, belongs to the past. We have to replace competition by cooperation.'

I remarked that past generations had been attracted to spirituality as well and asked him what was different now.

'Today people are not only interested in thoughts and ideas,' said Pir, 'but want to know through experience.'

I commented, 'This is why teachers who promise experiences, such as inner light and sound, are so successful despite the high fees they charge.'

'Yes,' he responded, 'because we are not yet in the New Age, we are just moving into it. For the moment people feel all religious approaches are good, which is of course better than the old narrowmindedness. Different ways are being tried. One of the main things about New Age people is that they want to find out about the others.'

Buckminster Fuller and his term 'otherness', for being aware of others, came to my mind.

'In order to become world-conscious, you have to experience other ways without getting bound by them,' Pir went on. 'You also have to understand the link between the various possibilities.'

'In the West there are more and more teachers, sects and groups,' I said. 'Many acknowledge the New Age as a time of unity. Yet we see only further division and separation.'

Pir Vilayat agreed, adding that quite a few teachers were concerned about this matter. The fact that so many students followed several paths at the same time and often mixed the practices forced teachers to come together and deal with each other. Only recently he had participated in a meeting of Sri Chinmoy, Yogi Bhajan, the Buddhist Lama Govinda and other gurus, each of whom answered the same questions coming from the public.

'But this is not yet enough,' declared Pir. 'We want to go further and discuss our systems among ourselves, in order to iron out our differences.'

'Is it really possible to find unity?' I wanted to know.

'Yes, and it is important, but we must be willing to invest time in it. Gurus are so busy nowadays, traveling constantly. From a guru's viewpoint, one evening without a public is already a terrible loss of an opportunity to give his teaching. But I feel the sacrifice is necessary for the coordination of the different approaches. It just depends on what one considers more important: one's own teaching or teaching in general.'

'Not all teachers look for unity,' I said.

'For me it is clear that anybody who maintains his way is the only one does not have New Age consciousness,' stated Pir Vilayat. 'The New Age consists in the integration of all ways.'

'What is the basic mark of a New Age teacher?' I asked.

'He includes all ways. He has roots in his tradition and branches in the new dimensions. But this is only the first step. The second is to find out how all these things can be coordinated. This the gurus have not yet done.'

The talk continued on various related topics, one of which was initiation. Swami Purna had told me that anyone on the spiritual path eventually has to take initiation from a living master. During the act the guru not only cleanses the disciple's body and mind, but also imparts spiritual force. A mantra and a meditation technique are given, by which power flows from guru to disciple. The student may receive a spiritual name. Vows are exchanged. The master promises to help liberate the student, and the student pledges to follow the disciplines imposed by the master.

The tradition of initiation is not intended for mass-quickness, Swami Purna had said. A real guru does not initiate without knowing someone well and considering him or her ready. It is a very intimate and sacred act. No two persons get exactly the same initiation, and there has to be individual teaching. But if the guru does not have time, and hundreds are waiting, it is very tempting to initiate everyone at once. According to Swami Purna, in the West the word 'initiation' is often used by the teacher to sell his product more easily than if he said: 'I am giving yoga lessons.' He told me that he himself had initiated only very few persons.

Unlike Swami Purna who firmly adheres to the classical tradition in which initiation is not given or taken lightly, Pir Vilayat discloses advanced techniques and practices in public places to those who have not been initiated. I asked him why.

'Because the need for training is enormous. The demand is so great that, unfortunately, I am unable to give individual guidance to everybody. In these circumstances all I can do is teach openly. If people aren't up to it, the practices don't mean a thing to them anyhow.

'Formerly the idea was to protect these teachings from anyone who wanted to use them for personal power and so forth. This is no longer a worry since most are now available in books. That's why I feel free to give practices in public, though I still keep secret the things not yet published. There is a certain frontier beyond which I don't want to go.

'I pass on these techniques because there are some people who can really make use of them but don't get them from their gurus. When they get them now, they are so very grateful. It changes their life. I think it very unfair that someone would have to join the Sufi Order before he or she could receive a higher teaching. That's like trying to make enrollments for the sake of numbers. The aim is not numbers but the training of people. Of course it is beneficial to become a member because initiation creates a tie with our tradition. The very fact that someone follows a teaching I give establishes by itself a link.'

'On the spiritual path, what is the purpose of having a new name?' I asked.

'It is a custom that developed in the past, especially in monastic orders,' answered Pir. 'It means you are changing. There has been a transformation in your life and you are no more the same. The fact is, one identifies very much with a name. People who think of you in terms of what you were, and call you by the old name, will hold you back. A spiritual name is a way of freeing yourself from the opinion of others, so it is important to utilize it in your life. That's what a spiritual name is all about. It is a fundamental human right to change your name, as you have done.'

In a new flow of thought I posed my next question: 'In your public lectures you say that in the Himalayas there are high beings who work for humanity indirectly and unknown. To what extent are you associated with them?'

'Well,' he replied, 'I feel that any leader or guru has the responsibility to maintain a connection with the living teachers, and also with those who are not incarnated but are still concerned with conditions on earth and are guiding us. If there were no contact with them, they could not give us guidance.

'I have scrupulously followed the message of the New Age by communicating with teachers of many different religions, for which I have been criticized by some people who maintain that I should visit only Sufis. Of course, most of the great teachers are unknown. They are living in caves or in small villages, like the dervishes, the Sufi saints. If some of their essence can come through me, then I act as a vehicle for what they have to give.

'One thing is certain. In every age there is a spiritual government, headed by a very high entity. He is unknown to the world and I don't know him physically or personally, but I have communication with him all the same.'

That led me to ask: 'Do these beings always work through persons who are aware they serve as instruments?'

'They work as well through persons who are not aware of it, but it is easier to work through those who are.'

We also talked about the spiritual community 'The Abode of the Message' founded by Pir in the Berkshire Hills near New Lebanon, in upstate New York, on the site of a former Shaker village. The Shakers were an American religious sect which originated in the 18th century and promoted communal, celibate and ascetic living. On 430 acres, bordering Massachusetts, they

established one of their communes. It amazed Pir to hear that, at
the age of 19, I spent my college vacation working as a counselor
in a summer camp in exactly the same village his order had just
purchased.

'Isn't it extraordinary! You were there! Just imagine, now we
own that property and are creating our own village, based on
New Age principles.'

With not more than a few minutes remaining before his next
appointment, I told Pir I still had not found full clarity about
myself after the experiences in India had so profoundly rearranged
me. I mentioned as well my confusion regarding Swami Purna.

'You see, what I think is this,' he began. 'You have to go
personally through the very things we've been speaking about. In
other words, you have to go through the thinking of the people
who have been caught up in a school, and then you have to free
yourself from it.

'And that is what the New Age is doing, because you cannot get
the experience without going through an authentic school. Then
you need the force to free yourself from the narrowness of that
school, while keeping the essence of it. In this way you are freeing
yourself from all forms and dogmas. So remember that when a
guru says something, it is not Bible truth.'

'I know that,' I said.

'The funny thing is that the same guru who can give you really
enlightened teaching can as well say something which is
completely wrong,' said Pir. 'A teaching he got from his own
tradition may be right, but what he says out of his limitations may
be false. I've been surprised to find one can get very high teachings
from people who are still bound in their tradition and say things
which really shock me by their narrowness.'

'Actually I'd like to return to India and retreat into myself for a
while,' I remarked, 'but being involved in worldly life and writing
about spiritual teachers – '

'Just imagine!' exclaimed Pir, interrupting me with a delighted
expression. 'What a wonderful opportunity.'

'It is wonderful,' I agreed, 'but instead of receiving bits and
pieces from many teachers, do you think it might be better to
work closely with only one?'

He answered immediately: 'I've made it a point to try and visit
all the great acknowledged teachers of my time. Not only those
known in Europe, but especially the ones in India. Also *rishis* in

caves. I've been very inspired by them.'

'I suppose that meeting teachers, to write articles about them, is part of the plan for me.'

'Yes, it's for your unfoldment. So I would go and visit them, just like the Buddha saw all the teachers of his time. Many won't even understand what you mean by New Age, but these contacts will nourish you, like a bee which takes honey from the profusion of flowers.

'Finally you will have to find the bridge between the different ways, put together all you have received, and make your own synthesis. It is the most difficult path you are on,' he summed up, 'the path of freedom.'

That was it! This was my path! With four simple words Pir Vilayat had put the process of my spiritual advancement into a proper perspective, helping me to understand the significance of my diverse encounters in and since India.

Although his words were directed only to me, I realized that ultimately they applied to all of us. The path of freedom is the road we all tread.

Maharaj Charan Singh
and Listening Within

A few days after enjoying the warm reception by Pir Vilayat Inayat Khan and still flying high from the fresh inspiration he excited in me, I read an announcement that another important spiritual leader, Maharaj Charan Singh, would soon arrive in Amsterdam.

Charan Singh was a guru of the Radha Soami faith, also called Sant Mat or 'the Teachings of the Saints', and belonged to the branch headquartered in Beas, in the Indian Punjab. Revered as the Sant Sat Guru, 'the Living Master' or 'the Lord in human form', he had a tremendous following in India as well as in Europe, the United States and South Africa.

The Dutch representative of the Radha Soami Satsang Beas, Lionel Metz, was not at home when I phoned. His wife took my message. To my request for an interview with Charan Singh she stated the group did not care for publicity and the Master did not usually speak to journalists.

I explained that my intended article was for a spiritually-oriented magazine. 'Oh, then it is something else,' she said. In the meantime, I could call another number for study material. Mrs. Prins, the spokesperson in Amsterdam, asked me: 'Do you want to be initiated?' My negative reply added no fuel to our exchange, but she nonetheless agreed to lend me some books.

From this information I saw that the Radha Soami method, also called *Surat Shabd Yoga*, 'the Yoga of the Sound Current', appeared in the late 19th century in the city of Agra. There, the Indian mystic Shiv Dayal Singh Soamiji Maharaj (1818–78) brought forth a new spiritual path after 15 years spent in continuous meditation. Next to his own inner discoveries, his main influences were the teachings of saints in the Sant tradition of North India, including Guru Nanak, the founder of Sikhism, and the 15th-century mystic-poet Kabir. They all followed an interior religion based on contemplation and the revelation of God.

Like most teachers, Soamiji Maharaj taught that the ego, controlled by the mind, presented the greatest barrier to our freedom from the cycle of birth and death. According to him, only one method existed for subduing the mind. This was to listen to *Nam*, the primal sound, the life current of energy, also called *Shabd* in Hindi. *Nam* corresponds to the term *Logos*, or 'Word', in the Bible.

Practitioners of *Surat Shabd Yoga* believe that the entire creation has evolved from *Shabd*, which is actually the Supreme Creator vibrating through all life. They reach the Divine by bringing their soul into contact with this sound current. Hidden in the temple of the human body, this current reverberates at the third eye where meditators can meet the higher, radiant form of their Living Master. It is the Master who, attuned with the *Shabd*, brings them into contact with the divine stream which is God in dynamic action.

The Radha Soami system emphasizes that students must be initiated and assisted by a Living Master of the Sant Mat tradition to enable them to hear the sound while meditating in the prescribed way. The master guides and protects the disciples on the journey through the various spiritual planes so they may reach the bliss of communion with the Supreme and attain the ultimate freedom. In true spiritual style, no fees are charged for either initiation or teachings.

During a well-attended gathering in an Amsterdam congress center, I heard more about this mystic path. Charan Singh, a cultivated middle-aged gentleman of Sikh appearance with turban and flowing beard, discoursed in a pleasantly tranquil manner for two evenings on the message of Sant Mat in relation to the New Testament, particularly the books of St. John and St. Matthew.

'You know I am no authority on the Bible,' he said, 'but I personally believe and feel that the teachings given by the Lord Jesus Christ are exactly the same as the teachings coming to us from the mystics and saints of the East.

'The main gist of the teachings of all the mystics is that worship of the spirit is worship of the Father. No other worship pleases the Father. No other worship can lead us back to the Father. And for worshipping the spirit, for worshipping the Holy Ghost, for attaching ourself to the *Shabd* and *Nam* within, we need the help and the guidance of a Living Master. This is the nutshell of the teachings of all the mystics, whether they belong to the East or the West. I will discuss with you the teachings of Sant Mat in the light of the New Testament, as this is your background.'

Then, explaining that much has been lost because the Christ's teachings were not written down until long after the death of Jesus, and have come to us only after repeated translations, Charan Singh embarked upon an interesting analysis which provided a new way of looking at the Gospel.

Maharaj Ji, as he was also addressed, used the words of the Christ to stress that, in order to get in touch with the *Shabd*, we needed the help of a Living Master: 'Christ said that the Lord is within, and if we want to search for the Father, we must worship Him inside ourselves. But', Maharaj Ji went on, 'Christ explains that no one by his own effort can reach the Father. God the Father is only accessible through a saint or master – not directly.'

A film followed. Depicting the Radha Soami colony in Beas, it included a scene showing a mass initiation of 500 new *satsangis*, as practitioners of *Surat Shabd Yoga* are called. When the auditorium lights came on again, it was announced that an initiation would take place in Amsterdam later in the week. It struck me to hear: 'Maharaj Ji will not attend this initiation in his physical form.'

The next morning I took part in a group meditation at the Hilton Hotel. Several hundred satsangis filled a large room. Charan Singh entered and sat on a raised platform, remaining in silence on his chair. Legs crossed, hands clasped, eyes open. Profiting from the presence of their Sant Sat Guru, who is regarded as the very embodiment of the divine sound, the satsangis meditated with closed eyes. After about ten minutes the master got up and left.

A young bearded Dutchman took the stage and enthusiastically repeated his guru's message of the evening before, that everyone needed a Living Master.

'Without initiation you can't get home,' the satsangi told us. 'That's the way it is; that's the law. There is no other way.' For him there was no route to salvation but Sant Mat, just as his master taught.

In Charan Singh's book *The Path* it is written: 'Without

constantly listening to the inner music of *Nam* or *Shabd*, no one can enter the kingdom of God.' And 'This is the only means of redemption . . . There is no second way.' Or, in other words, if we 'follow other paths, there will be no alternative left to us but to repent at the time of death for foolishly wasting our time'.[20]

My request for an interview with Charan Singh granted, I spent the whole day waiting in the hotel until finally, at four-thirty in the afternoon, I was able to see him. To my regret about 20 satsangis were also present. I remembered the change in Maharishi Mahesh Yogi's attitude when his students joined us during our interview.

After being introduced to Charan Singh, I was permitted to start. The climate of the encounter was evidenced quickly, from my very first question. The subject had been suggested to me by Swami Purna and, when I presented it to other gurus, had elicited interesting reactions.

'It is said that in the Himalayas there are high beings who work for humanity indirectly and unknown,' I commenced. 'May I ask, to what extent are you connected with them?'

'First try to search for them,' replied Charan Singh.

'Pardon?'

'First try to search for those masters who are hiding themselves in the Himalayas. Then ask the second question.'

His attitude was not particularly encouraging and I registered a sudden freezing up of the already cool atmosphere, as if my question had brought the ice of the Himalayas into the room.

'You mean I should ask the hidden masters to what extent they are connected with you?' I inquired, like a schoolgirl before the examining board.

'Yes. Why ask me?'

Lionel Metz interpreted for the group: 'The Master says, ask Brahm to break the stone. If he doesn't, I will do it.'

His esoterica escaped my understanding.

By this time I had the impression that the spiritual assemblage had transformed itself into a law court where I stood in front of the prosecuting attorney, and I remembered that Charan Singh was a lawyer by training. In certain journalistic interrogations a combative atmosphere might be normal, but I had hardly expected this during an interview with a Sant Sat Guru.

With sufficient egg on my face I mustered up all my courage and proceeded with a question inspired by certain thoughts I had found in *The Path*. Charan Singh wrote there:

Those who remember the Lord as Wah-i-Guru ... call themselves Sikhs; those who remember Him as Allah call themselves Muslims; while those who remember Him as Ram, call themselves Hindus. We become so intolerant that it becomes difficult for us even to meet each other. Where this wrangling over words is leading us never occurs to us. If today, however, we were to merge our thought-currents with the True Nam, all strife and discords would come to an end.[21]

I therefore asked him: 'Some spiritual leaders say we are moving into a New Age of higher values and principles in which life will be marked by an integration of the various spiritual ways. May I ask, what are you doing to contribute to this type of unity?'

'You see, naturally every mystic or saint in this world tries to unite us,' he answered. 'But it is very difficult to say the world will ever be united. Because the human mind is there. It always divides in one way or another. It is very difficult to bring the whole world on one platform. We can't reform the whole world. We can just reform our own self, so that we can be one with others. Others may not become one with you, but you can definitely become one with others.'

'Yes, but there seems to be a marked tendency now for a spread of consciousness, especially in the West. People call this awakening the dawning of a New Age,' I said.

'This is what one thinks and says, but I feel in every age there has been a spiritual awakening,' he replied. 'In every age the inclination of the soul is always towards its own origin, towards the Lord. And this is spiritual awakening. This has been everywhere in every age.'

'Are you saying that the phenomenon we are witnessing today is neither new nor important to note?'

'It has always been there, in one form or another.'

'Nowadays there are more and more teachers, sects and groups, especially in the West. Many acknowledge the New Age as a time of unity. Yet we see no unity, only further division and separation. I am wondering, is there the possibility of integrating the spiritual teachings through the cosmic sound?'

'Well, those who are connected with the sound are very near to each other,' he answered.

'Yes, but I mean, with the cosmic sound is there any possibility for a new kind of oneness in which all teachings could be integrated?'

'That would be a very limited way,' he replied. 'Everybody won't follow the same teachings.'

Inspired by the visionary thoughts of such teachers as Sri Aurobindo and the Mother, and impregnated by the spirit of the time, I was searching for any enlightened contribution to my dream of a New Age to come, and this is why the interview continued in the same line. Unfortunately I was not yet aware that the Radha Soami system has no interest in increasing the world's attraction as a place in which to remain, and even considers any efforts in this direction detrimental to *satsangis* because energies given to outer work cannot be utilized for inner progress.

I was relieved when one of the satsangis indicated my time was up, and I returned to the safer anonymity of being a simple participant in the gathering.

Among my papers was a printed form that had been handed to me. 'Application for Initiation into the Radha Soami Satsang' it read in three languages.

At the top of the questionnaire was written: 'The object of initiation is to be able to realize God within ourselves, and it is not for the purpose of seeking any material gain or personal advantage. The applicant should abstain from alcoholic drinks and the taking of intoxicating drugs in any form; should lead a pure moral life, and have a firm resolve to follow a vegetarian diet, free from flesh, fish or eggs. He should be prepared to devote at least two-and-a-half hours daily to meditation. Only those living by these principles and willing to follow this ideal may apply, having grasped the essence of this philosophy.'

Quite apart from the fact that I had not at all considered joining the group, this impersonal approach to potential initiates did not appeal to me. At any rate, my own guidelines of conduct were almost as strict as theirs.

After Charan Singh's last discourse, I hastened back to my desk to type out the interview with Pir Vilayat Inayat Khan. With teachers arriving in Holland in a steady succession, the increase in my work prevented me from ever writing an article on Maharaj Charan Singh.

I gave no further attention to Sant Mat until years later, when circumstances brought me to the roots of the Radha Soami faith in Agra. From there it had spread to form various branches, like the one at Beas, each with its own Sat Guru and own interpretation of the teachings. In the same house in Agra where its founder, Soamiji Maharaj, was born, meditated and transmitted his wisdom to the first satsangis, I had the occasion to stay for some time and to see other aspects of Sant Mat.

In Agra, Soamiji Maharaj and his wife Radhaji, who is also revered as a Sat Guru, came to life for me. I especially admired their example of spiritual partnership between husband and wife. Led by affection for them and by the intense devotion of a close satsangi friend, Charan Das, I stayed as well at the original Radha Soami community, Soamibag. From there I visited Dayalbag, an adjacent Radha Soami colony run on socialistic principles. But all this is a story for yet another book.

Vasant and the Agnihotra Sun Ritual

'Who is your master?' one of the satsangis had asked me during the Radha Soami gathering, also inquiring: 'Have you been initiated?' I gave some vague reply. How could I have admitted to her, or to practically anyone, that my guru was the sun, and that in India the sun itself had initiated me into higher dimensions of consciousness?

I carried this secret in my heart, like a closet sun worshipper. Do I have to say that I identified myself so much with the shining orb that anything to do with the sun immediately engaged my attention?

Scarcely a day or two after the Sant Mat meeting I received a note with an exuberant drawing of a sun. Tulia van Twist, the yoga teacher whom I had met during the visit of Swami Satchidananda in The Hague, wrote to me on bright yellow stationery.

'Dear Surya,' she began, 'an Indian teacher named Vasant whose mission is to teach the Fivefold Path (Kriya Yoga) to the people of our era is coming to my home. I am very sure it will be of great value to you, so try to come!'

Tulia's enthusiasm radiated from the colorful piece of paper. The letter felt almost warm in my hand. I read on: 'One of the main points of his mission is to teach people a fire ceremony named Agnihotra. This must be carried out by as many persons as possible, to save the world from pollution of the atmosphere. Many people in the United States and Germany are already doing it.'

When Denis and I arrived at Tulia's home, on a Sunday incidentally, about 30 men and women were already assembled. An air of suspense filled the room. Something important was obviously expected to happen. Looking around, I saw a copper container, shaped like an inverted pyramid, placed on a stone slab together with small pieces of wood. I had the inexplicable sensation of having returned to ancient times.

Soon a middle-aged bald-headed Indian man entered briskly and sat down in front of us. 'Time is fast running out,' declared Vasant. 'So I have come to talk about a few practical things. You do not have to believe any of my words. My only request is: please try to examine what I say to the farthest limit of your reason. The divine will is so strong at the moment that what yogis failed to achieve in many incarnations, you and I are going to get with little effort.'

Denis and I exchanged a wondering look. Were we going to hear about another easy short-cut to instant enlightenment?

Again we were told that our mind was the key to change. Only when we went beyond the reasoning intellect to the higher intuitional mind would reality dawn on us. Mental purity helped this to occur. Among the many causes of mental pollution, Vasant concentrated on the new troublemaker, our poisoned environment.

'Any disturbance in the atmosphere affects all life on the planet,' he said. 'Modern scientists know about the harm of environmental pollution to the body, but the ancient Indian science of bio-energy and bacteriology states that pollution has a highly damaging impact on *prana*. This vital energy, taken in through the breath, connects us to the cosmos and is needed by the mind for the thinking process. Purification of the atmosphere leads to purification of prana. Prana and mind are two sides of the same coin.'

Then he told us about Agnihotra, the Sanskrit for 'purification of the atmosphere by fire'. The process aided mental cleanliness by removing tensions in the mind caused by pollution. Gases formed from Agnihotra also stopped putrefaction, sterilized household dust and acted as subtle nourishment for plant, animal and human life.

'This ancient Indian technique was revealed to me by somebody great from the divine hierarchy which rules the world,' Vasant disclosed. 'I am the blessed stone sent to the West to explain Agnihotra. I am merely an instrument, like a postman bringing good news.'

The Agnihotra procedure consisted of burning specific varieties of wood, dried cow dung and clarified butter in a copper pot, at sunrise and sunset. 'The proper conditions within these phenomena of nature last only two minutes,' he explained, 'and during this short period you utter a particular mantra dedicated to the Sun God Surya and make offerings of raw rice.' I was intrigued.

Pure copper had to be used because only this metal had the required reaction. Preferably the container should be pyramid-shaped, because the form of an object affects the finer energy. We could buy the suitable pot after the meeting as Vasant had brought a supply from India.

Swami Purna told me later that the fire ceremony held in India by many Brahmins at sunrise and sunset used the same materials and followed the same method as Vasant's Agnihotra. The joint combustion of cow dung, clarified butter and certain types of wood created a special environment conducive to concentration. This could aid us when we wanted to attain a higher level of consciousness, for instance during contemplation or meditation.

If all of us were to perform Agnihotra, implied Vasant, we could counteract, reduce, perhaps even remove the massive pollution seriously undermining our present way of life.

Vasant's optimistic views did me good, but I simply could not imagine that Agnihotra alone had the power to solve the tremendous problems caused by mass pollution. Would not each of us have to change our daily actions, those which contributed to the deterioration of the planet? Vasant never once mentioned this.

When I met him for the second time, at the home of yoga teacher Carola Waterman, he again talked about the special conditions existing at the moment of sunrise.

'At that time,' he said, 'a flood of energy comes from the sun. It consists of electricity, ethers and subtle energies which have a purifying effect. The flood has a music, the essence of which is the Surya mantra that we chant.'

We also discussed Vasant's main objective: 'to fill the whole sphere with love, by spreading the message of the Fivefold Path.' Agnihotra was only one practice in a disciplined program of self-study, yoga, meditation, the performance of meritorious deeds and the purification of thought patterns.

'When the eternal principles are trampled down on a large scale, terrible resultant karma takes place,' said Vasant. 'But when things go extremely ill, a special divine entity comes to set things right, like a Moses, Jesus or Buddha, each with a task to fulfill in an allotted time. At no time in history have things been as bad as today. But a divine entity is here in physical body to do the task.'

Had I heard right? Another Christ or Buddha was among us? Before I could speak Vasant continued: 'In Buddha's time there was another great entity, Mahavira. His teachings of non-violence and the sacredness of life shaped the Jain religion of India. When he left his body, it was stated that the Wheel would again be set into motion after 2,500 years, a period completed this year. Later, the Prophet Muhammad said that the Message would be given again in 1,400 years, a period soon to be completed.'

At this dramatic point came a knock on the door and the anticlimatic announcement: 'Lunch!' Two young men associated with Agnihotra carried a dining table and chairs into the room.

I ate the fried buckwheat and vegetables in silence, listening as Vasant and his associates reviewed the exploding activity around the mission. He had already been to the United States, Germany and Scandinavia. Invitations were arriving from other countries, together with a stream of calls and cables from all sides. Vasant, in fact, would have to cancel next Sunday's lecture in The Hague and return early to Germany, his European center for spreading the message. There would be a quick trip to India before he had to fly to North America where Agnihotra enthusiasts had built a fire temple in the Virginia forest adjoining Shenandoah National Park.

'The film is running very fast now,' Vasant commented when we were again alone with him. 'It is fantastic. Beyond human intelligence. The time is coming.' Pause. 'You know, I am very happy to meet you, this meeting itself is part of the Plan.'

Evidently Vasant was referring to the article I would write. It became clear, however, that he was not interested in publicity for the divine entity. Although he told us fascinating details about the divine entity's birth, eternal links, supernatural powers, life and whereabouts, he did so on condition I would not publish this information.

'I do not want people flocking around because of fantastic miracles,' he indicated as the reason for the present secrecy. 'These things may confuse people now. It is not really necessary for people to know the divine entity's name, or meet him, or see his picture. They will experience him in the silence of their own home. He only says: "Follow the Fivefold Path." But his presence will be

known in this century. His message has been given to the
atmosphere. The atmosphere has been seeded with holy vibrations
of love. He will give everything by catching hold of the inner mind
of people, by influencing them on the subtle level.'

No wonder Vasant had stated that seekers of our era would
achieve easily and quickly what yogis had failed to attain in many
reincarnations of effort. For all the supposed confidentiality about
our new savior, I was surprised later to see his name printed in the
publicly distributed magazine of Vasant's organization. Parama
Sadguru (literally meaning 'highest among the true masters') Shri
Gajanan Maharaj was born on 17 May 1918 and lived in
Akkalkot, in the Indian state of Maharashtra.

When I asked what exactly was the mission of the divine entity,
Vasant replied: 'To protect the devoted and destroy the wicked.
Nobody aims at killing the wicked, but by their own karma they
will destroy themselves.'

Of course wishing to be included in the realm of the saved, I
requested Vasant to tell me what I could do to belong to that
group.

'Use your free will in the proper manner and you will
automatically receive light. You will receive the light in whatever
way you want,' he answered.

Where did Agnihotra fit into all this?

'Mind is subtle matter, and Agnihotra gives a push to subtle
matter,' Vasant explained. 'It is a great material aid to free us from
desires. Unless this is done, development is very difficult. So
Agnihotra helps the mind get unburdened and a person
automatically starts living a simpler life of less wants. There is
nothing spiritual about Agnihotra, but from it people get the
strength to follow a spiritual discipline.'

Vasant next made it clear that the Agnihotra Surya mantra and
instructions for the procedure were given publicly, with no
conditions or fees.

'I tell people to remain with their formal religion, organization
or guru, and to become better followers, disciples or practitioners,'
he added. 'Never form a sect, I advise them. You can get everything
in your own house. We don't have to meet. But people who do
Agnihotra are creating a few community places where 24-hour
silence can be observed and the fire ceremony performed. Anyone
can come, be silent in a purified atmosphere, and meditate.'

The Fivefold Path had no center and no branches, he stressed.

It was made a nonprofit legal institution in the United States merely to hold the Virginia property and to publish the magazine.

We had spoken several hours and the persons for Vasant's following appointments started to arrive. Before I left he sang the Agnihotra Surya mantra into my tape recorder 'just in case you want to perform Agnihotra later'.

On the train back to Amsterdam, Denis and I discussed our encounter with Vasant, who appeared to us sincere and dedicated. He truly believed that Shri Gajanan was the long-awaited savior of our time.

Glorification of a guru is not unusual in India and elsewhere, but if Shri Gajanan were really the world teacher, would not more people acknowledge him as such? According to Swami Purna, Shri Gajanan was considered to be just one of India's many spiritual teachers. On the other hand I thought that, should Jesus the Christ Himself reappear among us, he might very likely not be recognized.

Martinus, in the Light of the Christ

My spiritual path and my work were starting to blend harmoniously. The spartan lifestyle I accepted as part of my discipline. Never had I been excessively interested in material acquirements and now my limited finances helped me gain even more distance from the desire syndrome set up by the consumer society.

Anyway, I wanted to use things, not be used by them, to borrow Swami Purna's phrase. If certain machines or objects could genuinely help me, fine, I employed them, but was not troubled when they were not available. Those that could lead me to be lazy, wasteful or possessive, I resorted to cautiously or not at all.

My scant resources kept me pretty close to home, a situation causing me absolutely no pain. Amsterdam was in those days one of Europe's focal points of the burgeoning spiritual movement and practically every swami, yogi and lama who arrived in the West included the city in his itinerary. I was more than content to stay in Holland and let the Orient and the New Age come to me.

Still, I was delighted when *Bres* asked me to go to Denmark to interview the elderly Danish writer Martinus, called by Alexandra an extraordinary sage and teacher.

Reading about Martinus Thomsen, who preferred to be known just by his first name, I became fascinated with the idea of meeting him. Born in 1890 and raised by foster parents, he received only an elementary school education and worked at simple jobs until the age of 30. One day he underwent an unexpected transformation of consciousness permitting him to apprehend and describe the main spiritual forces, basic eternal principles and cosmic laws behind the manifest world. This led to the writing of a Cosmology which earned him a certain recognition in

Scandinavia and, eventually, study groups in England, Germany, Holland, Yugoslavia and the United States.

In 1932 the nonprofit Martinus Institute of Spiritual Science was established in Copenhagen to distribute his literature, and two years later a summer school was founded to teach the Martinus Cosmology. For one week in July, lectures in English supplemented the regular Danish and Swedish courses. Denis and I chose this period for our visit.

Gerard Oude Groen, a Dutchman from The Hague, awaited us at the bus stop in the small Danish town of Nykøbing, 60 miles northwest of Copenhagen. When we approached his car, an 18-year-old Vauxhall, he patted it kindly and said it had formerly belonged to Martinus. Gerard bought it a few years earlier, when the old sage abandoned the steering wheel for good.

Together we drove the short distance to Klint, on the Kattegat seashore, the location of the summer school. En route we passed through fragrant woods of pine and spruce. Then the landscape turned flat, and the Kattegat's clear waters and stony beaches appeared.

In a marsh close to Klint, in 1902, the famous Sun Chariot was found. This precious ritual object, now housed in the National Museum in Copenhagen, is a gilded bronze disk representing the sun drawn across the sky by a horse. Dating from the early Bronze Age, circa 1000 B.C., it gives evidence of sun worship in those times.

According to Martinus, Klint possesses a special atmosphere resulting from the concentrated worship of God which has taken place in its surroundings for thousands of years. He explained that the earlier religions were often primitive and involved animal and even human sacrifice, but these lower aspects had been transformed and only 'noble thoughts' remained, making the area distinctive.

When we came to a sign *Kosmos Ferieby*, Kosmos Holiday Center, I noted with interest that a stylized sun adorned the board.

Leaving the road, we entered a small private resort. Our home for the week turned out to be a rustic cabin nestled under a soothing umbrella of pine trees. A huge grass field spread luxuriously before our porch, with the sea to the left.

That evening, after dinner in the center's inexpensive vegetarian restaurant, Denis and I visited the library, food store and camping site. The next morning we sat in the spacious meeting hall to follow the first lecture: 'Martinus, The Man and His Work'.

Mogens Møller, who had studied the Cosmology for over 30 years, narrated the life of Martinus. Born on a farm in western Denmark to an unmarried woman, Martinus was brought up by his mother's half-brother and his wife, both of whom were barely literate. As a child he walked every morning over solitary plains to a one-room schoolhouse. From the age of 12 he herded cows during the summer, and by 14 was forced by the family's financial difficulties into full-time employment as a farmhand.

Martinus longed to read, but there was never money enough for books, not even a Bible. It was at school and later from the local priest that he heard Bible stories. Endowed with a deeply religious nature, he prayed to God every day and Jesus shone as his ideal and guide. In all cases of doubt he asked himself: 'What would Jesus do?'

Perhaps many people ask themselves the same question, but with Martinus the answer always came promptly:

> In the fraction of a second I knew how Jesus would have acted in a similar situation. And this led me on to the Father, to the very presence of God. By following the divine decree, thus made known to me, I got – taintless, safe and sound – through all difficulties, temptations and pitfalls.[22]

At 18, after finishing compulsory service in the Danish navy, Martinus settled in Copenhagen where he secured a clerk's post in a dairy. Twelve years later a strong yearning for spiritual knowledge seized him. A colleague at the dairy introduced him to Lars Nibelvang, a musician with a keen interest in religious philosophy, who lent Martinus a small theosophical tract from his collection.

Back at his home, inspired by this book, as he recounted later in his writings, Martinus tried meditating on the concept 'God'.[23] Suddenly he felt indescribably elevated and in the presence of something immensely sublime. In the distance appeared a small luminous point. It got closer and he saw that it emanated from a Christ-like being of dazzling white light spangled with shades of blue.

The fiery figure raised its arms as if to embrace Martinus. Eventually it entered him. At that moment he could see the entire world and how it rotated, with mountains and valleys, continents and oceans, cities and countries appearing continuously. The earth, steeped in the light now emanating from his own mind, 'was transfigured into the "Kingdom of God".'[24] A second experience brought him into the middle of an overwhelmingly brilliant golden light which he felt was 'the very consciousness of God, His own sphere of thought'.[25]

> *The veil that conceals the real world to us was removed from his eyes, and the truth, the longed-for goal of every one of us, was revealed to him. He found himself in possession of new senses enabling him to see not only the world visible to everybody but . . . the road leading to our goal, to the state of existence where each one of us, who is now living in conflict with his own self and with the world in general, shall awaken to conscious awareness of God's existence and learn to perfection the command of the Nazarene: Love one another!*[26]

In the ensuing adjustment period, Martinus suffered physical pains as his body adapted to the higher vibrations working in him. His knowledge seemed to have no limits. He discussed his revelations with Lars Nibelvang who, wanting to know all about the principles and laws of Creation and the universe, stimulated Martinus to elaborate and explain his discoveries in detail. Cosmic analyses, presented in strong, logical forms, were the result.

It took Martinus a full seven years to put coherently on paper the great mass of knowledge revealed to him. In the early days his sentences were so long they could cover an entire page. No wonder he had several times to rewrite the first volume of his magnum opus, *Livets Bog*, 'The Book of Life', which eventually comprised seven volumes. Within months of its publication in 1932, there were study circles in four Danish towns. Yet Martinus never built up an organization and had no disciples, only 'co-workers'. Thanks to the financial support of friends who recognized the importance of his work, he was eventually able to leave the dairy and dedicate his energies entirely to the spiritual mission.

After the lecture Denis and I returned to our cabin and were enjoying the view from the porch when Gerard came running. 'Do you want to go on an outing with Martinus?' he asked enthusiastically.

We were delighted. From the first phone contact Gerard had warned that seeing Martinus would be rather difficult, if not impossible. At 85, he wanted to reserve his energy for his writing.

On this beautiful Sunday, Martinus had suddenly decided to take a ride. 'He usually goes out once a week to relax and be together with people,' explained Gerard.

The group left in several cars, Denis and I driving with Gerard and his friend Flori Adler. For several years the personal attendant of Martinus, Gerard knew many particulars about him. He was hard to live with, we were told, 'because in his presence you always try to behave well, and that is difficult'. Martinus never had the ambition to give guidance to those around him or to be a guru to them. 'You just learn from his example.' He slept only four hours a night and wrote daily from eight in the morning until three in the afternoon. 'Martinus has no problems,' added Gerard, 'except to formulate in writing what he has to say.'

By the time we pulled into the parking lot of an outdoor pancake restaurant, Martinus had already left his car and was striding towards us. Although only recently recovered from a prostate operation, his every action was energetic and vital. The first thing I saw of him was a big grin. Then his broad hand grabbed mine and pumped it vigorously.

'Welcome to Denmark!' he declared in the few words of English he knew. I burst out laughing and Martinus joined in. Spotting the camera over my shoulder, he stepped back and sign-motioned I could photograph him. What a charming grandfather, I thought.

In good spirits we took places at a long table granting a magnificent view over the surrounding countryside. Below us lay a flower-covered valley, one of Martinus' favorite spots. Sitting directly opposite him allowed me to imbibe his force of personality, even if I could not understand his Danish. He talked loudly, with a musical Scandinavian lilt, waving his body and arms around for emphasis. When he initiated a long discourse and received the undivided attention of our gathering, I imagined he was expounding on a mighty cosmic theme. At a pause I leaned over to Gerard and asked what was being discussed.

'The beauty of the view and the pleasantness of today's weather!' he answered.

The others now joined in and a lively conversation developed. Martinus told many jokes, laughed easily, and infected everybody with his cheerfulness. A permanent expression of amusement seemed embedded in his deep brown eyes, framed by thick, bushy black eyebrows. His friendly face was outlined by a mass of strong white hair, combed straight back. I was amazed by the size of his ear lobes, certainly the largest I had ever seen apart from representations of Gautama Buddha.

Suddenly Martinus reeled backwards, his chair having fallen into a hole. He bellowed with laughter, which grew into a roar when he realized I had been photographing him that very moment. Then he asked Denis and me how we had heard about him and inquired about our work. With the same complete concentration he devoted to everything around him, Martinus listened to our account, translated by Gerard.

Hearing about my articles on spiritual subjects, he launched into a description of the book he was currently writing. It would sum up his discoveries of the laws and principles already presented in his previous works and offer solutions for the problems of our modern world. The book would as well include some of his one hundred 'symbols' – paintings which used geometric forms and color to make his abstract ideas more understandable.

For the text he was seeking another word for death, because 'there is no death. From the cosmic perspective, death is really a birth.'

Cheese sandwiches were served. Those of Martinus disappeared in large chunks, consumed with gusto. I relished his carefree enjoyment of the food. He was so simple it was hard to associate him with his grand universal visions.

I kept snapping photo after photo. Not at all disturbed by the camera, he even seemed to welcome my focus on him. In fact, I had to ask my willing subject not to stop and pose every time I aimed the lens. His cooperative attitude disclosed a generous heart.

While I was debating with myself whether I should request him to change places with me, so that I would not have to shoot into the sun, he was quicker than me and proposed the very same thing. So I could take better photos, as he said.

At the leave-taking, Martinus hugged me goodbye, stroked my cheek fondly, and declared happily that he had enjoyed the tea party. I was captured by this man who radiated so much love.

In the car Gerard said: 'You were really lucky to spend an afternoon with Martinus in this way.'

'He seems a very ordinary, uncomplicated person,' I remarked.

'Yes,' replied Gerard. 'Martinus considers it part of his mission to show that an ordinary person without education can have cosmic consciousness.'

Did I know the British writer Paul Brunton, who published many books on inner search in the 1930s and 1940s? He had met Martinus and wrote appreciatively about him, Gerard related. Moreover, at the beginning of the 20th century Rudolf Steiner, founder of the spiritual movement known as Anthroposophy, had told about his vision that a special individual would eventually appear in Denmark to explain cosmic laws clearly and logically.

'If people of such renown have admired Martinus, why is he so unknown outside Scandinavia?' I wondered.

'Martinus does nothing to promote his mission,' Gerard answered. 'Believing that attraction to the Cosmology will grow gradually and naturally, he advises the co-workers to continue their studies and prepare themselves for the spread of his teachings, which will not occur until after his death.'

The next day Tage Buch, a close co-worker for nearly 40 years, brought good news. He said that Martinus interpreted my coming to Klint as a favorable sign for an upsurge of interest in his work, and he agreed to my interviewing him.

Every day, for one week, Denis and I attended morning lectures and afternoon discussion groups on the Cosmology. We learned that the majority of the participants, middle-aged Danes and Swedes, had been coming here for years, valuing the chance for intensive pursuit of the studies in a conducive atmosphere. Those we talked to were unpretentious and friendly, just like Martinus himself.

Each echoed the same principal reason for studying Martinus: he was logical. According to them, the seven volumes of *Livets Bog* described in clear thought, comprehensible to everybody, the full course of evolution of all life. As Gerard put it: 'Martinus says that his main task is to give the eternal truth in a form adapted to the intellectual level of people today.'

It was impossible for me to investigate the much praised logic of Martinus personally. The complete analyses existed only in Danish. Of his nearly 40 published books, later to be known collectively as the 'Third Testament', only a few had been translated into English. I had no choice but to content myself with condensed summaries as presented in the lectures.

The most fundamental feature of the Martinus Cosmology is the conception of the universe as a huge, living entity in which everything is alive and has meaning and purpose. Life is simply movement. All matter vibrates and represents some form of life, governed by a perfect evolutionary pattern.

The Creator of the universe, a divine 'Something', is eternal, unlimited and beyond definition. This Godhead embraces everything with a love that continually expresses the Biblical statement: 'And behold, it was very good.' Each of the analyses supposedly confirms this truth.

Besides having a limitless love, God also has wisdom which manifests itself in cosmic laws and principles ultimately beneficial to all and everything. Any life-form can freely use the substance and energies of the universe according to its own wishes, of course always receiving the consequences of its actions.

Free will is counterbalanced by what Martinus calls the 'force of destiny', his term for karma. He says that everybody will gradually see that the consequences of their actions, words and thoughts revert to them, not as punishment but as instruction.

To reduce the accumulation of negative karma, people are urged to apply the ethical doctrines of Christ to their lives, to stop blaming others for their own problems, and to search their own characters for the true causes of their difficulties and sufferings.

Although Martinus never read any Eastern philosophy, he stated, like Sri Aurobindo, that humans are in a transitional stage of evolution, moving to a God-conscious state. The change of life on earth will not occur through dictatorships or miracles but through evolution in the minds of all of us. At present, according to Martinus, we are 'sphinx beings', half human and half animal.

Our evolutionary process is a working together of our own forces and actions and of the universal eternal laws, assisted by the spiritual energies. Martinus speaks about 'Providence', a group of spiritual beings who inspire us from other planes. To be in touch with this guiding Providence one needs humility and unconditional love.

The purpose of life as a whole, says the Danish sage, is to live it. Ninety per cent of our development results simply from life's lessons, only 10 per cent is effected by what we read in books. Suffering and illness are to aid our growth. Behind them is true love, God's love. Life's hard experiences bring up in us the longing for peace and harmony. This motivates us to drop our primitive qualities and to develop our humane side.

Eventually we will reach our ultimate destiny: to become a 'real human being'. We will be Christ-like, with unending love for all. When the masculine and feminine principles in us are in total harmony, we will enjoy a perfect balance of our intelligence and feelings. The power of intuition will fully enter our minds, and we will be inspired to serve as a tool of God, taking up practical tasks to help transform the world into a kingdom of real humanity.

Martinus sees the journey towards the real human being as part of a larger spiral cycle of evolution. In each cycle the living being experiences countless lives extending through six planes of existence: the vegetable kingdom, the animal kingdom, the human kingdom, the kingdom of wisdom, the divine world, and the kingdom of bliss. In his symbols, Martinus represents each plane by a different predominant color.

What happens when we reach the end of the cycle? According to Martinus, in the kingdom of bliss we remember all past incarnations in the six planes of existence of the passed spiral cycle. The 'principle of glorifying memories' operates, allowing us to see everything from our former lives. What at the time seemed like suffering is now recognized as a divine gift on the path upwards. We enjoy continual bliss, in constant awareness of God's greatness, perfection and love.

This is a goal of human evolution similar to the one expressed in Hindu and Buddhist philosophy, which talk about blissful union with the higher, transcendental consciousness, resulting in enlightenment.

But Martinus went further. According to him, eventually the 'principle of hunger and satiation' begins to work, causing boredom with the unbroken ecstasy. Because of the 'principle of contrast', existence in the physical world now appears very attractive. This longing initiates a new organism in a new spiral cycle.

In the cosmic view of Martinus, there is no repetition in the spiral cycle. Life is eternal and we continually advance to higher cycles. After the kingdom of bliss we incarnate as a planet. Upon passing through that spiral cycle we become a solar system, then a galaxy, and so on, endlessly. Our planet is therefore not only alive, but is a living being ahead of us in the evolutionary progression. Earth's most highly developed cells, her brain cells, are in fact ourselves, the people of this planet.

'On what do you base your knowledge?' I asked Martinus at our interview. We were sitting inside his summer house, just a short walk along the beach away from the main settlement. Tage Buch translated.

'I base my knowledge on facts,' Martinus answered, giggling. 'On cosmic experiences.'

'How can you be sure you are correct?'

'Because I have the world picture. All my analyses end in the result that everything is love. I have had these experiences and have worked with these ideas since 1921. They form one large whole.'

Martinus told us it was his special task to continue and complete the mission of Jesus. By introducing the concepts of karma and reincarnation he was to renew Christianity so it would become a way of living, with Jesus as the model of the man made in God's image. What people accepted in the past only on faith or by religious instinct, Martinus came to prove. His analyses explain the cosmic principles and laws underlying the doctrines of Jesus.

'People must know God as a reality they can experience in their own lives. This is possible through understanding and applying the principles and laws of life and nature I have outlined.'

To everyone who wanted to advance spiritually, Martinus suggested that they live these laws and principles and pray. He maintained that this combination would gradually lead people away from mere intellectual understanding of God towards genuine experience. Prayer was to him the best connection between the individual and the Godhead.

I asked Martinus which specific practice he could recommend on the road towards becoming a real human being. The only exercise he advocated was to concentrate for five minutes, morning and evening, with love and charity, on those persons you do not like or you think do not like you.

'This will help develop the qualities of charity, tolerance and forgiveness of which Christ is the living example,' he said. 'Then you will realize you meet only "mirrors" of yourself and reactions to what you yourself cause. In this way you are able to overcome many limitations.'

He did not advise people to meditate, not in our time, which he found lacking the proper guides. For help in daily matters, we could take a high being as model, as he himself did with Jesus the Christ. To all evidence, Martinus' identification with Jesus influenced his entire personality.

At the end of our interview, Martinus emphasized that he had never allowed any sect or cult to be formed around his work or his person. This explained why there was not a single photo of him in either the Klint or Copenhagen centers. Nonetheless I asked: 'Why do you call the Institute and the teachings by your first name?'

'It is easier to find in a phone book!' he declared, laughing. 'People called it that: it was the easiest,' he added.

I enjoyed the simple side of Martinus, which gave him an innocent, childlike appeal. For all his beatific experiences with Jesus the Christ and the consciousness of God, he remained by and large the unassuming farm boy from the countryside, apparently unhampered by any desire except to be exactly what he was.

In fact, another one of the tasks entrusted to him seemed precisely to be the shattering of the stereotype of a mystic. While he had reached an inner attainment of sublime level, concretely affirmed by his books and symbols, his natural approach aligned him with the person in the street.

Yet he had been lifted up, out of the multitude, through an illumination which abruptly revolutionized his life. Without preliminary studies or knowledge from any source other than the Bible, he was enabled to write comprehensive philosophical works and create unique geometrical diagrams demonstrating a profound perception of eternal truths.

The example of Martinus confirmed to me once more that spiritual experiences are real and can happen to anyone. Suddenly the transcendental may shine its light on us.

But for most people, says the Danish sage, cosmic consciousness is not attained miraculously, all at once. It comes gradually. As we progress on our journey, unexpected cosmic glimpses reveal life's hidden dimensions.

World Teachers: Maitreya and the Immortal Babaji of the Himalayas

After Denmark, Denis and I visited Swami Purna in London. Our slender budget delivered us to the force of circumstances and again I took everything as a test. By the time we left England, Denis and I had become so flexible we were sure we could stay in any place, under any conditions. This lesson would stand me in good stead later, during my long years in Asia.

On the days Swamiji had other engagements, Denis and I discovered the alternative London which crowded new impressions upon us.

One afternoon I retreated to the tucked-away oasis of Watkins Book Shop, a treasure trove of writings on the spiritual, truly a paradise for any esoteric bookworm. Digesting my way through many visions of reality encased in book form, I happened upon a loose-leaf binder containing information on local events.

One circular captivated me, speaking to my precious dreams of a better life on earth. Fascinated, I read that the Christ-Buddha World Teacher awaited by all religions was already among us. I could learn about 'Maitreya', as the heralded one was called, a few evenings hence at the Friends House meeting center.

I was puzzled. Only a few weeks before had not the divine messenger Vasant told that the Buddha-Christ Divine Entity of our time was named Shri Gajanan, who lived in a small village in West India? I therefore almost instantly dismissed this second candidate.

Yet my curiosity had been whetted. Over the following days an interest to hear Maitreya's message managed to invade my consciousness, where it received encouragement from my Pondicherry vow to remain open.

Maitreya having thus penetrated my logical defenses, Denis and

I some days later entered an intimate gathering around a white-haired, elfin-faced man sitting at a table in a small room. It was the Scottish painter and healer Benjamin Creme. In a soft voice he announced he would go into trance to receive Maitreya's weekly communication, deliverable only through him as a channel.

Closing his eyes, Creme was silent for a moment before he moved his lips to pronounce a statement being dictated to him on subtle inner planes. Creme's bearing had an eerie authority, and I anticipated important instructions from beyond, but the divine transmission from Maitreya contained no more than a vague entreaty for his brothers to have faith. There was no mention of his sisters.

After Creme emerged from trance, we heard he was not yet permitted to reveal the savior's whereabouts, though he tantalized us with several provocative clues. He was a man and would soon be coming down from the Himalayas to take up residence in a major industrialized city. At some propitious future time Maitreya would disclose himself to everyone in the world simultaneously. Until then he would work through Creme.

During the question period I asked Creme why the teacher of our era, incarnating for our needs and circumstances, referred mainly to 'brothers' and 'men' in his message and used the phrase 'mankind' instead of a wider term like 'humanity'. Should the new times not also be reflected in our language, making it responsive to changing social perceptions about the place and potential of women? Did we not require a tongue of equality which would make women more visible?

A few people in the room, including several older women, turned around to see who had dared to imply criticism of the mighty Maitreya. Creme, in a charming manner, suggested I not dwell on externals.

When I replied that the outer mirrored the inner, and that today a universal teacher had of necessity to use a non-sexist vocabulary, a man shouted out that I should not waste the group's time on unimportant points. It was clear we saw things differently.

To me the freeing of language from sexual and other biases is an extremely relevant issue, and it seemed impossible that a world renewer would use patriarchal terms. This had to have something to do with the channel, I thought. Unless a channeler is a realized being, he or she may bring through a partial message because his or her own understanding is still limited.

After the meeting Creme, a person obviously of sensitive vibration, very politely invited me to speak with him privately. That led to a talk, several days later, in his home.

The world was moving to the end of an age and the start of another, he told me, explaining that Maitreya is a member of the spiritual hierarchy of illumined masters which has always supported humanity in its evolution. Because the time is ripe for the revelation of an important new teaching, Maitreya will eventually make his appearance before the entire world community as the teacher for all.

Maitreya is the fifth buddha awaited by Buddhists, the Savior expected by Christians as the Christ, the Messiah prophesied by the Hebrews, the Imam Mahdi anticipated by Muslims, and the tenth incarnation of Vishnu, Kalki, described in the Hindu scriptures. All of these names, says Benjamin Creme, describe one and the same entity.

When identified as the 'Christ', this refers not to the entity's name but rather to a certain function, or office, within the hierarchy. The present 'Prime Minister' or 'President' of the hierarchy, so to speak, is Maitreya. By whatever name he is called, the World Teacher will make clear the changes we need to adopt in order to save ourselves and our world.

As intriguing as I found the story, I did not get involved with it, having in the meantime conferred with Swami Purna. His injunction very simply was: 'Beware those who make claims.' Swamiji stressed that highly evolved beings did not generally need to send out an advance force to propagate their existence. They just did the task they came to do, becoming known and proving their greatness through it.

'You grow through your work and it grows through you,' he said.

Over the years I have followed with interest the continuing emergence of Maitreya. To herald his coming, Benjamin Creme has been publishing articles and books and traveling throughout the United States, Europe and the Far East. To further spread the good news of the Master's presence and his messages, the Share International Foundation was established. Headquartered in Amsterdam, of all places, it issues a monthly magazine.

According to Creme, Maitreya left his Himalayan retreat in 1977 and flew to London where he took up residence. Since then he has been working behind the scenes to prepare people for the long-promised 'Declaration Day'. On that auspicious occasion Maitreya will emerge into public life by contacting everyone on earth simultaneously by mental telepathy, or more mundanely by international television hookup.

Among Maitreya's various priorities, he calls for a new social order based on the principle of sharing and redistributing the planet's resources in order to establish right human relationships. Maitreya, who travels widely, is frequently in London. There, as in other parts of the world, he meets with selected persons whom he is readying for the new times.

My visit to London in 1975 not only gave me my first news of Maitreya, it also brought me into closer touch with another manifestation of high spiritual energy.

One Sunday, with Swami Purna's absence from London, Denis and I took a long ride on the underground to attend an afternoon lecture on Indian philosophy at the Hindu Centre. Entering as strangers, we immediately received the typical Indian hospitality which regards the guest as royalty. Places were made for us in the front row.

Before the discourse began, my chair neighbour introduced himself as Dr. S. K. Lal from New Delhi. My own links with his city led us into a pleasant conversation. All of a sudden he asked me, rather impulsively: 'Have you read *Autobiography of a Yogi?*' Another time this magic title! Finally I could say 'yes', and my answer encouraged Dr. Lal to show me a photo of his guru.

When I held the picture in my hand, gazing at a beautiful young-looking yogi, I realized I had already seen this luminescent being. It was Herakhan Baba, whom devotees believed to be the Immortal Babaji of Paramahansa Yogananda's book. Clifford Smith had acquainted me with him shortly after my return from the East.

Denis and I joined Dr. Lal for dinner, and stories, of the supernatural occurrences taking place around Herakhan Baba. The day after hearing about Dr. Lal's encounters with Babaji, as this mysterious being was affectionately called, Denis and I related the details to Swami Purna. He expressed amusement at our latest adventure, joking that the New Age was producing Buddhas, Christs and other divinities like grapes in a vineyard.

Regarding Martinus, Swamiji found him an admirable, illumined person. But he stressed: 'Martinus is only a single individual, working alone.' He emphasized that the scriptures which form the basis of Hinduism, called the Vedas from the Sanskrit root *vid* denoting 'sacred knowledge', derive from the inner experiences of not one but of many enlightened sages, the *rishis*.

Explained Swamiji: 'Revelations received, understood and analysed by each *rishi* were related to the findings of other seers. Only after collective verification did truths come.'

According to Vedic tradition, the Vedas are revealed scripture or *sruti*, meaning 'that which is heard directly'. The final and climactic portion, named Vedanta because it is the *anta*, literally 'the end', deals with the discovery and realization of the eternal spiritual truths as expressed in the Upanishads, over 200 essays on various themes of divine knowledge and the meaning of human existence.

From the viewpoint of the Indian scriptures, which Swami Purna considered definitive but the Danish sage had never read, Swamiji differed with certain points of the Martinus Cosmology. He objected, for example, to Martinus' insistence that we usually reincarnate as the same sex in one spiral cycle.

'*Gun karm vibhages*,' recited Swamiji. 'According to your thought, according to your action, you will be born again. So teach the Upanishads, which form and express the philosophy of Vedanta,' he continued. 'Vedanta never said one remains the same sex throughout reincarnations.'

The Atman, the soul, of course has no sex. But until the soul realizes that its individual self is but part of an all-pervading Infinite Eternal, it is born again and again in a physical body. With this body it identifies, for the satisfaction of desires. Until liberated from identification with the physical form, as well as with the mind, ego and senses, the soul takes repeated rebirths of one or the other gender.

Making certain that I understood these and other points, Swamiji suggested that they should be included in any article I would write about Martinus and his work.

Swami Ranganathananda and the Tradition of Sri Ramakrishna

Swami Purna's comments about the fallibility of a single person's spiritual understanding were supported when I returned to Amsterdam and made acquaintance with *The Message of the Upanishads* by Swami Ranganathananda, one of the most prominent monks of India's highly respected Ramakrishna Order.

In this book I read that the *rishis* of ancient India noted and classified in a kind of teamwork their discoveries of the laws governing the inner world. Together they subjected their theories to rigorous scrutiny before accepting or discarding them. Today's reader of the Upanishads could follow this logical analytical process, wrote Swami Ranganathananda.

I had the opportunity to hear the swami on his annual visit to Holland. Often called India's 'traveling ambassador', Swami Ranganathananda had since the 1950s been lecturing and teaching on spiritual and cultural topics all over the world, many of his foreign tours sponsored by the government of India. At the same time he was a prolific writer.

His Amsterdam speech on the meaning of Vedanta philosophy for the West was delivered in an eloquent style, without any notes. This was all the more impressive because he enhanced his remarks with a profusion of quotes from great thinkers and philosophers, both Eastern and Western. What clarity of mind!

'There is one supreme truth which Indian philosophy and spirituality has discovered, propagated and upheld: the divinity of man,' Swami Ranganathananda pointed out. 'Behind our body-mind complex is the spark of divinity. Experience of this truth is primary; belief in dogma is secondary. The sages discovered the divine in their own hearts, they saw it in others and they preached it to the world. This is the central teaching of the Indian philosophy and spirituality known as Vedanta.'

Afterwards I thanked him for his inspiring address. With so much friendliness did he engage me in conversation, that I asked if I might see him again. He was staying at a study center near Baarn in the residential countryside, and invited me to visit him the following day.

From the moment I arrived there, I was made to feel very welcome. Answering my questions, Swami Ranganathananda showed the concern of a dedicated teacher who wants a student to understand at all costs. His readiness to explain the most elementary spiritual matters showed me anew the natural generosity I had come to associate with persons whose knowledge comes from both heart and mind.

At my request he told me as well about his life. Born in 1908 in Kerala state in South India, Swami Ranganathananda joined the Ramakrishna Mission at the age of 18. The monks of this international spiritual and cultural movement, founded in Calcutta at the end of the 19th century by the renowned Swami Vivekananda (1863–1902), strive for God-realization through service to humanity.

In a country where the government cannot meet all the needs of its poor masses, the nearly 100 centers of the Ramakrishna Mission provide free education, medical treatment and other social services for the economically weak of any creed, color or nationality. The Mission's branches in North and South America, Europe and Asia concentrate on the dissemination of India's spiritual ideas.

Ramakrishna Mission monks practise a disciplined balance of meditation, study and monastery duties. Swami Ranganathananda himself served in various capacities at Ramakrishna centers in India, Burma and Pakistan before becoming head of the Mission in Hyderabad, in the central part of his country.

While relating his biography to me, the swami made no hints or even vague allusions to links with high beings on other planes. There were no mysteries about him. Anything I asked him about his age or background, he answered clearly, in unequivocal language. How refreshing! I trusted him implicitly. He seemed to me a teacher who could be followed blindly.

With thoughts of Martinus and his remarkable transformation

still on my mind, I asked Swami Ranganathananda what experience had most influenced his inner life.

'There was nothing flashy, no fireworks,' he responded. 'My spirituality has been a continuous development, conscious and deliberate, in the context of work, human relations and the manifestation of the divinity within.'

His manner revealed a person who had proceeded step by step with calm certainty, probably the safest attitude when seeking the higher knowledge. Still I inquired: 'Was there no sudden or unexpected occurrence?'

'A great burst of emotion I didn't have because the whole spiritual process is rational, and yet it takes us beyond reason,' he answered. 'At the most, I can say that when I read for the first time *The Gospel of Sri Ramakrishna*, I realized a tremendous new dimension of spirituality so genuine and spontaneous that it transformed my whole life. This explosive event, which still carries me on, took place when I was 14 and chanced upon the great book.'

The Gospel of Sri Ramakrishna is a faithful and detailed account, by the close disciple 'M', of the doings and utterances of Ramakrishna Paramahansa, one of the most exceptional spiritual figures of 19th-century India.

Born in Bengal in 1836, Sri Ramakrishna experienced mystical trances as a young child. The first half of his life was marked by an insatiable craving for God, and with unusual rapidity he tried out in turn not only the recognized spiritual disciplines of his own Hindu religion but those of Christianity and Islam as well. Guided by a succession of gurus, he reached the highest attainment on all of these paths, enabling him to experience that each of these traditions ultimately led to the same goal.

Sri Ramakrishna had married to please his mother, who hoped thereby to cure his 'God-madness', but the marriage was never consummated. He and his wife, Sarada Devi, lived in celibate monkhood together. Under his tutelage she evolved into an exalted spiritual model herself, becoming known as 'the Holy Mother'.

By origin a poor villager who could scarcely read or write, Sri Ramakrishna spent the last 13 years of his life transmitting his wisdom to a large number of seekers who included some of India's most distinguished personages.

'How to understand the greatness of Sri Ramakrishna?' I asked Swami Ranganathananda.

'That is easy,' he replied. 'Sri Ramakrishna's teachings are couched in extremely simple language with very illuminating examples based on everyday circumstances. His message can be summed up in two parts. First he tells that the divine spark is hidden in all of us and we should try to manifest it through our work, our interhuman relations, our total existence. What inspired everyone around him was that he lived in a perpetual state of God-union. His deep spirituality often produced inner experiences for those who came into his presence, giving them insight into their higher self and transforming their outlook.

'While trying to unfold the divine dimensions within us, we will follow a certain spiritual path. This leads to Sri Ramakrishna's second teaching: we must not think ours is the only way. Other people may follow different methods to achieve the same result.'

'In other words, all religions are true,' I said.

'Yes. Paths may vary but the goal is one.'

'If more people could only grasp this!' I exclaimed, thinking of all the conflicts and wars on this planet over religious differences.

Swami Ranganathananda nodded in agreement, elaborating that to Sri Ramakrishna the core of religion was spirituality. 'To be religious is to realize God in yourself, nothing more and nothing less,' he said.

'Why is Swami Vivekananda so venerated?' I next wanted to know.

'Swami Vivekananda was the forerunner of all the Indian gurus who went West. When he represented Hinduism at the World Parliament of Religions in Chicago in 1893, he was the first to bring the Eastern religious tradition to America and England. Because of him, Vedanta Societies were established worldwide.

'As Sri Ramakrishna's apostle, he was the disciple specially commissioned to spread his master's message. But he preached it in a variety of ways. In India he had to arouse the people from age-long inertia and backwardness. In the West social and economic development already existed, but the inner life of people was empty. So here he oriented the philosophy of Vedanta towards bringing peace to the Western mind, by yoking it to the spiritual dimension.

'Swami Vivekananda explained Vedanta in two different ways in two different hemispheres according to the needs of humanity at the time. This is the sign of a great teacher. He doesn't prescribe the same medicine for every patient. He knows what suits a particular individual and what suits another.'

'What is the main prerequisite of a spiritual teacher?' I asked, knowing that in our ambitious 'Age of Enlightenment' people often set themselves up as teachers before being qualified.

'Naturally he must be spiritual,' responded Swami Ranganathananda, 'otherwise he cannot convey spirituality to others. It is not like any other subject, which can be memorized and passed along. It is not an intellectual, academic exercise either. It is being and becoming. Only those who have realized spirituality in themselves can communicate this mighty power and wisdom. If I don't know how to swim, I cannot save somebody else from drowning. I will drown and so will he. In spiritual teaching, the main thing is to stimulate the inner progress of the other person.'

'What does it really mean to be spiritual?' I inquired, feeling that the swami could give a very clear definition of this basic and important concept.

'We have our sensory life, perfectly natural and welcome, but there comes a point when we realize this is not the highest in man: there is a more profound dimension. Atman, the infinite Self, shines through everything.

'To understand, to be aware of, and to start living in this consciousness, that is spirituality. It should not remain the prerogative of a few ascetics or mystics, but can be an experience for anyone. That is practical Vedanta: to manifest our divine nature in the midst of our work and the world's various distractions.'

'Doesn't Vedanta say spirituality is everyone's birthright?' I asked.

'Yes, it is the possibility hidden within each individual,' he answered. 'We have not to beg or borrow for our spirituality, we have only to unveil it. As the tiny baby grows from playing with toys to attending school in search of knowledge, there is a natural growth from the lower to the higher state. Spirituality doesn't contradict but only overcomes sensual life, and reaches out to something finer. We don't condemn people who live at the sensory level, but we ask them not to be complacent there, or static. We encourage them to move on, to ask questions, to be seeking.'

In our talk of several hours, I saw again that the length of time one knows someone has nothing to do with the warmth and affection which may suddenly arise.

The swami took much interest in me and my work, saying he

set great store by the contribution of women to the collective effort for a more spiritualized world. Swami Vivekananda, he mentioned, was the first monk in Indian history to champion, without any reservations, the freedom and equality of women.

Before I left he wanted to know whether I was in contact with my parents. When I affirmed this, he inquired what they thought of my involvement in spiritual matters. I was surprised with this question but the swami, having Western students, obviously knew our problems.

'My parents measure success in life by material achievement,' I told him, 'and do not understand my preoccupations.' I explained they were not happy with my devotion to writing on transformational themes because of the meager income it brought. 'Of course they are concerned about my future,' I added, 'and I see their point. My inner riches will not pay my bills, but my determination is firm.'

Swami Ranganathananda went to his suitcase and took out a copy of his book *The Message of the Upanishads*, which he presented to me as a help for my work. Leafing through the volume, he pronounced 'Page 352' and drew my attention to a certain paragraph.

I read that it is the spiritual awareness one achieves, not power or position or pleasure, which is the real measure of educational success. The attainment of spiritual awareness is the end and aim of human life. 'Therein alone', wrote the swami, 'is true freedom for man. "What are you?" is a deeper and more meaningful question than "What have you done or achieved?"'[27]

Since that encounter I have had additional opportunities to meet Swami Ranganathananda, both in Holland during several of his annual visits and a number of times in India. In 1986, the year he received the first Indira Gandhi National Integration Award, I stayed for a while at the monastery of the Ramakrishna Mission in Hyderabad.

During one of our wide-ranging talks, Swami Ranganathananda became prophetic when I asked him what the religion of the future enlightened humanity would be.

'There will never be just one single religion throughout the world,' he replied. 'But there will be one loyalty to a supreme truth approached through different ways – the Christian, the Buddhist, the Islamic, the Hindu, the Jewish, all the various paths. Differences will remain and yet unity will come.

'People will sense that a non-dual spiritual truth runs through the heart of all nature and humanity, like the thread uniting all flowers in a garland. Religion will be a source of this awareness because it is based upon the vision of unity. The diversity is an expression of that unity.

'In the 20th century we have seen great scientific achievements. Those of the 21st century will be more in the realm of interhuman relations, with much more cultural and spiritual give and take. You can say that the 20th century is the seed time, and the 21st century will be the harvest time of interhuman cooperation and peace.'

Professor Henri van Praag
and the Reminder of Roots

'Awake! Attune to the divine purpose and work for it!' From the mission post of my desk, I burned to communicate this message through my articles. In so doing I hoped to inspire people to take an active part in the evolutionary process, their own as well as the planet's.

Within the magazine world, the market for transformational themes was in those days pitifully small. Library research had yielded the names of possibly appropriate journals, and to these I had sent letters inquiring if my material might suit their editorial requirements. Steadily the reading public for my texts expanded.

By the height of the 'spiritualized seventies', as some called the decade, I was contributing regularly to a number of publications in Europe, Australia, and occasionally America. Honoraria far below standard prevailed in this fringe circuit because budgets were limited due to low circulations, or so the editors apologetically said. Just as grains of sand compose a beach, however, all payments together enabled me to survive.

Naturally I was delighted when in Holland another magazine on spiritual topics made its appearance and offered me an assignment. It involved my traveling to England where, at the College of Psychotherapy in Tunbridge Wells, I interviewed its founder, Ronald P. Beesley, a pathfinder in the use of crystals, color and light for healing. An article about this pioneer of alternative medicine would not flow from my pen until we had met again, several years later. The first encounter left too many unanswered questions in a field still quite enigmatic to me.

I contacted *Prana*, as the new Dutch journal was called after the universal life-force, and told the publisher, Paul Kluwer, about my reluctance to write the article at that time. He suggested I phone the editor-in-chief, Professor Henri van Praag, and gave me his home number.

It took an interminably long time to reach him. The line was constantly engaged. Later on when I came to know him better, I learned this was a normal state of affairs.

'Van Praag,' eventually announced a pleasant voice on the other end. I introduced myself and explained why I was phoning. His first reaction startled me and reached into my hereditary past.

'Are you a Jewish woman?' he asked.

'How do you know?' I questioned back.

Then, without any inhibitions, Professor van Praag told me my age, missing it by a couple of years, and commented that I was very receptive to other people, sometimes excessively. What strange behavior for a magazine editor! It crossed my mind that the *Prana* article had perhaps simply been a vehicle to bring me in touch with him. When he invited me to his home to discuss the Beesley matter in person, I accepted the earliest date he proposed, twelve days later.

In the beautiful garden city of Hilversum, the national broadcasting center not far from Amsterdam, an older woman wearing a head kerchief welcomed me into the study of a modest corner house. Her husband would be with me soon. Long minutes passed as I took in my surroundings. Two walls of the room were lined with shelves of books packed tightly from floor to ceiling.

A grey-haired man of around 60 entered, shook my hand and, without saying a word, settled into a chair. And there he sat, his eyes focused on me. A friendly smile took my attention away from his balding head and large Semitic nose. Although my ordinary impulse would have been to speak, I returned his gaze and rather enjoyed the relaxing silence.

Unexpectedly he opened his eyes very wide and then narrowed them, whereby his distinctly Jewish face took on Chinese features. An other-worldly atmosphere blotted out the visual reality around us, leaving only the Chinese face. After a moment it vanished too, except for the eyes which became three, the additional one between and slightly above the other two.

Finally, Professor van Praag broke the spell, questioning me about my thoughts and feelings in regard to Ronald Beesley. Without much ado, he released me from my journalistic commitment. That matter solved, he gave me, unasked, an overall impression of my ideas and ideals.

I smiled and joked that he certainly made a very good fortune-teller, a remark which amused him and caused us both to laugh. When he confirmed that indeed he had some clairvoyant gifts, I wondered if he would perhaps want to impress me further with the accuracy of his observations, and I asked him to go on.

'Better let the *I Ching* speak now,' came the reply, and from the desk in the adjoining room he brought a modern rendering of this ancient Chinese book of divination. Already having acquaintance with the 'Book of Changes' as it is also called, I knew it was based on universal laws of change underlying nature and human life.

Written over a long period of time, by a succession of authors including Confucius, the *I Ching* divides all phenomena into negative and positive forces, yin and yang. Their interchange produces 64 symbolic patterns, or hexagrams, which anyone who has learned to use the *I Ching* can interpret for advice and suggestions.

Professor van Praag had me spontaneously give him six numbers and, after looking into the book, said they formed the pattern termed 'Deliverance'. The accompanying text dealt with the abandoning of comfortable surroundings in order to find new forms of deliverance.

'This fits you,' he declared. 'Didn't you leave your background in search of other ways?'

Then he wanted to know how far I was still in touch with my Jewish roots and what my thoughts were on Judaism. While I assembled a reply, he pointed out that he considered himself 'an integral Jew, a complete Jew', who tried 'to integrate every aspect of Judaism'.

Without wanting to hurt the professor, I said Judaism had never really touched my heart, a statement immediately provoking an inquiry into my childhood years. His gentle approach encouraged confidence, and memories of my early experiences in the synagogue, Sunday School and the Jewish community surfaced with ease.

'You were brought up in a milieu which lacked understanding of the divine background of Judaism,' he concluded, 'in an environment of Jewish folklore, of people who prefer honey cake to the Lord who gave the commandments. I have never been a Jew like that. I'm not interested in Jewish folklore and in Jewish jokes which have nothing to do with the depths of Judaism.

'Too many American Jews know only about beefsteak, money

and things, not about the spirituality of Judaism. A Jew who is concerned only with this world is not really a Jew in the true sense of the word.' A twinge of sadness colored his voice.

I remarked that today in most established religions the inner life was neglected, with preference given to the outer. He wholeheartedly agreed, but was glad to see that a large number of young people, especially in the United States, had difficulties with the emphasis on materialism. The attraction of Eastern religions was obvious.

'You belong to this category yourself,' he said, adding that my parents had surely not given me a Sanskrit name. 'Why are you Surya and not Sarah?'

There was no critical undertone in his questions and, noting his sincere interest, I related in detail my stay in India.

'Your experiences were authentic, real mystical experiences,' he commented. 'But now you must see them as a Jewess, which means you must also be able to laugh about all those great things regarding the salvation of humanity, and be a very normal person. Forget the nonsense aspects. Spiritual enlightenment must make you modest and simple.'

I asked if he had any idea why my experiences had happened in India.

'Because in India so many persons have awakened, the *prana* of awakening is stronger there,' was the reply. 'In Judaism, the *prana* of revelation predominates. When you are in a community of Jewish mystics, a real Hasidic community, then you feel it.' It concerned him that I had not come to the proper understanding of revelation 'which has to do with the personal god of Israel, Creator of heaven and earth'. I was, therefore, 'more Indian than Jewish'.

Then he explained that the gods of India are only emanations but the God of Israel is the 'original God', the God of Creation who is eternal, all-wise and all-powerful. He is YHVH, the masculine god one has to obey.

'Feminists have some trouble with this,' said Professor van Praag, 'but God's exhortation to follow His commandments is the first law of Israel: *Shema Yisrael*, Hear, O Israel.' The creed of Judaism was revealed at Sinai, when the voice of God was heard not merely by a single individual, the prophet Moses, but by the many thousands of Israelites in the desert with him.

'For the development of man, it is important everyone knows

what it means that God revealed His will in this way,' stated Professor van Praag. It had to do with the intentions of YHVH for Israel, the people of the revelation, and through Israel for the whole of humanity. The Jewish people have a predestined role to fulfill in establishing the kingdom of God on earth, a role connected with the coming of the Messiah for the benefit of the whole human race.

'What is your particular task?' I asked him.

'To help prepare people for the Messianic time,' he replied.

The professor wished to have a hand in drafting the blueprint for a new world. He explained we were moving towards a harmonious future in which all cultures would have a place. An important part of his work had been to compare different cultures and the mystical dimensions of the various religions.

'Because we are all entering the Age of Aquarius, the beginning of a New Age,' he said, 'it is impossible to bring man to the path of higher consciousness as long as he is not acquainted with the religions of other areas of the world. I am working for the meeting of East and West in every way, also in the religious field. So you will understand I also feel a great responsibility to combine the historical task of Judaism with the mystical task of the Eastern religions.'

In between, he told me about his work. More an educator than anything else, he was currently lecturing on sociology and the methodology of education at two Dutch universities and on futurology throughout Europe. He held three master's degrees and had taught in 12 academic disciplines. Psychology and parapsychology were especially dear to him.

Over 200 books bore his name, on such diverse topics as the Bible, Israel, India, China, the *I Ching*, education, mathematics, logic, psychology, parapsychology and acupuncture. Further, he had published over 6,000 articles and arranged an equal number of conferences. Of the 31 languages he had studied, he spoke '17 or 18'.

As if all this were not enough, he was president or chairman of numerous nonprofit humanitarian organizations, including the International Anne Frank Foundation and the Leerhuis European-wide study centers for the stimulation of dialogue between Christians and Jews.

Of course I asked how he managed to do so much.

'I don't know myself!' he replied, laughing. 'But I remember all

I have ever learned.' He had a 'very retentive memory but it was also karma'. And, his 'third eye was pretty much open'. Writing was only one tenth of his activities. When he wrote, generally by hand, it just flowed. Assistants typed everything up. He needed a minimum of sleep, usually retiring by three and arising by eight.

'I can state, and please understand that when saying this I am not egotistic,' he declared, 'that there is no other person in the world like me.'

Anyone who trumpeted his own glories raised question marks in me, yet Professor van Praag's supreme self-confidence was not of the arrogant sort. Paradoxically, there was even a good touch of humility about him. I saw him as a man of great inner abundance who simply knew the whats, whys and hows of his life. I liked him.

An invitation for another visit followed, to my pleasure. Between us existed a natural bond of affection. This was not put into words during our first encounter, but we both silently acknowledged it.

During our second coming together, Professor van Praag – or 'V.P.', as Denis and I called him between ourselves – made the surprising proposal to be, in effect, my guru: to teach me how to find my 'real inner depths and to see the connections between the various religions'. Also, to be a spiritual father to me. He said I was like the daughter he never had.

'I have the feeling I can help you find your way,' he explained, 'because I believe your process of development has something to do with the synthesis of Jewish and Eastern thought. Only few people have really integrated the fundamental ideas of Judaism and Eastern religions.

'Above all, I have a great sympathy for you because I feel you are really seeking the truth and need a deeper understanding. I thought the fact that you are Jewish may be both an advantage and a disadvantage for you.

'In addition, when I met you for the first time, I immediately thought you could assist me in my projects.' Currently he was setting up a private university in Luxembourg to produce 'change agents' who would contribute to shaping the world's future.

How many people was he helping to develop their personality and spiritual life, I asked. The reply was: 'Around 20', but he met with hundreds more, trying to give everyone special treatment.

'Of course they aid me too, also in my own development,' he

said. 'I don't believe in one-sided relations. This is why I always look to see what someone can do for me. Not out of selfishness, but because it is better when there is a mutual reciprocity.

'The fact is,' he emphasized, 'you recognized who I am. Most people don't. They perceive my intellectual capacities and my strong religious feelings, but do not see beyond.'

Once more Professor V P got out the *I Ching*, asked me again to say six numbers, and told me they produced a hexagram which read in part: 'When such a companion thus reveals himself in his true character, it is one's duty to meet him and to work with him.' He interpreted this to mean, 'When you understand who I am, then you have to work with me.'

Perhaps the professor *extraordinaire* had indeed been commissioned by the subtle worlds to serve as my spiritual father while revealing to me the esoteric secrets of Judaic truth. Yet his mission was obstructed by several difficulties.

First of all, next to the sun of course, I considered my teacher to be Swami Purna. Swamiji's path to a large extent harmonized with my visions. Was it wise to have more than one guide at the same time? I became more flexible on this issue when V. P. told me one day that, between 18 and 25, he had simultaneously had four masters: a Chinese teacher, a Jewish mystic, a Christian theologian, and a philosopher.

He, however, did not approve of my association with Swami Purna. After seeing a photo of him, he made negative remarks and advised me to cease contact altogether. As confused as I was in those years about Swamiji's identity and teaching methods, I easily came under the influence of V. P., whose counsel I accepted as derived from the higher spiritual planes.

'Abba', as he wanted me to call him by using the Hebrew word for 'father', actually did become a teacher to me. For years I went to see him in Hilversum, benefiting from his wealth of knowledge and depth of insight. Nevertheless, the thorough teacher–student relationship he constantly talked about did not take form.

This leads to the second, more serious obstacle. Abba's extremely busy schedule prevented regular contact. Whenever I pressed him to finally establish the reading program he promised within our study, he invariably put it off due to more urgent commitments. 'I am always involved in at least 50 projects at a time,' he assured me.

Never before had I met someone who made appointments not

only for meetings but for phone calls as well. His days were so exceedingly filled that, to make use of every available moment, he even arranged conversations during his train journeys. Once, when he was traveling back and forth between Holland and various European countries, I suggested I might accompany him on the two hours' train ride to the border.

'My dear child, that is not possible,' he replied, 'because I already have several people joining me on that part of my trip!'

Regarding my inner growth, Abba gave no importance to my carrying out spiritual practices. I did not need to meditate in the sense of concentration, he maintained, because I was concentrated enough. He was not a meditator himself and explained: 'Meditation is to empty the mind. My mind already is empty, and has been since my young years.'

'But we can hasten our development by consciously undertaking a program of spiritual practices,' I said, from the Indian standpoint.

'Develop to what?' he asked, reminding me that a seed of the tree contains its development. The seed does not have to think about becoming a tree, it just becomes it.

'What you are looking for is in yourself,' declared Abba, repeating the ancient message of all mystical traditions.

As to my inner progress, he advised me not to see it with ambition and to have patience. According to him, my development would happen naturally, as his did: 'I never think about my own evolution. I just live my life.'

This was underlined when he mentioned having at the age of 18 written a book called *They are Waiting for You*, as its title translates from the Dutch.

'When I wrote that book I was young and impatient,' he told me. 'I thought we have to hurry because they are waiting for us. Later I understood another meaning: don't hurry, they are waiting for us.'

He preferred that I should marry, have children, eat a normal, non-vegetarian diet and exchange my long dresses for shorter ones. With all due respect for his views, I disagreed on these points as on others, including his support for nuclear energy and dislike of peace movements.

Denis had a greater divergence of opinion with Henri van Praag than I. Although he highly regarded all the scholarly achievements, he said he missed the experiential side to the professor's spiritual approach. This was the main reason my fellow monk gave for discontinuing his own visits to Hilversum, after having accompanied me several times at the beginning.

As with Swami Purna, Denis took a position of reserve. He never let himself be recruited into any teacher's projects, wanting to focus on his own work. Undoubtedly his cautious attitude helped restrain me from taking up any of Abba's job offers, and kept me on my own path of freedom. With pen in hand and camera over my shoulder I continued to meet and interview a steady stream of teachers and New Age personalities.

It goes without saying that Abba's comprehensive wisdom nourished me throughout the years. His answers always gave food for thought.

Once I asked him what payment I could give in return.

'Oh, it is very easy,' he replied cheerfully. 'I tell you things, helping you to grow. Later, you will assist other people in the same way. What you do to another person, you do to me. You don't have to give it back directly; it's not ping-pong.' He himself never took money for his private counseling and earned his income from teaching, consulting and writing.

'An important point, and part of our assignment for the future,' he continued, 'is that whatever spiritual inheritance we have received from our experiences and our teachers, we must pass on to others as our debt to the future.'

In 1980 I went to Asia, and after I had been there over three years I received a letter from him. 'It is important that you meet me one more time before I am beyond oral reach,' he wrote on the first page. 'I think you ought to come back to see me once again before 1985, as it is possible I then have to go to carry out a silent task which my masters, the 36 just men of Israel, will give me.' I flew to Holland.

Abba spoke again about taking me into the heart of Judaic spirituality, saying there might not be much time left for our work together, at least not on the earthly plane. He wanted me not to return to India. Why go there when I could get any answer I wanted from him?

I saw it differently. I wanted to find my own answers, from within, and believed India was instrumental in this process. But Abba maintained that the God of the Bible was here: I did not have to go looking for Him elsewhere. In view of my roots, I had to deal with Judaism, this was Abba's repeated message. Besides, he made clear, it was important I integrate the spiritual heritage of Judaism and Eastern religions.

He was referring to my origins when he said: 'According to Judaism, there is no need to seek God, He seeks you. God is not an object, as in Hinduism, but a subject. One cannot understand Judaism until one grasps this. In Hinduism one seeks enlightenment, in Judaism not. Moses was not enlightened but had the light of God upon him. God chose to speak to him, face to face. In all his countless incarnations, Buddha never spoke with God. This is why in Judaism one has to learn to listen, listen for God.'

On this, as on previous occasions, India was to me like a past karma calling for completion before I could steep myself in the sourcebooks of revelation Abba van Praag offered to read with me. It is possible that this fact had been an additional obstacle to our lessons.

When, after five years in Asia, I did indeed give up my Indian residence for the very purpose of studying Judaism with Abba, his shortage of time once more permitted no more than occasional talks.

In 1988 Henri van Praag passed away, at the age of 72. The funeral was so heavily attended that there was not space enough for everyone in the Amsterdam synagogue where the memorial services were held. From the many tear-streaked faces I saw in the crowd of mourners, it was obvious that not only I felt close to him.

For quite a while afterwards I carried around with me a great sadness. Mixed with it was disappointment, because my studies with Abba had never really materialized.

Again I reflected on the reasons that prevented us from working out the plans we had held in common. I could not deny I had always been wary of mental methods to spiritual growth. On the path to enlightenment, talking and reading are perhaps good supports, but my experiences in India had convinced me that scholarly or therapeutic approaches to Self-realization could not bear the desired fruits.

After Abba's disappearance, I had to remind myself that everything worked according to our karma and the Master Plan. Abba's idea for me to go deeper into Judaism, and my own wish to do so, did not really matter, nor did the pressures that from time to time I exerted to try and force circumstances. It is not our wish or will that determines our course. My awakening in India attested to this.

'Does everything really happen automatically?' I had asked Abba in the first year of our association.

'Nothing happens automatically,' he answered.

'I mean, are we always guided to the right people and circumstances?'

'We are all guided by the spiritual powers,' he replied, 'but we have to listen, and to see the signs in our surroundings. When we are sensitive, we can receive and also follow the guidance.'

On Silent Retreat in the French Alps

In rapid tempo the journalistic work was moving me from one spiritual teacher, group or event to the next. Voluminous research notes and recorded cassettes were in fact accumulating faster than I could convert the material into articles. A profusion of words and ideas about spirituality had poured so quickly into my mind that I could not sort out, evaluate and assimilate it all. Inundated, I longed to stop the intake for a while in order to digest properly what had already been received.

Fortunately, I took comfort in one of the teachings India had given me: we get what we need when we need it. And, indeed, sooner than imagined, I was presented with an occasion to withdraw temporarily from my activities and to see them in a refreshed perspective.

A friend of Denis, David Grabijn, told us that as in previous years he was going to visit the summer retreat center of Pir Vilayat Inayat Khan in the French Alps. Located high in the mountains, the *Camp des Aigles*, 'Camp of the Eagles', offered a place of seclusion where one could retire for a short time and lead the life of a contemplative.

What could have been better! We decided to join the undertaking. A few days later our party of three arrived in the Swiss town of Martigny, the departure point of our adventure.

Here we boarded a small mountain train which chugged leisurely upwards through tranquil Alpine scenery, past picturesque villages and tiny chalets scattered up the green slopes. The darkness of tunnels cut through the rock contrasted with light-bathed open country. After changing trains in Chamonix, on the French side, we took the cable car at Les Praz to ascend the mountain.

Sombre clouds blotted out the sun and soon we were gliding directly into the mist. Swaying silently in the all-enveloping whiteness, unable to see above or below, nothing existed for us but this breathtaking moment of suspended time and space. I felt lifted above ordinary life.

When we finally stepped out, it was a different season and I shivered in my summer cottons. A round of hot chocolate at a local hotel, in addition to the winter clothes we had brought along, acclimatized us, and without tarrying we set out. Leading straight up, the path prevented rapid progress. Our baggage became heavier, our breaths shorter. We paused often for rest.

An animal ran along the mountainside. We stopped and listened, motionless, until the tread of its footsteps completely faded. Standing there in nature's soothing silence, I thought it must have been my soul's longing for peace which brought me to this place.

We walked on. Intermittent rain impaired visibility and I continually lost my footing on the slippery grass slope. By the time the camp came into view, exhaustion tempered my joy. We took shelter in the first tent we saw, by David magnanimously termed the 'dining hall'. Rows of long wooden tables stood in the slushy earth while a strong wind slapped the canvas roof and the rain rushed in from the open sides. I had not expected the Chamonix Hilton, but also not this. A large muddy pool covered the entire site.

After a bell rang several times, human forms appeared. Under David's guidance we followed them to a large round tent, taking seats on hard, cold rocks arranged to face a heightened platform.

A bearded person, looking like a fisherman in a green rubber rainsuit with high boots, waded in and slipped off his wet garment to disclose a flowing brown robe. It was Pir Vilayat! Settling in front of us cross-legged, he talked, how appropriately, about the ecstasy of overcoming our limitations.

Encouraged by his words, I tried to forget my fatigue. At the end of the discourse we went to register, only to hear that our ordeal was not yet over. To get to our destination, the actual retreat camp, we still had ahead of us another 30-minute climb! David, who was to stay at the base camp, wished us a good journey and said he would see us at dinner. I joked that if this meant going up and down the mountain, I would fast all week.

Twilight had set in, there was a thick fog, and to make things worse, a heavy rain started to fall. I forced myself up the narrow path thinking about what Pir had said. How perfect had been his statement: 'The ability to free ourselves from the idea of being unable to do a certain thing, gives us an intoxication.' Then, suddenly, the retreat camp emerged from the mist.

Our elation was short-lived. There was only one tent and it was cold, damp and filled to capacity. On its slushy earthen floor lay a multitude of planks on which about two dozen people, wrapped in heavy woolen clothing and blankets, were packed tightly together. With everyone performing one or other Sufi exercise of breathing, head circling or chanting, to an incredible din, the place seemed like a madhouse. What had we got ourselves into?

We were like intruders and remained at the entrance, perplexed. Many eyes observed our predicament but nobody came forward to help. When a man put a finger to his lips, signaling us not to speak, we realized the retreat forbade verbal communication. No talking!

Finally a woman pointed to a water-soaked plank at the side of the tent, indicating we could lay it down by the entrance, the only available space. Overtired and chilly, I resigned myself to this not very inviting proposition, which was certainly preferable to the only alternative – having to return down the mountain.

But first my bladder needed relief. Where to find the facilities? And how to ask this in sign language? In time I observed that some persons were exchanging written notes and, slightly amused, I prepared one myself. Our rescuer directed me right into the black and stormy night. I shook my head and wrote: 'I'll wait until the rain stops.' With a grin, she handed me her reply: 'It's rained since yesterday noon!'

Upon my return, Denis presented me with the message 'Three days and then out!' along with the information sheet picked up at the base camp. He pointed to the paragraph: 'People should be aware, but not afraid, of the vipers which occasionally show themselves. If you are bitten, send someone to the secretariat for the anti-serum which we have on hand. Do not go on long walks without having someone with you.'

Soon several young men entered the tent carrying large pots, plates and cutlery. Everyone stood up, formed a circle and, holding hands, sang a Sufi song of thanks. I could not join in, not knowing the words, but at that moment felt very close to my companions in misery all the same.

The brown rice, hot vegetables and steaming tomato gravy took the edge off our low spirits. Under the circumstances, the simple fare tasted especially delicious and, as it began releasing its energy, a pleasant warmth reinvigorated my body. When a huge bucket of camomile tea made its appearance, my gratitude knew no end.

By eight, Denis and I had disappeared into our sleeping bags. Outside, the rain reached its height. A howling wind pounded the tent, the cold mocked my protective coverings, and any hope of getting a proper sleep vanished. To judge from the restless tossing of my tentmates, I was not alone in my distress.

At six o'clock the next morning we were nevertheless sitting attentively around Pir Vilayat who, as our guide in the week-long retreat, was alone allowed to speak. He started immediately to chase away our drowsiness by teaching us a series of exercises designed 'to force the consciousness into relation with higher planes'. Eventually we were sent outside to recite a certain mantra while walking. We had to gather again when he shouted '*Allahu Akbar*!' ('God is great!')

In the fresh air, I awoke to the reality of our surroundings. Yesterday's stormy veils were rolled aside to display jagged ice-capped mountains rising like proud giants in the clear morning sunlight. Mont Blanc, nearly 16,000 feet high, towered over us. The breathtaking, wild grandeur simply exalted me. Of course the climb yesterday had more than physical significance, for this was a place of power, of heights beckoning those who wanted to transcend their limitations and reach a universal level.

'The beauties of nature can be very inspiring at the beginning of a retreat,' cautioned Pir afterwards, 'but they tend to be a distraction later on. That's why ancient Sufis did their retreats in caves.

'Now go and practise being nothing, but don't enjoy it!' he instructed us. 'To maintain a state of peace, you have almost to restrain yourself from getting excited about the heavenly experiences you are having. Otherwise you lose them, because emotion immediately works on your ego, and you are right back in your earth-consciousness.'

He returned at five o'clock for our written questions.

The first one read: 'Up here we can spend all our time doing our individual exercises and meditations, but how does this relate to raising group consciousness in the world?'

Pir Vilayat smiled. 'Suppose there was a tremendous peace

somewhere in the world. Or imagine you could see behind the actions of people. Or you developed confidence in your own powers. Wouldn't all this be a great help to the world? To unfold your higher qualities, you must be able to experience them. Then you return to society enriched. Our aim is to become more perfect instruments through which the higher planes may manifest on the earth plane.'

Every morning he led us through sunrise and light practices, breathing and purification exercises, mantras and contemplation. And each late afternoon, after his classes at the base camp, he climbed up to us for our questions.

Repeatedly we executed together with him a *zikr*, the invocation to remember God by reciting mystical Arabic words while breathing in a certain way and circling the head. One day this lasted five solid hours, Pir's enthusiasm carrying us through 3,000 repetitions of the sacred phrase. When he got up to leave, he was reeling.

In those hours of intensive practice I received more insight into the mystical essence of Sufism than any amount of intellectual explanation could have afforded.

That afternoon a ferocious thunderstorm brought violent rains and angry winds. Our tent faced collapse as the ropes loosened from their pegs. Without words we all rushed to secure falling poles and flapping canvas. The rain thoroughly drenched most of our planks, sleeping bags and clothes, but we kept the tent standing.

Promptly at five, Pir Vilayat turned up in his fisherman's outfit. 'Of course!' he exclaimed when some of us showed surprise at his arrival. In the lower camp, both the dining and large round tent had given way. That we had managed so well, amazed him.

'I warned you that in Chamonix we are up against the forces of nature, didn't I?' he said, adding: 'When in a retreat you take a vow of silence, you may expect that the most extreme things come to tempt you to break it, like this storm today.'

Throughout most of the week there was no lack of temptations to have us interrupt our silence, if not to leave the retreat altogether. Life on the mountain seemed one big test, to determine whether our thoughts were tuned upwards with the eagles or rather down below with the hot chocolate. Perhaps because the hardships of our arrival topped any which followed, Denis and I came to accept the low nighttime temperatures, the heavy rains, and the scorching afternoon sun.

While our tent population numbered about 25 the first night, it was only 12 the next, and the thinning-out increased as the weather grew worse. Frigid nights drove many people to the main camp, where it was warmer. I held out, learning to sleep in the cold.

Daily we arose before dawn and, if the storm god had not yet joined us, we watched the sky grow from grey via pale blue to brilliant gold. Each of our days duplicated more or less the schedule of the previous one. Any changes we were experiencing came mainly from within ourselves.

Whenever we assembled before Pir Vilayat, we basked in the gentle and kind atmosphere surrounding him. What I loved was his continual readiness to share with us the pathways to the inner bliss he had found.

'In India they try your patience,' he said one day. 'You can go on for years with only one or two practices. But I have revealed many esoteric secrets to you. When old-time Sufis criticize me for this, I answer that times have changed. If I can teach you something that is really going to transform your life, why shouldn't I?'

During one of our sessions he told us: 'My main purpose is to give you a cosmic experience, to transport you beyond yourself. I offer you the opportunity to experience what I myself experience in a retreat. I will help you force the door.' Showering us with practices of Sufi background and teachings of various traditions, he aimed to get us into a state in which 'you won't know who you are or where you are'.

If I cannot remember all his words, I will never forget his intention. He almost desperately wanted us 'to experience the miracle of what you are'.

Our other teacher in the retreat was nature in all its severity, which similarly pushed me to reconsider my concepts, go beyond my limits and reach deeper into myself. As for the mountain, it encouraged me to explore its unspoiled beauty barefoot, out of respect. It reminded me that nothing on earth belonged solely to the realm of matter. Many of the ancient traditions say that our planet with all it comprises is a living, spiritual presence.

As the week progressed and the zone of quietness in me widened, I recognized the silence to be the retreat's third teacher. In so many ways it made its lessons known.

Having to converse by pen and paper, I noticed that I reflected before communicating, instead of saying whatever immediately came to mind. I understood that much of our talk is compulsive, unnecessary and drains energy. As in the material field, I could do more with less.

The ban on speaking also prevented me from classifying people superficially by the answers received to such questions as 'Where are you from?' and 'What do you do?' I was forced to relate to my companions beyond words, through feelings and understanding. In my silence I characterized people by their qualities of inner nature, on which our real identity is based.

Last but not least, I saw that retiring into silence can open us to the perfect peace within, the endless calm inaccessible to the mind. At the center of our self is the connection with all that exists beyond words and concepts.

On the retreat's last afternoon Pir prepared us for our return to civilization. 'Others will never realize what you have gone through in these days,' he summed up, 'and you cannot communicate it. Just try to carry out in your daily life what you have reached here.'

Before leaving the camp, each of us had a private *darshan* with him. At my turn, Pir asked first how I had liked the retreat. I confessed that I had not known beforehand what it implied.

'You needed the quiet,' he said softly.

'True. I was so busy before I came here, I was nearly overwhelmed.'

'I want to give you two *wazifas*,' he declared. 'One for solitude, one for outpouring.'

A *wazifa* is an Arabic word or phrase that denotes one of the qualities of God. Through repetition of the wazifa, practitioners invoke that quality and try to bring it to life within themselves.

'The outpouring of all qualities is good for the work you are being asked to do at the moment,' he continued, 'whereas the solitude is your real being. Recite them, alternately, 33 times every morning. They will help balance you.'

'Before I knew about the spiritual path, there was always so much activity in my life,' I said. 'Now I am wondering why it is still so hectic.'

'This is the sacrifice you must make,' explained Pir simply.

Then I mentioned that I wished to go to India on a long retreat, doubting whether to do so. Many interviews were waiting to be written. He advised me I could always go to India later. Now I had to fulfill my mission.

'What is my mission?' I asked.

'To make the spiritual known to the public,' he replied.

Along this line I told him I felt obliged to document the emerging age of transformation. Sometimes I had the impression I annoyed others by taking notes, making tape recordings and shooting photos at whatever gathering I attended. 'But I think I cannot do otherwise.'

Pir agreed. Those around me might not always understand. Still, I had to carry on in the same way. That was partly what he had meant the previous year by saying I needed courage because I would suffer much.

'But the suffering is as well in yourself, it does not always have to do with outer circumstances,' he now clarified. 'Part of it comes from the confusion of who you are. Compared to last year, however, you have made tremendous progress. You are coming out of the forest.'

'You can see this?'

'Yes, there is a great difference. Let go of time and really experience yourself as the visitor to earth who is now conscious of who she is.'

I knew much was changing inside me, I told him, yet I had observed I hardly needed to do anything special for it, such as meditate.

'Yes, there is a time to meditate, and it's like being in kindergarten,' Pir replied. 'As Hazrat Inayat Khan said, first you pursue meditation and then meditation pursues you. You don't have to do it any more because you receive it from above. That's the stage you are in. The only thing is to be in your higher consciousness, not in ego consciousness. Then meditation is no longer required.'

'Do you mean I can continue as I am? I feel that I am being guided and that all is unfolding in accordance with the divine plan.'

'Of course!' affirmed Pir. 'For God's sake, don't worry,' he added. 'It couldn't be better, what's happening to you.'

The talk with Pir Vilayat reassured me I was moving ahead in the right direction, in tune with the time scheme ordained for me. My confidence having been hoisted to the peaks, I was so high I literally floated down the mountain to the main camp, a vivacious community where everyone seemed to love everyone.

'*Allahu Akbar*! God is great!' I shouted out inside myself. How better to express my thankfulness for being alive? In the exhilarating milieu of the Camp of the Eagles I could uninhibitedly sing and dance and throw my arms wide to the heavens in gratitude. I looked forward to savoring this special place for a few days as a transition.

Denis, however, insisted we leave immediately. He saw the camp as a 'social club'.

'Most of the guys and gals were just fooling around, having a good time,' he complained to me on the return journey to Amsterdam.

'But they went through the same ordeal we did,' I said.

'With all those communal activities and dancing and singing together, they were just gratifying emotional and psychological needs,' he responded.

I commented that music and dance were used in Sufism to induce ecstasy.

'Fine,' Denis agreed. 'But how many of the campers had the urge for the real thing?' he asked.

That urge, to press unceasingly inwards and onwards until totally illuminated, both Denis and I had. Or, rather, it had us, possessed us, drove us on like two crazies. It was the shared aim around which our monkship revolved.

If we were to get involved in 'spiritual fun and games', or in joining a group, or in taking one workshop and seminar after another as many persons did, so Denis reminded me as the train brought us back to Holland, we might possibly get pulled off our one-pointed course. At the least, we would get delayed on our way. For these same reasons we also avoided the supernatural, magic and other occult phenomena – sidetracks filled with danger.

Ever looking to Gautama Buddha as a model, I saw indeed that he and all the notable spiritual pathfinders had, before their enlightenment, only one motivation: to know the Ultimate Truth. Until merged into this state, nothing else held importance.

'The great guys and gals were "urge people",' as Denis always joked.

Similarly obsessed myself, I was ready to cut my attachment to everything between me and my destination. My zeal kept me on the lookout for any teaching which could possibly speed me there. But Denis usually stepped in to prevent my spontaneity from taking me too far onto trails that would not, as he warned, lead me to where I really wanted to go.

Regarding the various spiritual groups, I saw that Swami Purna was correct. A group can help prepare a student towards Self-realization, but once the aspirant reaches a certain level of readiness, he or she usually needs individual instruction and guidance from an attained teacher.

In the classical guru-disciple relationship, the teacher's task is to lead the student towards the Ultimate.

Since the kind of teaching I envisioned for myself was not possible at that time, after the week of silence under Pir's Vilayat's able direction I decided I had only one route: to go inside myself. This, after all, was where my sunlit path of freedom had begun.

Besides, I was more convinced than ever that the all-encompassing spiritual apprenticeship I sought could happen only in the Orient. There, in *Bharat Mata*, I had been opened to the divine and given a larger, liberating vision. There I had understood that virtually all aspects of life can be a *yoga*, a uniting with the cosmic order and with God, or the Goddess. And only there, or so I thought at the time, could I dig down to my roots, not the ephemeral ones existing because of my birth into a particular religion, but those eternal roots connecting me with the source of all religions.

My idea was not to go East as a tourist for a number of weeks or months, but to live there for an indefinite period. This I eventually did. Storing away my possessions, subletting my apartment, making my farewells and leaving everyone and everything behind, I flew away from Amsterdam not knowing when, or if, I would ever return.

PART IV

The Continuity

Swami Purna and the Law of the Sun

My further adventures after the mountain retreat, covering a span of nearly 20 years, could fill many sequels. The first installment of my odyssey contains only the very beginnings of what may eventually flow from my pen.

Step by step I have traveled the path of freedom, seeking to reconnect more completely with my spiritual origins. Intensive experiencing and learning has led to a fuller blazing of my inner sun, and my life has come to a middle way between ancient and modern, East and West, yin and yang, body and spirit.

Perhaps my story, with a sun who speaks and a spiritual Prince Charming coming from a sun order of monks, may seem like a fairytale. It is very real, however, filled with fact not fiction, a part of the divine cosmic *lila*.

Today I view with quite different eyes some of the actors and actresses in my cast of players, and this particularly applies to Swami Purna. Better understanding our link, I feel I have to update what I have written about him.

When I set off to live in Asia, Swami Purna was one of the persons I left behind. The systematic training in consciousness that I failed to get from him, or from any other teacher, I assumed I could find in the East.

Although His Holiness had in principle agreed with my oriental pilgrimage, he showed cool indifference to the news that my journey would not start in India, as he suggested, but in the meditation monasteries of Thailand and Burma. Yet Swamiji had not tried to impose on me an itinerary of his own design. Following the approach of a true guru, he never told me what to do.

Recently I reread a page of notes scribbled down after a phone call with him in late 1979. We had apparently talked about my proposed Vipassana retreat in Rangoon with Buddhist meditation master Mahasi Sayadaw as my guide. Without mincing words I had let Swami Purna hear the main reason for my departure from Europe: his failure to give me systematic spiritual teachings.

'You have to be on the higher level before you can receive the higher teachings,' Swamiji responded, with unusual directness. I recorded his exact phrases: '. . . not ready . . . not fully prepared . . . not yet qualified'. I must admit his words hurt. In those days I hardly realized that a priceless spiritual training was always going on, spoken and unspoken, in endless ways, through the relation between my Rama and me.

Swami Purna also said: 'I give generously, but people must be sensitive enough to understand my guidance. I neither dictate nor do I infringe on anyone's free will. As you yourself know, you follow my guidance only when you want, when it fits in with your own thoughts and opinions, when it is convenient to you.'

Quite right he was, but good reasons existed for my reluctance to follow Swami Purna's pointing finger. It is true that at my initial sight of him on the Lauriergracht stairway I had immediately recognized H. H. Swamiji as a higher being. Not long after that, alas, questions about his identity started to plague me.

From the spiritual perspective, of course, someone's background does not really matter. It is the attainment in the present which counts. Furthermore, a renunciate leaves the past behind.

His birthplace, I had been told, was Mithila. In that former kingdom of northeast India, bordering Nepal, both Gautama Buddha and his contemporary, Lord Mahavira, the founder of Jainism, were born and grew up. Mithila is the very same place to which Lord Vishnu, in the form of Prince Rama, went to marry Princess Sita of Mithila, the beautiful daughter of King Janaka, as described in the *Ramayana*.

The name Mithila, by the way, derives from the Sanskrit root *mithi*, meaning among other things 'friend'. This same root also generated the name Mitra, used by an incarnation of the Sun in long-ago India.

It seems no coincidence that the transition point for Mitra's descent into the world was at Mithila. For in Mithila, as mentioned in the *Vishnu Purana*, there existed a branch of the *Surya-vansa*, the Solar race which sprang from Vivasvan, the Sun.

From this Solar dynasty, reigning at Mithila, came my Prince Swami Complete. According to Swami Purna, he descended from a line which included no less than Janaka, Mahavira and Gautama Buddha.

What is more, he said I belonged to that past myself, otherwise he would not have chosen to tell me about it.

'I let you know these things because in time you will have to understand all this,' he had once explained to me. 'You are also part of my past and I am reminding you of it.'

I could not help but ponder: who was Swami Purna really? And what was his role in the Plan?

In those early days my power of spiritual insight was lacking. I had grown up in the materialistic West and still looked at life through my conditioned mind and my karma. This limited perception of reality at times blocked me from seeing the inner essence of things, situations and people. Furthermore, I had no criteria by which to know what is a guru or a high being or *lila*.

Although Swami Purna had never made any concrete promises to me as such, my fantasy and imagination had led me to believe that I was disappointed with him, and that I could not trust him entirely. Incidents hinting at his yogic powers, such as his invisibility at the airport or his sudden materialization inside my apartment, were blotted out of my memory by his sometimes peculiar and occasionally shocking acts. Also I was influenced by Denis, whose negative views sowed in me further seeds of doubt and suspicion about Swamiji.

Despite my misgivings, in most cases I gave a positive interpretation to Swami Purna's presence in my life and I remained ready to help him in his work. In fact, I considered it a privilege to lend my pen to his correspondence, articles, and other writings. What did it matter if, in exchange, I did not receive the classical method of consciousness training for which I so longed? Had not Sri Krishna instructed us to perform our actions without expecting reward? Was not service an important part of spiritual life?

I intuited that there was more to the sun monk than appeared, but was simply unable to pierce through Swami Purna's masks. Just as Arjuna in the *Bhagavad Gita* lacked the mystical, supernatural eye to recognize Sri Krishna's transcendent form, I was blocked by the veils of my own ignorance and could not see Swamiji's totality.

During my intense five years in Asia, Swamiji and I did not hear from each other. After I had arrived back in Europe we met once more, in London. That confrontation failed to remove the wrappings of enigma I still saw around Swami Purna, or whoever he was, and I decided not to seek further contact. Shortly afterwards I left another time for India, returning to Amsterdam only two years later.

I began to regard Swami Purna in a clearer light only after starting this book, when the challenge to put my autobiographical account onto paper brought me greater clarity of inner vision. By the manuscript's end, I understood why he had advised me to meet many spiritual leaders and teachers.

At last I realized that of all the living masters I had known over the years, Swami Purna was my earthly *sat guru*. I remembered as well what Swamiji had told me several times: I had a mission to accomplish and to help me with this was one of his purposes in coming to the West. The words of Dadaji rang in my ears: 'If the *sat guru* appears and is not recognized, we might not be granted such an opportunity again in the same life.'

Without further delay, in late 1992, I wrote to Swami Purna in New Delhi: 'Years have passed, karmas have burned . . . . I would very much like to see you.'

He cabled back quickly, giving the date of his next return to the British capital.

A few weeks later I took the boat to England. A crisp December day with occasional sun invited me to sit for a while on the open deck. Gazing out over an expansive blue waterscape, I reflected on the 20 years since my awakening, and delved into memories associated with the 'high guy from the Himalayas'.

A picture of Swamiji arose in my mind. His head was tilted to one side, his lips wore a Mona Lisa smile. Then quickly flashed in front of my eyes another figure, as well with beard and white robes. It was not until days later that this appearance would be explained to me.

In London, an attractive young woman ushered me into Swami Purna's reception room. Within minutes he entered, looking just as I had remembered him.

Before he could say a word, I bent forward and placed the palms of my hands on his bare feet. Never during all the years of our association, save in jest, had I touched his feet in the traditional Indian way of paying respect.

He sat down, and I chose the chair across from his. In the

beginning we discussed his most recent stay in India, where some of the nation's top decision-makers were taking his guidance. I recollected a photo I had seen years back, of Swami Purna sitting together with Sri Morarji Desai, at that time Prime Minister of India.

Swamiji showed me a report he had had drawn up for the present Indian Prime Minister, Sri Narasimha Rao. Covering a range of topics, the paper dealt with concrete suggestions for bringing India into a balance between spirit and matter. Especially dear to me was a section emphasizing the many practical uses of solar power: '. . . this force which our Vedic ancestors revered above all else and of which they understood the value'.

The sun – as heat, light, wind and wave – Swamiji mentioned to me, can provide energy sufficiency for all countries willing to develop and apply the appropriate technology. 'No nation with access to solar energy, of any form, need be poor,' he declared. 'Sun power is the fuel of the future.' Because of his direct intervention, he said, Prime Minister Rao officially declared solar development a top priority in India's 8th Five-Year Plan.

Swami Purna's mission had decidedly assumed a wider significance, for his guidance was now also being taken by leaders in many countries, including my own birthland. He had, he jokingly told me, become a steady commuter between Europe and America.

After the young woman left the apartment, I felt free to confront Swami Purna with the purposes of my visit.

Without any preliminaries, I asked him: 'Will you forgive me?'

'Certainly,' he answered.

'For my ignorance, stupidity, disrespect, arrogance, pride, ego . . . and everything else,' I went on.

He pronounced some words which sounded like a mantra. An extended silence followed in which much was said. Earnestly we looked at one another. Sometimes both of us, simultaneously, broke into a smile. He seemed to mirror whatever I did.

Eventually I spoke: 'I am recalling our last meeting, before I left for Asia. We were at the train station in Venlo, in Holland. I told you that I had the feeling I would not see you for a very long time. Do you remember?'

'Of course.'

'We have not really been together for 12 years.'

'Well, it could also have taken 12 months,' he said, laughing.

'Twelve is the number of the sun, but did it have to take something twelve?' I asked.

'Twelve seems to be very significant,' he remarked, continuing to laugh.

'What about my visit to you six years ago?'

'That was only half way, you came half prepared,' replied Swamiji. 'You did not come in love and faith but still as a question mark. Unless all your questions are answered, and you have stability of mind and intellect, you cannot advance to the next stage of attunement and communion. While doubt and confusion persist, the student must work on clearing the mind.'

Then he recited in Hindi and translated: 'O bird, you can fly away from me, the boat in the ocean, but I know you will return, because there is no other boat.'

Swamiji laughed again and I joined in.

'During the 12 years you felt my influence and my link,' he explained. 'You were like the bird in this song by Surdas.'

I nodded, recognizing the name of the 16th-century saint-poet of India's Bhakti renaissance.

'His song is very beautiful,' commented Swamiji. 'O my mind, where will you have peace? I know you will run around the whole world and then you will come back. I know, because wherever you go, you will not have that bliss and that peace you long for, except here, but you do not yet understand. O my mind, where will you have peace?

'The bird flying away from the boat finds nothing but the vast ocean, and finally returns to the boat. This is the mind, wandering all over. It does not take refuge in the Beloved. But I knew the bird would come back one day and find the ultimate bliss.'

Such a tender smile he gave me.

'I knew that sooner or later, when you would have more tranquility and peace, you would realize this. Until then you had to go through so many things, as part of your growth.'

Agreeing, I told him that in the 12 years I had met countless gurus, but no one had ever replaced him in my heart. In addition, I felt my path of freedom had narrowed into a razor's edge, and I might not be able to reach the highest state on my own. The help of a living master was required, just as Maharaj Charan Singh had so insisted.

'You have been contemplating?' asked Swamiji.

'Yes, but it was more than that,' I responded, telling him that in the past year certain significant desires had burned away. After they disappeared, I realized they had been obstructing my spiritual advancement.

Swamiji nodded and said: 'The problem with many Western seekers is that they want to fulfill all their desires and at the same time reach enlightenment. The teacher must make them understand that as long as they are in desire, they cannot gain spiritual knowledge and liberation. At a certain time they have to go beyond desire and say, "That's it. I have gone through it, and that's it."'

'Why did our separation take 12 years?' I inquired anew.

'Twelve is a symbolic number,' answered Swamiji, 'associated with the 12-year period of *sannyas*, with purification and stability. In the tradition of *sannyas*, the teacher gives the knowledge and then lets the disciple be free to wander and to go through various processes, sometimes applying the guru's teaching, sometimes not. I knew you needed to go out and do some things in your way. It has been a rich time, helping you to understand and see more clearly.'

'Certainly everything I have been through is a living out of my karmas,' I commented, 'but in hindsight, some of my adventures seem merely to have cost me time.'

'Nothing is a waste,' replied Swamiji. 'All your experiences helped you get where you are. You could not have learned in the same way from books. I knew when you came out from under the cloud of confusion, you would be strong. Remember I urged you: "Meet every spiritual and religious figure. That will be the best education for you. Then you will know me more."'

Again we reverted to a speechless communion. I was reminded of saints and mystics I had encountered in India. Some of them either spoke a language I did not comprehend or, having taken a vow of silence, did not speak at all. To sit in their presence is to reap the benefits of *darshan*, for they continuously transmit spiritual energy.

My former tribulations with Swami Purna in regard to his indirect style of communication also entered my thoughts, and I questioned him about this.

'It was part of the training, to help you tune with me and get the essence rather than depend on my verbal expression,' he explained. 'This technique develops inner communication. When I was vague or did not want to talk, that was a sign you should take the message from my silence,' he explained.

'But in silence how can students be sure they are getting the message of the teacher and not of their own thoughts?' I queried.

'That is why students have to elevate their level,' he answered. 'Before you were always demanding phone calls and letters, or lectures like a philosophy professor would deliver. But the guru does not speak or act in styles to which the student is accustomed. This is to break the mind's patterns and give the mind the flexibility required for inner progress.

'Not until your demands and expectations disappeared would a higher state prevail. Then you could understand without words and receive my messages on a subtle plane,' he said. 'The clarity you sought about our connection was actually obstructed by your own mind.'

Swami Purna disclosed other details of his teaching method and admitted what I had always suspected: he had played many games with me. This belonged to his *lila*. Sometimes he had behaved like a very ordinary human being; other times he had been sublime and mystical. The confusion created in me about his identity grew because of my limited perception and my ego. Finally I had come to understand that a teacher of Swami Purna's level could be the 'other half' of anyone open to tune with him.

I now also understood, for example, that the iriscopist's negative remarks about Swami Purna's photo had been part of a process to determine whether I knew Swamiji by my own heart or by the opinions of others.

'You went through a trial of your faith, love and strength,' explained Swamiji. 'The student has to undergo all kinds of tests but the guru, again unlike the university professor, does not say "I will give you an examination tomorrow." The student should be unaware of the testing.'

'I certainly failed many of your tests!'

'That is part of the process of learning and growing,' he said. 'It may take a long time before the student reaches the final stage in his or her preparations. Only then can the actual training begin.'

'Denis and I were so critical of you,' I declared.

'I always advised both of you not to react immediately but to watch and observe,' came the response. 'With limited vision one does not see the motivation. That is another lesson for the student: to get the overall view you need patience. Only at the completion of something can you come to understand what is what.'

Swamiji illustrated his point with a story about the Tibetan yogi-saint Milarepa. During his training period he was told by his guru, Marpa, to build a house. When the house was ready, Milarepa was told to destroy it. This happened several times. Milarepa, who saw no sense in building and destroying, thought Marpa must be insane.

'Milarepa had no faith: that is why he questioned,' explained Swamiji. 'He doubted, he judged. But when, in the end, he realized why Marpa had acted so strangely, the picture looked very different. Among other reasons, Marpa did all this because Milarepa had accumulated much bad karma. Unless the karmas were consumed, Marpa could not start teaching him.

I realized I too had built and destroyed many houses, symbolically, of course, during my own process of karma burning.

'Just see how extreme and outrageous the guru's acts can be,' Swami Purna continued. 'Still more complicated, the guru does not explain every statement or act. That would be like defending; if you defend, you are no guru.'

'Isn't it necessary for a student to have some critical faculty, and not be like a sheep?' I asked.

'What is important is positive discrimination,' responded Swamiji. 'Seekers have to become able to discern who is a true teacher. Once they decide this teacher is the way to the goal, they need to carry out the teachings which are imparted. But you did not give the teacher a chance. All the time you were questioning whether the teacher was capable, or whether he would help you or not.'

'I guess this shows the absence of a humble attitude.'

'Yes, the first quality of a student is to be humble.'

'And to be clear about what you really want,' I said.

'In any relationship you have to know what you want to get and to give,' he stated. 'If it is spiritual knowledge and enlightenment you're after, you need not only a qualified guide, but to know what you want from him or her.'

It has become evident to me that for many years a dark outer energy tried to keep me separated from Swami Purna. This sunless force had worked through certain persons, close to me, who tended to look at life through a negative lens. Now I regard my personal battle against destructive thoughts and actions as part of a training to help me face the greater resistance to spiritual work which exists in the world at large. I had to struggle to develop my own independent eye and mind so that I would be able to see the truth and know what is right.

I had another important question for Swamiji. To my surprise it was answered before I had said a word.

'Also as part of the training process,' he explained, 'you had to be made more aware of the workings of your own body and mind, desires and wishes. In order to push you to greater awareness, I sometimes had to resort to "shock therapy". It is like when someone needs to be reanimated and is given a shock to get the heart working.'

When Swamiji had to answer the telephone, I nibbled on the Indian sweets presented me upon my arrival. For quite a while he listened to his caller's problems and gave advice.

'It cannot be very pleasurable for you to descend from your usual high state to be at human level,' I said after the phone talk ended.

'Obviously I do it for some purpose,' he replied.

'And not just the purpose to create confusion?' I asked, teasingly.

'The purpose is upliftment,' he told me in a serious tone, 'to elevate those who have been preparing, not only in this life or in this century. People will be given the opportunity to enlighten themselves. They in turn will work to bring awareness to others.'

The time is approaching, Swami Purna told me, when the commercial phase of spirituality will finish. 'Imagine a forest abundant with fruit trees from which anyone may take,' he suggested. 'When so much fruit is accessible, you simply gather it and eat. There is no necessity to buy.'

Swamiji spoke of a nearby future rich in the free availability of the eternal knowledge. Already among us, he confirmed, are high beings who have come to renew on this planet what has been spoiled by human ego, greed and arrogance. Nothing less than a true teacher and a true teaching, he reminded me, are needed to arrive at the spiritual destination. Teachers of the highest level most often carry out their blessed work quietly, without audience or applause. To transmit the grace energy freely is one of their main tasks.

'What is the larger purpose?' I asked him.

'It is time to restore the Law of Aditya,' he answered.

'Aditya?' I was struck. Aditya is one of the names of the sun, from the Sanskrit. Instantly I felt that this word, Aditya, was a sign and a signal. Would Swami Purna now start to teach me the Sun-knowledge?

'Yes, we need to restore the Law of the Sun,' said Swamiji, 'because everything on earth is based on the sun and its twelve principles.'

Very briefly he explained to me the Law of Aditya, the Law of the Sun. All-embracing, it rules everything in the cosmos, including the laws that control the forces of nature governing our planet. These natural laws regulate the life of the rivers, the mountains, the trees, and so on. In contrast to these natural laws are the human laws, created by the human mind. Usually unenlightened, limited and lacking foresight, our mind does not give us the vision to see the larger consequences of our acts.

'The problem is, humans have been making laws that contradict or oppose the Aditya principles,' Swamiji continued. 'That is the blunder.'

Listening to Swami Purna speak about the Law of the Sun, I sensed that my reunion with him marked a new beginning for me. I saw that his visions for earth's bettered future belonged not simply to utopias we could discuss animatedly until the wee morning hours, as in our earlier years together. In those days the rise of a spiritualized earth civilization seemed a very far away and distant possibility, but now Swami Purna was starting to share with me concrete suggestions for improving the world.

Some of these transformational ideas are already being put into practice in countries where Swamiji has been giving personal guidance. I found it significant that he based his earth-improvement program on a joint effort between humanity and the sun.

Before the Law of the Sun can be restored fully on earth, Swami Purna added, human beings need to get the global house in order: 'Disasters are occurring today to warn society to sort out its mess. And, as the global situation worsens, the world community will realize the need for guidance. Then the hidden masters will make their presence known to the larger public. At that time, no matter their native language, people will have no trouble understanding our message.'

'Don't the masters first have to be recognized?' I asked.

'People may know us in different ways,' he told, 'but when the time comes, they will see who we really are.'

'What do you mean?'

'Some persons who are entwined with only one identity will then know its many forms.'

For a long moment I pondered his remark.

'Are you saying you yourself have many forms?' I finally inquired.

'Yes.'

'So you are not solely Swami Purna?'

'That's right,' he said, laughing. 'This entity has many forms.'

A high being can have several physical bodies, he explained. Some of the bodies may bear resemblance to each other, while some may look quite different. They can, for example, be made to appear and disappear.

As he spoke there came to my mind the sight of him suddenly materializing before me in my Lauriergracht apartment, when he had entered my house without a key. Now I understood more about the message he had delivered to me with that miraculous appearance.

'A high being uses several bodies not as a gimmick,' Swamiji stressed, 'but only under certain circumstances and for a purpose.'

'Most people will find your statement unbelievable, that you can change your form,' I commented.

'Because they do not know the principle and law of spiritual transformation,' responded Swamiji. 'Where all the physical laws end, spiritual transformation begins. To comprehend this, people have to evolve their higher minds.'

As the mind develops, just as Swami Purna had repeatedly assured me from the very beginning of our association, what is difficult to fathom at the time eventually becomes clearer. That is why after many years, at last, I perceived deeper meanings to Prince Swaniji's gnawing riddle: who is he, and what is he to my life that is more than a guru and more than the Beloved?

When the solution started to dawn on me like a Pondicherry sunrise, again I came face to face with my nameless identity. Only now it was the inner sun which did the reflecting, and it bore the features of a moustached man looking like Swami Purna.

Knowing the Sun Master: Maitreya

To penetrate the veils covering the identity of H. H. Swami Purna was not the only purpose of my Channel crossing. Other faces also drew me to Britain.

One was that of 'Maitreya', as I had seen it a month earlier on a photo published in *Share International*, the magazine edited by Benjamin Creme. The photo was presented as Maitreya, as he appeared 'out of the blue' at an open-air prayer meeting in Nairobi, Kenya, on 11 June 1988. 'He was photographed addressing (in their own language) thousands of people who instantly recognized Him as the Christ.'[28] Finally I saw the features of the mysterious Maitreya whose very existence had for so long been a question to me.

Denis, or Denish as he is now called, pointed out to me that Maitreya resembled a spiritual teacher already well known to us. Launching a serious investigation, we compared the *Share International* picture with photos I had taken of that teacher years back, and we discussed what we knew about his person and his work. Now we suspected him to lead a double and perhaps even a multiple life. That he had never claimed to be Maitreya we took as a positive sign. Because we held him in high regard, we were able to consider the extraordinary idea that 'the holder of the office of Christ within the Hierarchy of Masters' was indeed living among us.

Was this possibility any more far-fetched than the one which says that our sun is an alive being who can speak? I took for support the sentence pinned to my workroom bulletin board: 'Faith sees the invisible, believes in the incredible, and is rewarded with the impossible.' Would my faith once again be made real?

The name Maitreya, by the way, is another derivative from the

Sanskrit root *mithi*, and is usually defined as 'the loving one' or 'the kind one'.

Exactly one week before the yearly feast commemorating the birth of Jesus of Nazareth, I had an appointment with the Master whom Denish and I conjectured to be the World Teacher of our present time. I entered a well-furnished sitting room in London. Although the 'Savior' may have come down to us from the Himalayas, this British interior reflected European good taste.

With the finest of manners, he invited me to sit in a comfortable chair. A light snack and drink were served me which, however, I did not touch. Nothing could divert my attention when here I was facing 'Him'. Certainly he resembled the magazine photo.

The initial moments, spent in silence, allowed me to absorb the energy-filled atmosphere and to observe intently the man before whom I sat. He was dressed in robes, had the mandatory long hair, beard and moustache, and fitted altogether the classical image of an Eastern guru having set up spiritual shop in the West.

Looking at his face, I saw it as if for the first time. A huge wave of respect came up in me for this being. I was therefore not play-acting when I asked, in a quite formal way: 'Your Holiness, are you Maitreya?'

He laughed and stated enigmatically: 'You will know at the proper time.'

Apparently my approach was too direct. Later on I got a better chance to inquire about his name.

'There is a book called *Vishnu Sahasranam*,' he said. 'The Lord Vishnu had thousands of names. Similarly, Krishna and Rama had many names.'

My ears perked up.

'At the higher spiritual levels you are recognized in diverse ways,' he told me. 'Different names are given you, dependent on the observer's evolution. Some of the close disciples of the Buddha did not call him "Buddha". They called him instead "Tathagatha". As individuals or seekers grow, they know you by different names.'

His remarks about Gautama Buddha came unexpectedly to me, like the emergence of the sun on a cloudy day. Eagerly I seized the opportunity.

'You just mentioned the fourth Buddha and what he was called,' I said. 'Now Buddhists are awaiting the fifth Buddha, whose name is Maitreya.'

'Yes.'

'Do some persons or entities call you Maitreya as well?' I asked.

'Yes,' he replied, 'on that level some people know me.'

'Those who would call you by that name would most likely have to be quite high themselves,' I commented.

'Yes, of course,' he agreed. 'Masters and very evolved beings would not call me by the names normally used.'

'Are you working together with the other high beings?' I next asked.

'Some of the masters are still remote, not really involved with humanity in general, but a few are in the world,' he said.

'The masters give power to teachers and energy to those individuals who can tune with the subtle level,' he went on. 'This transmission has nothing to do with religion, race, gender, country, particular tradition or culture,' he added. 'It has only to do with one's ability to receive the grace energy and to benefit others.'

Behind the scenes, he disclosed, he had been 'preparing people to be instrumental in helping to transform their respective country as part of the total renewal of Mother Earth. . . . specific things have to be accomplished . . . . certain persons have a particular role to play.'

His ideas sounded like those attributed to Maitreya in *Share International*. Nonetheless, I considered it important to capture with my tape recorder his fully unveiled identity. I hoped to hear him say in words, his own words, exactly what he represented.

Naturally I asked him about his manifestations in public. According to *Share International*, Maitreya appears unexpectedly and then after some time mysteriously disappears, vanishing into thin air. As easily as most of us walk through a doorway, Maitreya apparently moves through time and space at will.

'People know me by various appearances and names . . . ,' said the being before whom I sat. And then he added: 'But when the time comes they will perceive I am Maitreya.'

Maitreya! He had pronounced the magical word.

Thoughts of Oma Mimi and her visions of the luminous Christ came to my mind. I had no further questions – at least for now.

'At the highest level,' Maitreya started to explain, 'Krishna, Christ, Maitreya and all the other great beings are the same. They are all manifestations of the same grace energy. This energy may be manifested in one, or two, or more different forms. How people recognize and name the energy, depends on their soul evolution and cultural background.'

By request of the spiritual hierarchy, he went on, he had come to guide humanity and the planet to renewal. When I mentioned that the Share International Foundation announces that the World Teacher left the Himalayas in 1977, Maitreya said that 1977 'was only a year chosen to initiate the unfoldment of the Maitreya Principle for the world. I was down here in the civilization long before that, time and again actually.'

Maitreya's faith in the truth of himself and his mission seemed unshakable.

'Whenever there is a rise of elements which severely disturb the cosmic laws,' he said, 'interference comes from on high.'

According to Maitreya, the time is ripe for divine law to be restored on earth. This has, however, nothing to do with establishing a new religion.

'Religions harm humanity when they follow the dogmatic approach,' he declared. 'Look around. Many of the world's present conflicts have a religious background.

'Each religion must return to the eternal truths which inspired their path,' said Maitreya. Launching into an explanation, he spoke first about Judaism, and its gift to humankind in the form of the Ten Commandments. The ancient Hebrews provided the discipline and order without which the peoples of the Old Testament would have been directionless, he said. Modern Judaism, struggling with divisive internal forces, has to reconnect with its ancient wisdom.

'A return to roots is required for all religions today,' said Maitreya, going on to talk about Buddhism and its conflicting factions. Buddhists, too, need to leave dogma behind and find common unity in the origins of their faith. A refocusing on Gautama Buddha's basic teachings of wisdom and compassion will benefit all Buddhists as well as humanity in general.

Referring to Islam, Maitreya pointed out that despite the outer warring between various groups, a harmony of inner purpose can be felt in Mecca. There, where the same holy call brings together all worshippers, the invisible energy of Oneness exerts a strong positive force. If Muslims will seriously follow the Prophet's teachings about the duty of Oneness and the equality of men and women, said Maitreya, they can assume a dominant role in leading the global community to bettered relationships. As a beginning, Muslims would be wise to embrace the Sufi realization that at the core of all religions shines the same light.

Hinduism too, said Maitreya, can make an important contribution to solving the problems of our time. Hindus have to grow beyond rites and rituals and spread the message of Vedanta, with its emphasis on Self-realization and freedom from all bondages. They have to put into daily practice the Vedic truth of *Vasudev Kutumbakam*, the realization that all human beings belong to one global family.

Then Maitreya mentioned Christianity, calling for it to be based on the teachings of the Christ rather than on the life of Jesus. Let people celebrate kindness and service, he suggested, not the details of the master's birth and death.

Maitreya's remarks about Christianity especially interested me because, in *Share International*, he had been making miraculous appearances as a Christ figure.

'Why, in our time, are you stressing Christianity?' I asked him.

Very simply he replied: 'If those who love Jesus can be inspired to elevate themselves from the institution of Christianity with all its dogma, narrowmindedness and intolerance, they can set an example. Other religious groups will follow suit. All institutions of religion must transform themselves or dissolve.'

Maitreya's confident tone instilled me with hope.

'Will the Great Transformation occur soon?' I inquired.

'It is possible, if enough people work for it.'

'What is necessary?'

'That the pioneers, the teachers, and all those who are trying to help others, should be more aware.'

'More aware of what?'

'More aware of the transformation taking place. But everything on this planet, including spirituality, has become a business, a big show, a facade. All this delays the restructuring process.'

'Regarding the transformation of the economic system, what are the main changes that have to be made?' I asked.

'The decision-makers, the politicians and the economists have to make a new economic system relating to the world as a whole,' Maitreya answered. 'Life on earth must be seen as a totality and based on balance. Every person,' he declared, 'is entitled to the fulfillment of five basic needs: proper food, appropriate clothing, good shelter, health care and education.

'At the moment the world economy is based on artificial

values,' he said. 'House prices in the Mayfair district of London, for example, do not reflect real value. Half a million pounds for one apartment? An apartment is not made of gold. These are values created artificially, to keep prices high for the benefit of certain vested interests.

'The huge gap between the rich and the poor, the North and the South, is intolerable. Some people are starving and others in the same world are wasting so much. Sharing and proper distribution of wealth must prevail, not the dictatorship of monetary gain.'

His words corresponded very much to his statements in *Share International*. Maitreya considers the market forces of the present economic system to be 'forces of evil'. Controlled by the negative energies of greed and competition, and putting financial profit before anything else, these market forces lead to social and environmental havoc. Any government which bases its policies only on the blind following of market forces is leading its citizens to ruin.

'If the appropriate changes are not made, the present system will break down,' he declared.

'If that happens, there will be even more chaos and confusion,' I noted.

'Perhaps, at that time, humanity will accept the necessity for guidance.'

'Is that when you would emerge openly?'

'It is possible. I have been asked to take a very big task, a global task. And I have been saying that when the time comes . . . when the right time comes . . . .'

'Just what is your purpose?'

'*Ekohum bahusyama . . . sambhavami yuge yuge*,' he recited, quoting from Indian scripture. Then he translated from the Sanskrit: 'I am One, but I manifest as many, and I descend from time to time . . . .'

Discussing the importance of timing, he said: 'The 20th century has witnessed a speeding up and an increased intensity. These are some of the signs it is time to go to the next phase of our evolution. This period is very critical, as when a child is being born and it is a difficult birth. The child can die if not handled properly. This is the present stage of the earth. Certain things have to be done or humanity will suffer so much it will become almost impossible to do anything.

'We are not only at the change of century, but also the change of age. We are at the juncture of transformation, where we can leave the Kali Yuga behind. That is the critical birth, entering the next age.'

'Is this one of the reasons many disasters have been occurring?'

'These are all signs of the transition,' Maitreya answered. 'The signs are also warnings,' he went on. 'The new civilization will be built on the preceding one, but those things of the past which are negative and corrupt have to transform or die off. More disasters will occur until people accept the transformation, the new cosmic order.'

'What does this new cosmic order involve?'

'Human laws have failed,' stated Maitreya. 'Now the law beyond has to run society,' he said.

'The law beyond?'

'Many of humanity's present-day problems can be resolved,' declared Maitreya. 'The power to do this is within us and among us. People have to see and accept and introduce this force into their lives.'

'The power is within and among us,' I repeated. 'Isn't that the old spiritual message?'

'No, what I am suggesting is very concrete,' said Maitreya. 'Every day we are affected by a mighty energy whose meaning and message we still have not understood. The answer for our world problem is staring us right in the face.'

'Are you saying that the answer is before us but we do not see it?' I asked.

Maitreya replied: 'For instance, you have an energy which you are not utilizing in a proper way,' he began. 'Instead you pollute the earth by use of minerals,' he continued. 'Why destroy the world when you have readily available the power source which is clean, effective and has the solution for many of humanity's problems?'

How to express my joy at the words I was hearing!

'There is only one energy I know which meets this description,' I burst out excitedly. Light danced in Maitreya's eyes and I said to him gaily: 'Are you by any chance talking about . . .?'

'Yes, exactly,' he replied with a smile.

Imagine my delighted surprise when he revealed: 'That is one of my tasks – to bring humanity to the sun-fold.'

Naturally I asked him the obvious: 'What exactly is the sun-fold?'

Quite matter-of-factly he told me: 'Sun-fold is when you follow the path of the sun.'

'What exactly is the path of the sun?'

Maitreya's explanation was simple: 'On the sun path you align all your being with the sun principle, that the sun is affecting you physically as well as spiritually. So first you enjoy the physical gifts of the sun, and then you tune yourself in a spiritual way.'

Then ensued a lively conversation about the sun as the basis of all life on earth and the necessity for us to attune with the sun. Maitreya pointed out that by following the sun a person gets not only spiritual solace, but also material and economical advantage.

One of Maitreya's projects is nothing less than to remove exploitation from the world and to solve the global pollution crisis through the use of solar energy. He described how the path of the sun would bring prosperity to all people, and lead to the real recognition of the sun. 'Human beings should be able to recognize the Source,' he said.

Returning to Maitreya's use of the term 'sun-fold', I commented that some people might think this expression indicated a group or a cult.

'The "sun-fold" refers to the laws governed by the sun,' Maitreya clarified. 'And now there are teachers, world teachers, who are here to introduce and explain the sun laws.'

'Are you referring to the Law of Aditya?' I wanted to know.

His face lit up and he said, 'Yes, you can say Aditya.'

When Maitreya pronounced that meaningful name, I understood I was where I was supposed to be, in the right place with the right timing. Despite his human appearance, the one who had just said 'Aditya' might indeed be none other than a divine personification of the Sun itself.

As a journalist of the spiritual, I grasped the significance of this moment and posed the crucial question: 'Mr. Maitreya, are you . . . The Sun Master?'

Maitreya laughed and said: 'Well, my work is sun-related . . . so whatever you choose to call me . . . .'

'How long will you stay?' I made sure to ask.

'When the purpose is achieved, when the work has been accomplished, then I will leave.'

'How can we help the mission?'

'Those persons who have been prepared will be given tasks to bring about concrete results.'

'What about those others who want to serve but do not yet know their task?' I inquired.

'They will know in time.'

'Until then, what do you advise us to do?'

'People have to amend their ways, their thinking processes. Break the old conditioning. Leave destructive thoughts and actions. Have positive consciousness. Work on themselves so they can be ready to receive the grace energy. This is the time to wake up and transform.'

Sufi Mystic Irina Tweedie and the Voice of the Silence

By the time I left Maitreya, I realized that the manuscript I had written about my spiritual odyssey still needed two additional chapters: one describing my reunion with Swami Purna, and the other to show that 'Maitreya' is not just a name but someone of flesh and blood.

With work on the German translation in its final stages, I literally had to beseech my German publisher, Verlag Hermann Bauer of Freiburg, Germany, to squeeze at least one of the new chapters into the book. I am very grateful to publisher Friedrich Kirner and editor Karin Vial for their flexibility in making last-minute production changes to allow this. Readers of Der *Ruf der Sonne* ('The Call of the Sun'), published in the autumn of 1993, did learn about my return to Swami Purna but heard not a single word about my recognition of Maitreya. This unfortunate state of affairs was rectified in the next foreign edition, *Als de zon spreekt* ('When the Sun Speaks'), brought out in December of 1994 by open-minded Dutch publisher Willem Franken of Uitgeverij De Ster in the Netherlands.

The unfoldment still continues, and even after the appearance of the expanded Dutch edition, I sit in my Amsterdam retreat writing more new pages. Once again I see that the unveiling of the Plan, 'which is already planned', has its own timing which can neither be rushed nor slowed. Patience is a primary requisite for everything in life.

Since my reunion with Swami Purna, the borders of my mind have been gradually widening, and finally I have come to perceive the deeper significance of several other meetings I had during my extraordinary visit to England. This applies first of all to Sufi mystic Irina Tweedie, in whose inspiring presence I came to understand so much more about myself.

Mrs. Tweedie was the first Western woman trained within the ancient yogic lineage of Naqshbandi Sufism. Known as the Silent Sufis, this branch of mystical Islam practises a silent rather than vocal *zikr*, repetition of one of the many names of God.

The Sufi's goal is to return to 'the Beloved'. God, or Allah, or Truth, is to the Sufi the ultimate lover. Progressing in the spiritual direction, the Sufi comes to know that the Beloved lives nowhere else than in one's own mystic heart. To move safely along the specific path of Naqshbandi Sufism – or along any spiritual road into the inner world – one requires an experienced travel guide. The 13th-century Sufi mystic Jalal ad-Din Rumi, founder of the Mevlevi Order of dancing dervishes, expressed it as follows:

> *Without a master this journey is full of tribulations, fears, and dangers. With no escort, you would be lost on a road you would have already taken. Do not travel alone on the path.*[29]

Irina Tweedie has been a spiritual guide for some three decades already. A large group of aspirants look to her as their spiritual elder, and some students have become spiritual guides themselves. For years she offered *satsang* at her London home. *Satsang*, from the Sanskrit *sat* meaning 'truth', and *sang*, 'coming together', is the voluntary assembling of people on the path for spiritual upliftment, preferably in the company of a guide who has already made the journey.

Irina Tweedie is known as a mystic, someone who experiences oneness with the One. This union with God, or Truth, or however the Supreme Absolute may be named, occurs when we transcend our personal self and experience our divine, higher identity.

Once we are in union with the All-Knowing, the decision-making faculties of our mind become passive, allowing us to receive guidance on a higher level, from within. 'Intuitive knowing' takes place because the mystic lives not in the past nor in the future but in each single moment of the now. Mysticism is not a yoga of thinking and doing but of being.

> *The perfect mystic is not an ecstatic devotee lost in contemplation of Oneness, nor a saintly recluse shunning all commerce with mankind, but 'the true saint' goes in and out amongst the people and eats and sleeps with them and buys and sells in the market and marries and takes part in social intercourse, and never forgets God for a single moment.*[30]

For mystical reasons not then visible to me, Mrs. Tweedie started to occupy my thoughts and, after I obtained her London address from a Sufi friend, I wasted no time in writing to her.

I introduced myself as a journalist – even mentioning that I was a member of the Dutch Association of Journalists as well as of the International Federation of Journalists – and explained that, since my spiritual awakening, I had devoted myself exclusively to themes pertinent to new consciousness, transformation, yoga and meditation. Together with a selected bibliography of my articles on spiritual subjects I enclosed a synopsis of my book manuscript in its form at that date.

Because this first book included my meetings mainly with men teachers of spiritual wisdom, I envisioned the preparation of another book which would give attention to the great women teachers I had met – as the Mother of Pondicherry, Sri Anandamayi Ma, Mother Krishnabai, and others. I told Mrs. Tweedie that no work on contemporary teachers could be considered complete without a chapter on her.

Some of Irina Tweedie's biography was already known to me. Although she sometimes lectured in various parts of Europe and the United States, she stayed mainly in her adopted country of England.

Born in Russia in 1907 and raised partly in Bulgaria and Austria, Irina moved to England in the early 1930s as the worldly young wife of a British banker. After his death during the second World War, Irina was living in Italy when she fell deeply in love with an English navy officer and married for the second time. In 1954, when her adored second husband died, the grief-stricken widow no longer wanted to live. Life had lost all its color.

A book on reincarnation, passed along by a theosophist friend, changed her perspective. Mrs. Tweedie joined the London branch library of the Theosophical Society, the international organization which teaches that all the great religions spring from a common inspirational source. Reading one theosophical book after the other, she became acquainted with the mystical thought of the organization's co-founder, Helena Petrovna Blavatsky (1831–91).

New Age pioneer from the very beginning, Madame Blavatsky was the first person to reveal to the modern world what a small group of spiritual initiates had known over the ages: high up in the Himalayas live an enlightened group of *mahatmas* (*maha*, great; *atman*, immortal soul). These 'great souls', some of whom come from exactly the same Source as all human beings, represent the most sublime levels of human and spiritual perfection. The shackles of ignorance which once bound them to the wheel of reincarnation have fallen away and, discarding the painful hair shirt of mortal life, they have acquired the shining garments of inner immortality. Death can no longer claim them.

Instead of leaving the physical plane for a well-deserved holiday in some blissful heavenly hereafter, these spiritual elders of the human race remain on earth and consecrate their vast faculties and powers to the welfare of the Whole. Self-realized and indifferent to worldly rewards, motivated only by compassionate love for others, they serve humanity in an indirect and subtle way from the heights of the mystical Himalayas and other unpublicized localities.

Yet at certain times, when standards of life on earth sink to destructive lows, and the distraught world civilization may have the ears for divine guidance, one or more of the immortal masters appear in society. The task is to transmit, in an unadulterated state, a new revelation of the long-forgotten wisdom.

It was the mahatmas who inspired the founding of the Theosophical Society in 1875 in New York. Through their envoy H. P. Blavatsky, they implemented another step in their Master Plan to uplift humanity and usher in a golden age. In our time the Plan calls for the descent from the Himalayas and emergence into the world of the selfless immortal masters led by one of their number. This, the Master of the masters, the World Teacher for the coming era, is none other than Lord Maitreya.

Such were some of the heady esoteric teachings in which Irina Tweedie steeped herself for seven years, before her spiritual search took her in 1961 from England to India. There, in a small northern city, she was led to the home of the Sufi master Bhai Sahib, 'Elder Brother'. Recognizing him as her *sat guru*, she surrendered herself to his spiritual guidance. The diary Mrs. Tweedie kept from her first meeting with Bhai Sahib in 1961 until his death in 1966, as published in its abridged form *Chasm of Fire*, I read while awaiting her answer to my request for an interview.

Two months passed. In the meantime I had written the already-mentioned fateful letter to Swami Purna in New Delhi. After I received his telegram announcing his return to London within a fortnight, I decided to be there upon his arrival. I seized the opportunity to make appointments with several other spiritual teachers in Britain.

Still lacking any response from Irina Tweedie, I telephoned her. A woman answered and we introduced ourselves. Elisabeth Linder, who lived in the same house, informed me that the elderly Sufi mystic was now 85, very weak and tired, hardly slept at night, and mostly meditated. All her students had been sent to her successor, Llewellyn Vaughan-Lee.

Elisabeth knew about my letter, but to her regret she had to tell me that Mrs. Tweedie was no longer giving interviews. As if to console me, she added that Mrs. Tweedie saw only a few close people. She was in retreat from the world, preparing for her death.

'That is exactly the subject I would like to talk to her about!' I exclaimed.

Quite unmistakably Elisabeth made clear that Mrs. Tweedie's 'No' was definite.

'Nothing is definite with a spiritual teacher,' spontaneously flowed from my lips. There was a slight pause and Elisabeth suggested that I phone again, after my arrival in London.

The next day I mailed Mrs. Tweedie a second letter, respectfully asking her to reconsider my request to meet. 'You are, after all, a very important inspiration for seekers of our time, especially women,' I wrote in all sincerity and expressed my hope that she would grant me the unique chance to talk with a highly conscious person about death and dying. We all need more understanding about 'the journey to the other side'. When I had raised this important subject during my interview with J. Krishnamurti, it had apparently upset him.

Furthermore, I also mentioned my recent meeting with Indra Devi, the Russian-born yogin who helped to make yoga a household word in her adopted country of Argentina. *Mataji*, respected mother, was already 93 when I was able to see her in Antwerp. Two years hence, she told me, she wanted to leave her body consciously.

In the last lines of my letter to Irina Tweedie I dropped all journalistic disguise and revealed myself as the fervant *bhakta* that I am. 'With all humility, as a dedicated servant of the divine,' I declared with passion, 'please may I come and meet you, pose a few questions, tape the answers.'

A few weeks later in London, on the day of the full moon of December, I mailed an audiotape to Mrs. Tweedie. An accompanying note, addressed to Elisabeth, explained that rather than phone again with my request, I had recorded it.

The sound of my voice, I hoped, might persuade Mrs. Tweedie to see me. Perhaps she would hear the sincerity, devotion and commitment which filled my words and, on an even more subtle level, possibly tune into my vibrational frequency. That would enable her to receive a message which words could not convey. Or had the Sufi mystic, to tune with me, no need for intermediaries such as cassette tapes and letters?

Following my inner guidance, I turned my attention away from her and spent the week immersed in interviews for the anticipated book on feminine spirituality. Recharged by memorable meetings with Dadi Janki of the Brahma Kumaris and Swami Bhavyananda of the Ramakrishna Vedanta Centre, I felt impelled to contact Irina Tweedie anew. Not that I refused to take her 'No' for an answer, but my inner voice kept encouraging me to persist in this mission.

When I phoned, Elisabeth relayed that Mrs. Tweedie had been too busy to listen to the tape. Moreover, she had confirmed that she was bowing out of life and would not give any more interviews. Elisabeth did not think Mrs. Tweedie would change her mind. 'She has orders to step backwards, and she always obeys.'

But twelve hours after my reunion with Swami Purna, which had taken place in between – I had noted the exact time in my diary – the telephone rang and I heard Elisabeth's voice, filled with excitement. Mrs. Tweedie had apparently thrown away my letter and the tape but Elisabeth had told her that I wanted to talk about death and the beyond.

'And you know what Mrs. Tweedie said? "Then I want to see her!"'

Elisabeth sounded really joyful when she announced these glad tidings, which came so unexpectedly to me. 'So I searched frantically for your phone number!' she added.

Mrs. Tweedie offered me an appointment at her home on Sunday – how perfect – at ten o'clock in the morning. Needless to say, I accepted with much gratitude. I was convinced that this happy turn of events was connected with my return to Swami Purna.

Two days later, in North London, on my way to Irina Tweedie, I stopped at a grocer's shop to purchase some fruit. Nestled in my shoulder bag were already a few other small presents I had brought for her from Holland, including a golden-coloured sun. In the spiritual tradition, one does not visit a teacher with empty hands. Depending on one's means, taste and loving heart, one brings a guru some kind of gift, fruits, sweets, flowers, or a money donation.

From Swami Purna's living example, as well as in my talks on this subject with several spiritual teachers, I had learned that true gurus never ask anything for what they impart. It was Kriya Yoga master Swami Hariharananda Giri who explained to me the responsibility of students to give to the teacher, also on the material level, in exchange for what they will receive from him or her.

At the exact appointed time, I rang the doorbell.

'Some people are so punctual!' a woman's voice exclaimed with great energy as the door flew open. There stood Irina Tweedie looking quite robust, a big smile on her shining face.

What a pleasant welcome! The Irina Tweedie who was preparing for her death was not a fragile old person propped up on pillows in her sickbed, but an energetic elder who radiated a tremendous force. While I was recovering from my surprise, Mrs. Tweedie helped me out of my cape and apologized for 'putting me off'.

Finally I sat before the woman who, despite the obstacles she had placed in my way, had in fact drawn me to her. Through the French casement doors which opened onto a garden, the December sun lit up the day for us. I began by asking Irina Tweedie what she had meant just before when she had said that she had 'stepped back'.

'There comes a time in life, my dear, where one is bowing out; it's the end,' she replied in an English colored with an East European accent. 'I am nearly 86. The body is tired, and I am tremendously lucky because I have somebody else who continues the work. He is in the States, by the order of Bhai Sahib. So I stopped everything, and unfortunately I was not very courteous to you. You wrote me a long letter and I did not even answer. I intended to but, well, you know, the way to hell is paved with good intentions.'

We both laughed.

'And then, quite frankly, I forgot. Because my memory is very, very unreliable now. So I have stopped lecturing and giving seminars. But when you phoned the last time, Elisabeth told me that you wanted to speak about life after death and the moments of dying. That is a subject which is very dear to my heart – actually my favorite subject. Sounds funny, but that is because everybody seems to be terrified of death.

'But death is a part of life, really a friend, and it is truly simple. I'm looking at you, right? I turn my head and look at the door. That's all that death is. Your attention is directed somewhere else. It is true. It is so final. That's why people are afraid of it.

'We have to shed our physical body, which can be trouble because the physical body has a life of its own and will fight, and wants to be alive. But it's nothing else than that your attention is directed somewhere else.

'When we die we function on another plane. In order to function, or to be on another plane, we have to acquire the body of that plane. So there we acquire a spiritual body and this', said Mrs. Tweedie pointing to her physical frame, 'has to fall away.'

Unfortunately, space does not allow me to squeeze into these few pages each wise word I heard from the voice, and the silence, of Irina Tweedie. It is my faith, however, that those readers who are mystics themselves will understand the deeper import of the material extracted here.

To return to Mrs. Tweedie's opening soliloquy on death and dying, I must say I listened with rapt interest and no questions arose in me. Then came her remarks about people like clairvoyants and other sensitives, who can contact the subtle dimensions. She said that they sometimes have difficulties in living in our physical world and can become unbalanced.

'Something like being pulled between the worlds,' I commented.

'It is natural that when you are with a teacher things begin to happen,' Mrs. Tweedie went on. 'That you develop something which you have always had. We are born with it. The innate wisdom that we do not learn. Every human being has got it. We all have this ability to know more than our brain allows us to know. We don't need a teacher. Life is the greatest teacher, and every outer teacher will point to the inner teacher. That's what my teacher did to me.'

'All of us have the ability,' I agreed. 'Yet usually one does need a teacher, to show us the right direction. Mostly we do not have the capacity on our own.'

'Some people have,' replied Mrs. Tweedie. 'There are some people who never have a teacher. Actually, we always have a teacher but we may not know it. You see, there is someone, at the other side of life in the beyond, appointed to help us. In the Christian religion they call it the guardian angel. They do exist.

'The spirit evolution – angels and jinns and ghosts and all those – is a parallel evolution to human beings. They do exist. And they can be seen. But when I began to see and to know such things, my teacher took this away from me. "Are you after child's play or are you after Truth?" he said.

'I have no clairvoyance, no clairaudience, I know nothing. If I am *told*, I know. Told by whom? By my teacher. Because the relationship with the teacher remains forever. He is not in the world any more; that does not matter. One can always reach the teacher, always.'

'Is it the guidance that you have received from him that tells you it is time now to prepare for going beyond?' I asked.

'Yes. I don't think it will be very long.'

'I see. Are you planning to leave your body consciously at a certain time? Or do you leave it, as it were, up to the divine caretaker?'

'The divine caretaker? That is a very nice expression,' said Mrs. Tweedie, pronouncing it twice. Was she avoiding my question?

'Now that leaving your body is your most important next step,' I went on, 'what is really your innermost thought about this process? Are you resisting, are you allowing yourself to go, are you sad about this, happy about it, are you scared?'

'Does it sound very funny if I say I am looking forward to it? And all the people around me know that this is true.'

'Why are you looking forward?'

'Life becomes so difficult. I am so breathless, I can't do gardening any more,' explained Irina Tweedie, going on to list her numerous physical ills, including edema, angina, kidney problems, arthritis.

In meditation, however, she soars above all her bodily woes. She told me that meditation took up most of her nights, and explained that she slept only two or three hours. This confirmed my own experiences that the more one meditates, the less sleep is required.

Continuing the subject of meditation, Mrs. Tweedie described to me that in deep meditation she experiences what there 'is'. In deep meditation she just *knows* that there are various planes of existence – for instance, the one where there are 'blue distances, tremendous freedom, no breathlessness'.

With emphasis she said: 'Where you want to be, there you are. Here we have to take a plane or a car or a bus or whatever to get somewhere. There you don't need to do that. You just think and you are there.'

Then she spoke as well of a lower plane where there is 'a lot of sorrow' and narrated a dream, 'or rather experience', that kept recurring to her since her childhood.

A street curves to the left, with high buildings of 'four–five–six stories – buildings like they have on the Continent, in Vienna, in Hungary, in France, with balconies'. In one of the houses are many problems and she is there washing children, helping people. 'There is a lot of crying . . . . a kind of boo hoo hooo, boo hoo hooo,' said Mrs. Tweedie, demonstrating the sound for me with considerable acting skill.

She was describing 'the grey zone', the plane of power where witches work. It seemed to me, that grey zone bore a great similarity to the realm of suffering which is our planet earth.

After a short pause she said: 'There comes a moment in this experience, or dream, where the sun invariably is rising behind me, and all the many windows in all the houses are lit, and reflect the sun. And I just turn quickly and say, "Look! It is exactly *that*!"'

'And I wake up. The dream never finishes. There are some activities going on and there is an important moment which has to do with the sun, rising behind me.'

Intrigued by the role the sun plays in Mrs. Tweedie's dream-experience, I immediately asked: 'How do you interpret the dream?'

'I don't interpret. Why should I? It just is. It is like mysticism. You cannot explain mysticism. You cannot learn it. You either are, or you are not. It is a state of being. And Sufism is also just a state of being. We do not teach. I am not a teacher. I am just, I hope, a disciple of somebody very great.'

There was no picture of Bhai Sahib in her book, said Mrs. Tweedie. He did not like his photo to be taken because people tend to worship pictures. 'We do not bow before anything except the Most High,' she said, pointing out that in this respect Sufism could be compared with Islam. Followers of Judaism know the same injunction, I mused, seeing myself as a young girl reciting the Ten Commandments. Also I recalled what my Abba van Praag always used to counsel me: 'Remember what happened at Sinai.'

Mrs. Tweedie's statement would have interested me as a student of spiritual evolutionary history, but I refrained from picking up this thread of thought lest our conversation divert onto a religious sideroad. Quite consciously I returned to the main subject that, to all intents and purposes, had caused Mrs. Tweedie to be at home for me. I asked her if she had experienced what it means to 'go beyond death'.

Again she spoke of wondrous realms she had visited in deep meditation, about a superior plane where time, space, and the state of consciousness are one and the same. These subtle things could not be explained, she said, because human language is 'very coarse'. Besides, the mind, which gets all its impressions from outside, cannot understand this plane. 'But once you have seen it, even in a split second, you *know*.'

When she was just about to quote illuminating words on the deeper states of meditation by a certain Saint Gregory of Nyssa, whose name I had never heard before, she abruptly stopped and said: 'Sorry, my mind went completely blank. It happens sometimes. Let's change the subject. I will come back to it. I tried to make an important point. My mind is very weak now. I think I suffer from geriatric senility.'

It did not occur to me to question this diagnosis: I accepted her statement for what it was. Only now, her words strike my ears quite differently. I think that they belonged to the divine world's masterly way of offering me hints and clues intended to bring me more awareness about myself.

When listening to the recorded tapes of my conversations with Irina Tweedie, I became intrigued. Why had she stopped so suddenly at the mention of Saint Gregory? My research books informed me that Gregory of Nyssa was a 4th-century Christian mystic whose fame rested on his voluminous writings.

While reading about him, I had the curious feeling that a close contact existed between us. Although he had been dead for over 16 centuries, he was no stranger to me at all. This experience was quite extraordinary and I cannot escape the thought that there is more to it.

In any case, Saint Gregory had provoked Mrs. Tweedie to suggest geriatric senility, which shifted our talk to more earthly matters and, in turn, made me ask her what she was doing as a preparation to leave the body.

'I leave it in the hands of God,' she said. 'I don't prepare. You see, the most important part of any spiritual life is surrender. Once you are surrendered, well, you are surrendered. You don't want anything anymore. You have no desires. I don't want anything. I just fulfill my destiny, what comes before me, trying to do it the best I can.' And she added: 'It seems to me that however little I know of what is there in the beyond, there is no need to fear.'

Later she defined 'complete surrender' as follows: 'You do not surrender to the teacher, you do not surrender to anything that is created, you surrender to the light within you, which is the Light of God.'

When I asked what she anticipated to find in the beyond, Mrs Tweedie again mentioned Gregory of Nyssa. He, a contemporary of Saint Augustine, had described the higher spiritual planes which she had experienced. Gregory called God the dazzling absolute darkness. 'Absolute darkness is absolute light,' he had written.

To my question whether, at her present stage, the knowledge she had taught as a spiritual teacher still occupied her thinking mind, she replied that it simply had become part of her being. Her mind sometimes did not work at all. 'But when a certain string is touched in my heart, as by the questions you are asking me, wanting to know the truth, then I have to answer. My esoteric name is "the bell-ringer". I ring the bell in your heart, whether you want it or not. That is the job of every teacher.'

By sharing this detail with me for my readers, Mrs Tweedie shed more light on the role of the spiritual guide. Now her words touch me at my very core. The symbolism of my bell ringing at the sacred Vishvanatha Temple in Benares suddenly becomes more clear to me. I also remember the words of Sri Sinha when he, in reply to my 'Surya' poem, wrote to me: 'You are fine, and taken the right road. The poem rings the bell, repeat bell . . . .'

Another task of the teacher, said Mrs Tweedie, is what in Christianity is called vicarious atonement. 'This is what Jesus did, taking on himself the sins of the world. Every yogi does it. Every yogi takes upon himself a little bit of the darkness of the human being.'

When I wanted to know whether, because of this, spiritual teachers sometimes develop serious physical problems, she said, among other things, 'Nobody ever dies. They only work on another plane.'

Eventually I asked: 'At this point you are probably seeing your life and work of over 80 years in review. What do you consider to be the most important thing in your life?'

Her answer was: 'The most important moment in my life, which is called the second birth, is the moment when I met my teacher. And now I can say – now I know – that all my life was a preparation for that. It is the way of return.'

The 'way of return' was 'a long, long subject which would take days to explain', she added. 'We are born with a certain destiny and we have free will and we have karmas. The karmas can be explained easily? Well, let's try.'

We both laughed and Mrs. Tweedie gave a short explanation which elicited several comments from me and meaningful answers on her side. Then I said: 'We were talking about destiny and that some things cannot be changed. Things like where you work or where you live can be changed, but meeting the teacher, that is destined.'

'The teacher will find you,' declared Mrs. Tweedie. 'It is like lighting a lamp in the darkness. Somebody will see it from afar.'

'Because you have been with that teacher before.'

'Of course. It is from life to life, Bhai Sahib said. "The relationship with the teacher is from life to life, and there is no divorce." Those are his words. He even used the word "divorce".'

With Swami Purna on my mind I said: 'It is possible that you meet your teacher and that, for some reason, you are separated again, for a period of time.'

'Yes, there are such cases,' agreed Mrs. Tweedie. 'And sometimes the teacher will send you to another teacher also. You see, one cannot make a rule. Those things are always moving. The teacher has no fixed habits.'

Guru-disciple relation, transfer of energy from guru to successor, her present work, detachment – these subjects and more came into our dialogue before Mrs. Tweedie volunteered: 'There is a certain knowledge which is not imparted. It is reflected, into the tranquil mind of the yogi. So this line of yoga is not transmitted orally, it is not transmitted mentally, it is not transmitted by anything. It is direct reflection from heart to heart. It is a very mysterious yoga and we meet every night as a group, with the teacher.'

Bhai Sahib explained the same point very well in *Chasm of Fire*:

*In our system, it is the soul which attracts the soul and the soul
speaks to the soul. We need nothing. We are not limited. Music is
bondage. Ceremonials, worship, when done collectively, can also
be bondage. But we are free. We go to the Absolute Truth in
silence, for it can be found only in silence, and it is Silence. That
is why we are called the Silent Sufis.*[31]

Paradoxically, the 'Silent Sufi' who is Irina Tweedie spoke at
length to me. In her elevated presence I was not always able to
hear the deeper meanings of what she said. From her answers I
could see, however, that Mrs. Tweedie had the authority of
someone who derived spiritual truth not secondhand from other
people or books but rather from her own inner experiences and
visions of the spiritual worlds, those subtle realms normally veiled
to the human eye.

Her journey had already brought her to the top of the luminous
mountain where the reunion with the Beloved takes place – inside
one's own surrendered mystic heart. Standing there at her higher
level, she could see me winding upwards on the path.

I even imagined that she could see me not only in my present
identity, but as all the persons I had ever been in the past, and that
she was shining light on my way to help me advance. As part of
this, it was necessary for her to tell me more about her guru, Bhai
Sahib. His wise and mystical sayings filled her book, she said.

That made her book particularly valuable I told her, adding that
I thought it very beautiful. 'That's why it is sold out. I couldn't buy
one and had to borrow a friend's copy.'

Elisabeth, who had been silently in the room since my arrival,
interjected that she still had a spare one upstairs.

'I have one as well,' said Mrs. Tweedie immediately. Instead of
the shorter version which I had read, she presented me with the
unabridged edition called *Daughter of Fire* and counting no fewer
than 822 pages. I asked her to sign the book for me.

'Then you will have to leave it overnight,' she answered with a
laugh. The amused look on the face of Mrs. Tweedie reminded me
of a mischievous Krishna at play. It goes without saying that I
gladly accepted her proposal.

My first visit was nearing its close. Elisabeth had instructed me
that the interview would have to end promptly at 11.30, because
of lunch. That deadline approaching, I had no choice but to
suggest to Mrs. Tweedie that we finish for today.

'That's all right,' she replied. She did not seem to worry about the time. 'You see, when one is with a human being, it is timeless. Timeless in many ways. People come for all sorts of reasons. There is always time.'

Now that I no longer had to watch the clock, I tried to explore Mrs. Tweedie's personal connection with the sun, but in vain. Instead she focused the attention on me, asking that I tell her my own story.

As it turned out, our conversation continued well into the afternoon. This gave me the opportunity to ask, among other questions: 'When you say that Bhai Sahib "told" you, does this mean on the inner planes, in your meditations?'

'If I say "he told me," it is a lie,' replied Mrs. Tweedie, 'because that would be duality. At the end of the training, so it is said in the Hindu scriptures, the higher self of the disciple and the higher self of the teacher are one.'

'You mean guru, God and Self are one. So at that point you do not ask, you do not receive, you just are. Then why do you keep saying that Bhai Sahib told it to you?'

'How should I say it? That I know it?'

'Because you would then think it has something to do with the ego?'

'Exactly. Because this is not *my* knowledge. I know that it comes from somewhere, the infinite source of all life. If I say "Bhai Sahib told me," it is very simple. Everybody will understand.'

Finally Mrs. Tweedie announced: 'Now I will show you the picture of Bhai Sahib, and then, I think, it is enough for the moment. Because I have a pain in my heart.' But very kindly she reassured me: 'That's all right. This is one of the signs. The doctor says if I have this pain it is angina; I have to stop what I am doing.'

Her pain in the heart served to remind me just how misleading appearances can be. Mrs. Tweedie had said she suffered from quite a number of physical ills. Yet outwardly she looked like a fit elderly woman. Or was *maya*, that inner veil of ignorance, again playing games with me?

Mrs. Tweedie not only looked beautiful for her 85 years, she had replied to my questions with the great energy of a person standing in the midst of life. Besides, she expressed herself in a captivating theatrical style and kept me focused on each of her words and every accompanying gesture. Sometimes her answers had a dramatic impact on me, for instance when she narrated her recurring dream-experience with its final image of the sun. At other moments she whispered sentences so softly that I had to turn up the volume control of my tape recorder. Even when, in between, we sat in silence, she held my undivided attention.

As strange as it may seem, and despite Mrs. Tweedie's 'geriatric senility' and angina pain, I wondered what importance to give to her statement that 'it won't be long now'. For some unknown reason I asked myself: was she really preparing to vacate her body in the imminent future? Not that a teacher of the Truth would ever tell an untruth, but she or he would certainly be an expert at playing *lila*. 'One important quality required on the path is never to judge by appearances,' Bhai Sahib had said.

In short, I had the distinct feeling that Mrs. Tweedie was . . . play-acting. I had to think of Swami Purna. During our early years together, the shutters over my inner sight had been dense indeed. Many of my numerous imperfections I had difficulty in seeing. To shock me into greater awareness, Swami Purna had more than once resorted to behavior joltingly different from his usual calm, self-confident equilibrium. This feigned behavior was so extreme that I usually spotted it as 'acting'. I came to understand that spiritual masters are never attached to the ordinary ways and means of the world.

Irina Tweedie as well seemed to me to be play-acting a role, that of a mortal human preparing to shed her body and 'die'. My intuition suggested that she was not planning to leave her body at all. On the contrary, she would *never* die! My inner voice told me that death could not claim Irina Tweedie because she . . . is immortal . . . and so am I.

This line of mystical thinking carried my thoughts upwards to the silent Himalayas, and to the 'high guys' (and gals?) who reside there, unknown and unsung by human beings down below in the world.

Attuned with the Immortal Himalayan Masters

My encounter with Irina Tweedie seemed to have more purpose than just my writing a book on women teachers. When I returned to the mystic's home, this impression of mine gained more substance, since our second meeting took a course quite different from the one I had anticipated.

Elisabeth had cautioned me before that I could stop by only to collect the book, because visitors were to come. But upon my arrival there was, to my good fortune, no sign yet of the expected guests, with the result that Mrs. Tweedie invited me into her sitting room. She lovingly placed the book in my hands, and I was delighted to read her dedication, along with an old Sufi proverb she had quoted: 'Only what you cannot lose in a shipwreck is yours.'

'In a shipwreck you can lose even your life, so what does belong to you?' asked Mrs. Tweedie like a Sunday School teacher in front of the class.

'Your soul,' I answered right away, and we both burst into laughter.

'Exactly!' she declared. 'You've got it right.'

I felt so attuned with her! Without my having had to pronounce my astonishing thought that she and I were 'immortal', Mrs. Tweedie had responded to it with a Sufi proverb which put to rest my mind's imaginings about the Himalayan masters, at least for a while, and placed the subject of immortality into a comprehensible frame of reference.

'So clear, so clear,' said Mrs. Tweedie in a very sweet voice. 'This is the only thing. Our soul is the ray of the spiritual sun. That is what we believe.

'And our relationship with God is the same as the relationship of the ray to the sun. The sun cannot help but radiate, and the ray cannot exist without the sun. Only something so evanescent, something which you cannot even touch and hardly understand, only that is the real us, nothing more, nothing less.'

With the book *Daughter of Fire* pressed to my heart, the many wise and mystical statements of both Bhai Sahib and Irina Tweedie recorded on my cassette tapes, and uplifted by the spiritual energy of Mrs. Tweedie's atmosphere, I would have been quite content if I had been dismissed then and there. Reminded by her that it is the soul which is immortal and certainly not the physical body, I would have wished her a blissful last journey to the other side, whenever that journey might take place.

But apparently a divine higher hand altered the schedule set up for that afternoon. The awaited guests never arrived, so that my dialogue with Mrs. Tweedie was allowed to continue on until the evening. We discussed many subjects under the mystical sun, including her guru Bhai Sahib and the diary he had asked her to keep, which was to form the basis of her book.

I became aware that it was actually not 'a diary of a spiritual training' as the front cover announced, but a record of the *preparation* for the training. Surprisingly, this training did not start for Irina Tweedie until after the physical 'death' of her guru. Then she 'met him somewhere in deep meditation, and the training really began, in a completely different way from what I had imagined. It came as direct knowledge to me.'

This experience occurred at a Gandhi ashram in the Himalayas. In meditation Irina Tweedie saw Bhai Sahib, felt his energy, felt attuned.

'He had no human shape any more,' explained Mrs. Tweedie to me. 'He was a center of energy. When you sit in deep meditation, you don't see it with these eyes. The knowledge just was me. I knew it was my teacher, and the mind was so obedient at that time. It didn't rebel, it didn't create a barrier, it didn't create doubts. It just was.

'For instance, like I speak to you now, it is so simple really. It does not need an explanation. Somewhere in your heart you know. It's so simple.'

'But that's because all the barriers had been removed,' I said. 'You were completely open and receptive. You could receive and hold those energies which led to the higher manifestation.'

'Correct. You just put it beautifully into words, better than I could,' declared Mrs. Tweedie.

I hastened to give the credit for those words to my teacher. When she wanted to know if I saw him often, I replied that I had not been with him for 12 years. Only recently had we been reunited, I told her.

Mrs. Tweedie asked me to give him her respects.

'He knows that I am with you now,' I mentioned.

'I am sure he knows,' said Mrs. Tweedie enigmatically, and added: 'Just tell him, "respect from heart to heart".' As she pronounced these five words, I had the quite improbable thought that with them she was sending Swami Purna some kind of secret message.

Redirecting my attention to being in the moment with Irina Tweedie, I brought our mystical teach-in back to her experience at the Gandhi ashram, which I termed a revelation.

'A *great* revelation,' she agreed. 'And I didn't quite understand it then. Because I came to him in deep meditation, always asking for others, never for me because we are not allowed to ask for ourselves. We can only ask for others. And gradually it dawned on me that, my goodness me, my horizons had somehow widened.'

'You started to see how things were fitting more easily into place and flowing more harmoniously.'

'Exactly.'

'As if many hindrances were falling away.'

Mrs. Tweedie complimented me again on my ability to express myself and modestly said that for her book she had very much struggled to find the right words. It had to be edited by a dear friend, Jennine Miller, living now in France.

I told her that my words flowed easily in her presence, perhaps because she was helping me to understand the recent developments in my life.

This led us to talk about my forthcoming book which, similar to hers, was also the story of a preparation for a real training. In some way my London reunion with Swami Purna resembled Mrs Tweedie's spiritual meeting with Bhai Sahib after his supposed death. I asked how much time had passed from the revelation at the Gandhi ashram until the start of the teaching.

She replied: 'There's one sentence in the book which says it,' and she opened *Daughter of Fire* at page 793. 'It takes time to make a soul pregnant with God,' she read aloud in her expressive manner. She continued for a page or so, permitting me to take some photos.

By the way, when in the presence of a spiritual teacher, I can never photograph her or him until I have first received my own inner green light to go ahead. This green light does not come from the voice of my ego or from my thinking mind, but from the voice of the silence within me.

Mrs. Tweedie read another section, telling more about her profound experience at the Gandhi ashram in the Himalayas. Looking up, she said: 'You see, it is in between the lines. But if the reader has had a similar experience, he knows exactly what I mean – that there was an encounter on a higher plane of energy.'

'How long did it take until you received what in India is called "final *diksha*?"' I asked. *Diksha* is the final transference of wisdom (*jnana*) or power (*shakti*) from master to disciple, which brings the teaching period to completion.

'I do not know,' she answered. 'It's a gradual process, a widening of the horizon, a little bit here, a little bit there. For instance, in our line of yoga we have no initiations. The widening of the horizon is initiation in itself. A little bit here and a little bit there and a little bit there.'

To be in the company of Irina Tweedie was obviously part of my own widening process, and with a fully open heart I told her later on: 'You are a great blessing for us, and for me, especially at this moment, because you are confirming so many things and helping me to see more clearly. I feel it was a great grace that I was sent to you, that you so graciously received me. Even if I may not yet fully understand the significance of our meeting.'

At another point in our conversation I asked Irina Tweedie how she first got into touch with her spirituality. She replied: 'By getting in touch with the Theosophical Society, and then going to the British Museum, and by having the vision.'

This material was not included in her book, she said, 'because the book begins at the moment I was born, when I met the teacher. When the teacher for the first time looks at you, this is the second birth. So how did I get in touch with my own spirituality? I cannot tell you that now.'

The story would be far too long to be told in one sitting. A number of cassette tapes would be needed to record it. I offered to return once more and Mrs. Tweedie agreed. She let me know that we would have to start with the death of her second husband, and with her joining the Theosophical Society.

'I think all this is really interesting,' she said. 'I could write another book about it. How I lost God, and how I had the vision about the great masters in the Himalayas, and how I knew I was working for them.'

'It sounds very important indeed,' I commented, not yet aware of just how important.

'*Very* important, because I knew, somewhere I knew . . . .'

What Mrs. Tweedie *knew* was clearly revealed to her seven years after she had joined the Theosophical Society. A lecture she attended at the Society set the stage. The subject was the immortal mahatmas who founded the Theosophical Society through the attuned person of H. P. Blavatsky. It was then that Irina Tweedie first heard about *The Mahatma Letters*, written between 1880 and 1884 to A. P. Stinnet, an English civil servant in India. They discuss various esoteric matters and were set onto paper by no ordinary hands but by the two immortal mahatmas of Tibet whom Madame Blavatsky acknowledged as her mentors: K. H. (Koot Hoomi) and the Master M. (Mahatma Morya).

These letters are safely stored in the British Museum, and Mrs Tweedie went to see them. 'Reading the original letters, some written on packing paper, some on rice paper, I got the vision of the immense chain of mountains, and suddenly I knew I had worked for these masters before.

'I just looked at these letters, and I saw the signature of the master K. H., and I put my fingers as in an oath on his signature, and I said to him: "I know I worked for you before. And I want to work for you again. Somewhere I know I must not put any conditions. But because I offer myself so absolutely, without reserve, I feel I can put one. Do not let me forget that I belong to you, ever."'

While Mrs. Tweedie related this event, I started to remember a past of my own which had been dormant until then. Meanwhile I continued hearing her voice in the distance, telling me about her love for the Beloved, and how that love kept her young. Was Mrs. Tweedie again hinting at her immortality, or was I once more reading too much into her words?

'I am just as much in love as when I first met my teacher,' she went on to say. 'And it is as fresh and as young as when I was in love at 16. I am old and the body is going, but the heart is just as young. "We Sufis, we die young," he said to me.'

Listening to the Silent Sufi speak of her love for the Beloved, I felt uplifted. Mrs. Tweedie's energy transported me to the holy

Himalayas, the snow-clad abode of those divinized mahatmas who live in 'bodies of light' not visible to the ordinary human eye.

I told her that as she was talking about the oath she had made over the signature of Koot Hoomi, I heard in my mind the Sufi proverb she had written in my *Daughter of Fire*: 'Only what you cannot lose in a shipwreck is yours.' Probably there was a link between her mention of the Himalayan masters and those words, I suggested.

'Of course,' she confirmed.

'Because I too belong to this Himalayan Hierarchy,' I said intuitively, experiencing the truth of this statement. With a Madame Blavatskyian sense of mission, I added: 'And we are here to do a work.'

'Of course.'

'And that is why I am brought before you.'

'That is very obvious,' said Mrs. Tweedie, giggling as if she knew a secret I had not yet discovered. 'That is why I have time for you!'

After our dinner together, prepared exquisitely by Elisabeth thanks to her flair for gourmet vegetarian cooking, I rode the underground back to Wood Green where I was staying. During the journey I realized that the conversations with Irina Tweedie already provided more material than could possibly fit into merely one chapter of any book.

Early the next morning, just as I wanted to dial Irina Tweedie's number, the phone rang and it was she on the line. Would I be coming to her place today to continue the taping?

Of course I was anxious to tell her the thoughts, or rather inspirations, I had received the previous evening. It seemed I was being asked to write not the chapter I had proposed, but rather a full-length manuscript about her. Yes, her teacher had said that there would be a second book, Mrs. Tweedie told me, but someone else would write it.

Without hesitation she accepted my proposal: I would return in January, after taking some weeks in Amsterdam to study the first set of tapes. Could she think of other points which should be included in our book?

'I act according to the moment,' she replied, 'never premeditated. Just instantaneously, in response to the moment. That is yoga.'

We arranged that I would phone her from Amsterdam on New

Year's Day to fix our next appointment. Christmas greetings were exchanged and we were ready to say goodbye. It felt perfectly natural for me to tell her 'I love you.'

'I too,' she replied warmly, 'but I must say, not on the human level. I can love only through the Beloved.'

While writing these last chapters now, I experience a strong contact with Irina Tweedie and Bhai Sahib. In some mystical way they have been sending me messages. 'Himalayan Master' is one of the phrases I heard; 'continuity of the work' another. One morning she woke me up, out of a dream, the sound of her voice saying into my ear: 'Surprise!'

Shortly afterwards, when I was going through the typed transcript of our conversations, I unexpectedly came upon a very revealing section of the dialogue which for some reason had slipped my mind. I had raised the subject of the immortal mahatmas by saying: 'Of course you have a connection with the Himalayan masters.'

'I have . . . .' she responded. 'Bhai Sahib . . . . He was one of them.'

I was speechless.

'And he was a Sufi, he is the link,' continued Mrs. Tweedie, but then stopped.

'Could you give some more details?' I asked.

'No, it's esoteric,' she replied. 'Bhai Sahib said to me: "Yes, I belong to the Hierarchy, but we do not speak about it."'

I nodded in understanding.

'It's a very esoteric subject,' she continued. 'And whenever I questioned his disciples about that – I also wanted elaboration, like you – they always changed the subject. So I'm changing the subject too.'

Yet it is a fact that knowledge destined to come to us will eventually make its appearance. While I was perusing the materials for these new pages, two readers of *Als de zon spreekt*, Magnolia Huijboom and Els Dijkstra, presented me with a book they wanted to bring to my attention.

With the most perfect timing I thus made acquaintance with a book that was indeed most helpful to me. *Life and Teaching of the Masters of the Far East* by Baird T. Spalding relates the experiences of an American scientist who, at the end of the 19th century, together with eleven other researchers, spent three-and-a-half years in the close company of several Himalayan mahatmas.

In the first of his five volumes, Spalding gives very clear descriptions of the mahatmas who accepted him in their midst, and often renders their statements directly. At a gathering of the masters on New Year's Eve of 1895–96, one of the female mahatmas explains to the group of scientists that the immortal masters

> have so perfected their bodies that they are able to take them into all the Celestial Realms and there receive the highest teachings. They have all lived a certain time here in visible form, then passed on and taken their bodies with them, to a place in consciousness where they are not visible to mortal eyes; and we must raise our consciousness to the Christ Consciousness to converse with them. But those that have so perfected the body that they can take it to this Celestial Realm can return to us and go away at will. They are able to come and instruct all who are receptive to their teaching, and appear and disappear at will. It is these that come and teach us when we are ready to receive instruction, sometimes intuitively and at times by personal contact.[32]

When I met Irina Tweedie in London, my consciousness was not elevated enough to catch all the clues and hints sent through her to me on an esoteric plane. Only now am I understanding what I think have been the main messages transmitted by the 'bell-ringer'.

Coming from the land of silence, such messages cannot be expressed in human language. They can only be heard inside ourselves, when we have become indifferent to the demands of our ego and our mind is no longer 'the great slayer of the Real'.[33] When we are able to commune with the beyond, the hidden knowledge is revealed, that ageless wisdom which no lips can convey.

At Mrs. Tweedie's, while we were scaling together the spiritual summit, she all of a sudden went mute and signaled me to do the same. Her living room ceased to be of this world. A profound peace reigned, a quiet energy filled the space. I was awed, as if in the presence of a power extending far back into time, to the Source.

A few minutes later Irina Tweedie whispered very softly in this rarefied atmosphere: 'Bhai Sahib was here.'

Illumined beings who have mastered the laws of nature, can move in and out of various planes of existence at will. Whether we recognize these great souls with our mortal eyes or not, they are inspiring those who are ready for the higher message, knowledge and task.

In this light I see the oath of Irina Tweedie, renewing her commitment to work for the Himalayan masters. Her words, I am sure, belong to a pledge of continuity many more of us will make.

Reflecting on Bhai Sahib's unexpected visit, I realize that the Silent Sufi was giving me a sign with his invisible appearance. The high beings in the Himalayas, belonging to the spiritual hierarchy that supports humanity's evolution, are reaching out to widen their circle with all of us who are receptive.

The New Millennium

My true Self was first shown me by my precious Sun. Of course I was not the only one in the 1970s to glimpse the interior sunrise, and to make a radical turnabout in thinking and patterns of action. Considerable numbers of us, as if activated by a widespread invisible power, saw the emergence of a new day. Our vision focused on the light of Consciousness, which we recognized as inherent to everyone and everything.

So many of us in the 'spiritualized seventies' had our perspectives profoundly altered that there sprang up, naturally and without any leadership, an international movement – to this day continually growing – centered around the phenomenon of transformation. Without having to join, we spontaneously and automatically become members.

To us, the heightening of our own awareness is related to a greater process, involving all human beings, the planet and even all life. At a certain point in our soul's journey we perceive the larger Plan, and realize that our own individual destiny is tied up with the fate of all.

I see more clearly now that the important stages in my own spiritual story are the same as in that of any aspirant. This observation applies as well to the aspirant which is humanity itself, the totality of human beings.

Humanity as a group seeker is being readied to enter higher mental and spiritual realms and to progress to the next phase of evolution. In Sri Aurobindo's enlightened understanding, the human being is a transitional life-form on the way to becoming an illumined species with bodies of light.

For the Hindu, time is cyclic and unrolls itself in a recurring succession of four ages: golden, silver, copper and iron. The last three are marked by progressively deteriorating values and virtues on earth, as humanity is ever more immersed in matter and distanced from the divine.

We are presently evolving through the last, and most degenerate, of the four periods. This is the Kali Yuga, the Age of Iron, when the quality of planetary life rusts away. As rapidly as science and technology advanced in the 20th century, the decadence of society accelerated.

Many of the teachers quoted in this book confirm that our planet is in transition away from the Kali Yuga. Our Spaceship Earth is heading towards the new Golden Age of Truth, Satya Yuga, an upbeat era characterized by our conscious relationship with the Whole.

Preparations began long ago. In the recent past, the 1960s and 1970s were especially meaningful decades. Those years sowed, for a later flowering, many seeds of Light Consciousness. A wider view of reality, embracing such concepts as 'wholeness' and 'unity', infiltrated mainstream society.

Substantial contributors to the shift in awareness were the Asian teachers who arrived on our shores. Although the antics of a flamboyant few tended to prejudice the public against groups and leaders outside the established religions, it cannot be denied that many of the oriental gurus inspired people on a grand scale.

We may throw stones at several of the gurus for their business tactics and multimillion dollar enterprises, yet in a secular culture so blind to the sacred, they mass communicated the eternal truths and opened inner eyes. Thanks to many of them the word 'spiritual', representing the soul's deepest longing, came into general usage.

The idealism of the 1970s was somehow dimmed in the following decade with its strong accent on the outer, but the dawning continues. Growing numbers of people are discovering birth's deeper purposes, realize more fully what existence comprises, and perceive that life on earth is nothing but a school, to foster knowledge of Self.

Mental peace is increasingly being seen as more valuable than material wealth, and more persons are making conscious efforts to liberate themselves from a solely materialistic view of life. The freer we become of the conditioning which imprisons us to a narrow, lower perspective, the more we are open to the subtle, spiritual dimensions.

Unlike the 1970s, when the spiritual revival was confined to young, middle-class, 'alternative' Westerners, today people of all ages, backgrounds and religions are receiving and utilizing transformational energies.

Over the years we have witnessed a popularization of the 'New Age' phenomenon which has become a network of business enterprises making money out of the human desire for spiritual unfoldment. Although financial rewards may automatically come to one who passes along spiritual teachings, moneymaking must never be the goal. People who sell the higher knowledge, do not have higher knowledge. But spirituality has become a business, and many people have come to associate the New Age with commercialism.

Despite all this, there is a true New Age, of spiritual significance: the Aquarian period of sun forces and positive change on the rise. All heavenly bodies are being affected by the inflood of transformative energies, and the Piscean time inaugurated by Jesus the Christ is ending.

As Martinus and many others have declared, Mother Earth is a living creature, a live entity within the vast organism of the solar system. Like us, she will soon make an evolutionary leap forward from the rule of Pisces into Aquarius, from Iron once more to the Golden Age of Satya Yuga.

Coming under the influence of the constellation Aquarius, Mother Earth and humanity are together evolving towards a sunny era where life on this planet will be distinguished by the Aquarian values of respect, cooperation and unity.

Preparing to leave the Kali Yuga behind, Mother Earth is undergoing a metamorphic purification, releasing powerful energies. These potencies affect not only all nature but also the thinking and lifestyle of every one of us. Whether we like it or not, this process includes disorder, upheaval and collapse. Humanity, the world disciple, is somewhat like the student Milarepa, having to destroy the old to make way for the next creation. Inpurities are being discharged while healing and renewal take place.

Behind outer appearances, a modern miracle play is being enacted. What seems to be a general breakdown in society is actually part of a large transformational scenario. With this understanding, we are less affected by the fear and confusion brought about by catastrophic circumstances and are enabled to see the light in the darkness. Our doomsday mentality ceases as we become detached from negativity and yoke ourselves with the world's purpose.

We are here to bring to birth a beautiful planetary lifestyle, based on needs and not greeds. It is up to our free will whether we act voluntarily, or are forced by tragic events, to bring our lives into a healthy balance between matter and spirit.

But when most human words and ways have failed to inspire humanity to make the changes we all know are essential, how to proceed with our mutual task?

It is time to get our inspiration from the sun, and to view life from a higher vantage point. Looking down at our planet as if through the enlightened sun-eye, what do we see but one interconnected whole?

Further advanced along the evolutionary path than any human being, the sun simply is. Without any personal wishes and wants, our sun unselfishly radiates out the cosmic forces which allow everything in our solar system to exist. Even if clouds fill the sky, our heavenly friend is always there, showering us with life-giving light and warmth.

What is more, the sun's energies are clean and non-polluting, inexhaustible and free to all. A perfect example of total generosity, our sun makes its wealth unconditionally available to everyone.

As my experiences revealed to me, our sun is alive. Not only alive but also conscious, and more evolved in spiritual development than any individual of the human race. He, or she, is indeed the most perfect reflection on earth of the one source of all life. Yes, the sun that we perceive is of course only a reflection, just as we are, of the Eternal Light.

Behind our sun is a spiritual sun. One with the Source, the spiritual sun represents what no sword can cut, no air can blow, no fire can burn.

The spiritual sun and the physical sun are two expressions of the same Universal Light. Sometimes this Supreme Light sends down to earth a reflection of Itself in a human body. Rama and Krishna, the Buddhas, Zoroaster, Moses, Jesus the Christ, and Muhammad, are sun beings who gave their benevolent assistance to humanity during periods of planetary chaos and conflict.

At present the very survival of humanity's home, of Mother Earth, is at stake, along with the existence of all life-forms connected with her. Even clean air, clean water and clean soil are threatened with extinction.

Yet we are not alone in this urgent plight. To help us help ourselves, not just Maitreya but a number of other sun masters descended from the heavenly heights to be among us. Already they are moving in our midst. But do we recognize them? Those who are receptive to their guidance, are being trained and prepared to help usher in the Sunlit Age.

As the cosmic sundial signals the new millennium, it is time to link efforts in our common cause. We all need to seek, and find, the inner essence of life as well as the source of that essence. The future of our planet depends on our accepting our divine identity and fitting into the Plan.

To put our global house in order, we will have to attune with the grace energies. This will fertilize our environment with attitudes, values and actions based on the sacredness of all. Cooperating for our mutual goal, we can bring to blossom a global garden brightened by environmental purity, by the sharing of resources, and by divine luster.

Our positive approach can speed and smooth our transition into a higher state of expanded awareness. Without any delay each one of us needs to ask: Am I actively participating in the larger transformational process? Are my thoughts and my deeds contributing to our planet's well-being? Am I helping to create a spiritual world society?

All is one under the sun. What is more, when we look up at the glowing orb in the sky, we all see the same light. That light, both physical and subtle, inspired the origin of all true religions and spiritual paths.

In the Light without begining or end, whose essence is ever existent, we all share a common source. From that Oneness we evolve, life after life, until at last we reach our ultimate destination, which is in fact our source. Each one of us, a ray of our parent Light, is born with the urge to return home to our celestial origin.

By attuning with the sun, link between heaven and earth, we draw to us a consciousness much greater than our own. This feeds the flame of wisdom aglow within our depths, helping it to become the glorious blaze of spiritual illumination. Our veils of ignorance melt away, and our eyes are opened to what lies beyond apparent reality.

Perceiving the true nature of people, situations and things, we greet our sun as a spiritual elder ready to give to humanity the sun knowledge and teachings. Whether we hear the almighty Sun speak to us directly, have contact with sun masters, read divinely inspired books, or in whatever way we are readied for our Task, the time has arrived to recognize and to put into practice the guidance of the Sun. She, or He, continually showers our surroundings with purposeful signs and messages that can lead us to the fulfillment of the Plan.

What a blessing to look at the sun and to see ourselves! With our minds shining bright, and our hearts radiating love, let us be as suns here on earth. 'Hand in hand to make this land a better world to live in.' Together we can flower into a future which is all right, all Light – the Age of the Sun.

Notes

1 Cheiro, born as Count Louis Hamon in 1866 (d. 1939), became internationally famous for his divinatory gifts, especially his unequaled knowledge of palmistry. For 40 years he toured the world lecturing, teaching and reading the hands of countless people. He also wrote several highly regarded books on palmistry, numerology and astrology. His *Language of the Hand* is considered a classic in the field.

2 'Utopian Living on the Bay of Bengal' by Kasturi Rangen, published in *International Herald Tribune*, Paris, 25 October 1971.

3 Anecdotes told about the Mother by Sanskrit scholar Dr. Hari Upadhyay, international lecturer on diverse subjects including Indian philosophy and mysticism, at a seminar on Sri Aurobindo and the Mother sponsored by the School for Oriental Studies of Bussum, the Netherlands, and held in January 1989 at the International Theosophical Centre in Naarden, the Netherlands.

4 *A House for the New Millennium: Essays on Matrimandir* by Ruud Lohman, published by Alain Grandcolas, Pondicherry, India, 1986; p95.

5 *Gotama the Buddha* by Ananda K. Coomaraswamy and I. B. Horner, Cassell & Co. Ltd, London, 1948; p1.

6 *How to Know God: The Yoga Aphorisms of Patanjali*, translated with a new commentary by Swami Prabhavananda and Christopher Isherwood, New York, Mentor Books, 1953, third printing; p45.

7 *Ibid.*

8 *The Sufi Message of Spiritual Liberty: The Mysticism of Sound and Music* by Hazrat Inayat Khan, Volume II, revised edition, published by Element Books, Shaftesbury, England, in association with The International Headquarters of the Sufi Movement, Geneva, 1991, p1.

9 *Ibid.*

10 *The Sufi Message and the Sufi Movement* by Hazrat Inayat Khan,

published for the International Headquarters of the Sufi Movement, Geneva, by Barrie & Rockliff, London, 1964; p16.

11 *Ibid*, p17.

12 *Ibid*, p21.

13 *Ibid*, p23.

14 *Ibid*, p28.

15 *The Sufi Message* by Hazrat Inayat Khan, Vol V, Servire, Katwijk, the Netherlands, 1982, third impression; p192.

16 In a telephone conversation with the author on 4 May 1996.

17 *Towards the One* by Pir Vilayat Inayat Khan, Harper Colophon Books, Harper & Row, New York, 1974, first edition; p204.

18 From the article, 'The Beaming Faculty of Women' by Yogi Bhajan, from *Women in Training*, published by 3HO Transcripts, Eugene, Oregon, 1979; p51.

19 *Born in Tibet* by Chögyam Trungpa, the eleventh Trungpa Tulku, as told to Esmé Cramer Roberts, Penguin Books, Baltimore, 1972; p259 (© 1966 George Allen & Unwin).

20 *The Path* by Maharaj Charan Singh, Radha Soami Satsang, Beas, India, 1970; p96.

21 *Ibid*, p46.

22 *On the Birth of My Mission* by Martinus, The Martinus Institute of Spiritual Science, Mariendalsvej 96, DK-2000 Frederiksberg, Copenhagen, 1957; pp24–25.

23 *Ibid*, pp27–28.

24 *Ibid*, p28.

25 *Ibid*, p29.

26 *Martinus* by Erik Gerner Larsson, The Martinus Institute of Spiritual Science, Copenhagen, 1963; pp13–14.

27 *The Message of the Upanishads* by Swami Ranganathananda, Bharatiya Vidya Bhavan, Chowpatty: Bombay, 1971; p352.

28 *Share International*, English language edition, Share International Foundation, Amsterdam, November 1992; p2a

29 Jalâluddîn Rûmî (d. 1273) quoted by Eva de Vitray-Meyerovitch in *Rumi and Sufism*, The Post-Apollo Press, Sausalito, California, 1987; p117.

30 Abu Sa'id ibn Abi'l-Khayr (d. 1049) quoted by Llewellyn Vaughan-Lee in *Sufism, The Transformation of the Heart*, The Golden Sufi Center, P.O. Box 428, Inverness, California, 1995; p15.

31 *Chasm of Fire* by Irina Tweedie, Element Books, England, 1979.

32 *Life and Teaching of the Masters of the Far East* by Baird T. Spalding, De Vorss & Co., Los Angeles, 1924 and 1937, Vol 1; p151.

33 *The Voice of the Silence* by H. P. Blavatsky, The Theosophical Publishing House, Adyar, Miniature Edition third reprint, 1978; p16.

Glossary of Terms

ahimsa avoidance of injury in thought, speech and action

Allah the name for the one and transcendent God of Islam

Arjuna the Pandava brother who, in the *Mahabharata*, hesitated to go to battle with his enemies, who were also his kinsmen. His self-searching questions to Sri Krishna, and the latter's replies, form the teachings of profound spiritual wisdom recorded in the *Bhagavad Gita*

ashram residential community for spiritual aspirants, usually functioning under the guidance of a guru

Atman the soul, a person's true identity, the core of divine consciousness everpresent within someone whether she/he knows it or not; identical with the Self, the Supreme

Aum see **Om**

Avalokiteshvara the bodhisattva who represents the principle of boundless compassion

avatar the divine descended into physical form for the world's welfare; Hinduism recognizes ten main incarnations as embodiments of the essence of the god Vishnu

baba 'father,' respectful word in India for an older man, especially a spiritual figure

Beloved term used in some spiritual paths to indicate God, the Absolute, Truth; also represents the great high being who comes to earth to play *lila* with selected disciples in order to help them unite with the Absolute

Bhagavad Gita 'Song of the Divine One,' the bible of Hinduism, a portion of the *Mahabharata*, in which Sri Krishna teaches the spiritual knowledge leading to Self-realization

bhakti devotion, overwhelming love for the divine

Bhakti renaissance upsurge of devotion in India, 12th–17th centuries, with inspired outburst in poetry, music, dance and drama

Bharat Mata 'Mother India', ancient Sanskrit name for India

bodhisattva someone who voluntarily delays full buddhahood and repeatedly takes rebirth in order to help others progress towards liberation

Brahmin member of the most elevated of the four Hindu social classes, charged with the duties to study, teach and perform priestly functions

buddha a realized being who represents the highest stages of knowledge, wisdom and harmony that a person can attain

Buddha, the Siddhartha Gautama (Gotama), the Hindu prince who in the 6th century B.C. attained full enlightenment after years of renunciation and seeking after truth; fourth buddha in a succession of buddhas of which Maitreya is the fifth

chakra center of subtle energy in the human system

darshan sight of, or audience with, a deity or a saintly personage

dervish Sufi ascetic; may engage in mystical practices which include sacred dancing and whirling or vociferous chanting

dharma in Hinduism, the eternal law of Truth governing the universe; one's personal duty

Dharma the spiritual teachings of the Buddha Gautama

duhkha suffering

Four Noble Truths the Buddha Gautama's condensed teachings: the nature of existence is suffering, caused by ignorance, attachment and craving, and can be brought to an end by following the Noble Eightfold Path

Ganga (Ganges) India's most sacred river, also personified as a goddess

Gayatri Mantra ancient, purificatory Sanskrit verse calling to the sun for enlightenment; daily repetition erases the mind's negative tendencies

ghat steps leading down to a river

guru *gu-* 'darkness', *ru-* 'light'; the teacher who guides the aspirant from the darkness of ignorance to the light of spiritual knowledge

Hare Krishna, Hare Rama mantra calling to the Supreme for spiritual energy, protection and transcendence

Imam Mahdi 'divinely guided one', Islamic term for a Messianic figure who, at the end of this present age, will establish peace and justice on earth

jinn in Islam, spirit-beings which belong to an intermediate creation between humans and the angels and are considered able to influence humankind either for the positive or the negative

Kali Yuga the dark or Iron Age; the present, last and most degenerate of the four periods belonging to the Hindu system of world cycles

Kalki awaited tenth avatar of Vishnu, expected to lead an awakened humanity from the end of the Kali Yuga into the Satya Yuga of truth and purity

karma action, the law that governs all actions and their inevitable effects on the doer; the fruit of one's actions

Kashi ancient name of Benares (Varanasi), Hinduism's most holy city

Krishna eighth incarnation of the god Vishnu, personifying divine love and bliss in a human body

Kumbha Mela ancient spiritual gathering held in India every three years on four sacred sites in succession

kundalini the cosmic energy which sleeps within a person until awakened during the yogic process leading to Self-realization

kurta collarless, long-sleeved shirt

lama learned monk or lay person (Tibetan Buddhism)

lila the loving play of the divine or the guru with devotees

lingam rounded, vertical shaft symbolizing Shiva as the consciousness of the universe, usually set into a circular base or *yoni*, the female symbol

lungi long skirt consisting of a cloth wound around the lower body, worn by men

macrobiotic Japanese dietary system based on the principle that good health depends on balancing the *yang* and *yin* energies of food

Mahabharata ancient Hindu epic narrating a dynastic struggle and war between cousins, the virtuous Pandavas and the hostile Kauravas, who symbolize the forces of light and darkness, respectively; contains the *Bhagavad Gita*

Maharaj(i) 'great king', title for a respected spiritual personage

maharaja title for a ruling prince in pre-Independence India

maharani 'great queen', wife of a maharaja

Mahavira 'great hero', popular name for the Indian saint Vardhamana (c. 599–527 BC), founder of the Jain religion

mantra sacred syllables or words of power whose repetition can have material or spiritual effects

maya inner veil of ignorance which prevents human beings from seeing their divine nature and the true reality

Mecca city in western Arabia where the Prophet Muhammad was born and received his divine revelations; most sacred site and main pilgrimage center for all Muslims

Middle Way path taught by the Buddha Gautama, balance between self-denial and self-indulgence

Milarepa (1052–1135), ascetic with an unsavory past who, under the guidance of his guru Lama Marpa, transformed into one of Tibet's greatest saint-yogis

Mogul refers to the Muslim conquerors who established an empire in India (1526–1857)

Muhammad (Mohammed, Mahomet) 'the illustrious one', (570–632), the Prophet of Islam whose divine revelations form the main contents of the Koran (*Quran*), the authorative scripture for Muslims

namaskar (namaste) traditional Hindu hand-clasping salutation which silently expresses: 'I honor the light within you'

New Age (Aquarian Age) a state of expanded consciousness arising in humanity in the present era

Noble Eightfold Path eight virtues taught by the Buddha Gautama as the means to end suffering: right understanding, thought, speech, action, livelihood, effort, mindfulness, concentration

Om (Aum) Hinduism's most sacred syllable, represents the Totality and symbolizes the divine Source

Om Namah Shivaya powerful mantra used by those who worship Lord Shiva as the supreme form of God

Om Suryah Namah mantra invoking the sun energy which is within oneself as well as without

pandit scholar, teacher

pir Sufi master

prana vital life-force emitted by the sun, taken in through the breath

prasad food or any other item blessed by the guru or deity

puja worship ceremony

purna perfect, full, complete, whole

Radha spiritual consort of Sri Krishna, considered by some schools of Hindu thought to be his 'other half'

Rama (Ram) the god Vishnu in his seventh incarnation, a prince with divine qualities who represents the highest moral and ethical standards of ancient India and who saved the world from the demon Ravana

Ramayana Sanskrit epic describing the life of Rama and his exploits as benevolent ruler, brave warrior and faithful husband

rasayana the alchemy practised by yogis to change the chemistry and functioning of the body and the mind

rishis inspired seers of ancient India who wrote down the inner truths revealed to them

rupee basic monetary unit of India

sadhu (sadhwi) a man (woman) who lives the renunciate life without necessarily belonging to a monastic order

samadhi deep state of meditation; burial tomb of a saint

Sangam Yuga Age of Confluence, transition period between Kali Yuga and Satya Yuga, when the old and the new exist concurrently

sannyas the relinquishing of all ties and attachments for a life devoted to the ultimate liberation

sannyasi (Hindi), **sannyasin** (Sanskrit) one who has taken sannyas

sansara circle of birth–death–rebirth, fraught with suffering, which arises from our ignorance of the true nature of reality

sanskaras latent impressions of past karmas which emerge to bring about further developments

Sanskrit ancient religious and literary language of India

sarangi Indian string instrument with a mellow, moaning sound, used primarily to accompany vocalists of Indian classical music

sari traditional outer garment of Indian women, six meters of draped cloth

Sarnath ancient pilgrimage site near Benares where the Buddha Gautama preached his first sermon

sat truth; existence

sat guru the true guru, the guide who helps the disciple to know *sat* (the truth)

Sat Nam 'The True Name', Sikh salutation symbolizing the immanent presence of God

satsang assemblage or function for spiritual upliftment, held preferably in the company of a spiritual guide

Satya Yuga Golden Age of Truth

Shabd the inner, spiritual sound

Shaivite one who follows the path of Shiva, the path of Advaita (non-dualism)

shakti the creative force of existence, regarded as feminine

Shankaracharya Hindu spiritual leader of exceptional prestige in India

Shiva the all-powerful Vedic god of both destruction and re-creation who destroys for the sake of progress, represents the Ultimate Reality

Siri Guru Granth Sahib principal scripture of Sikhism, considered the embodiment of the eternal guru

sitar lute-type Indian instrument, most popular musical instrument in India today

sri (shri) Indian title of respect used for men, spiritual personages of either sex, and gods and goddesses

Sufism mystical path of Islam which aims at immediate and direct experience of the divine Beloved

suhka pleasure

Surdas (1483–1563), great Bhakti poet of Vraj (Vrindavan and environs) whose melodious songs are collected in the *Sursagar*

Surya the sun, Vedic god of light, symbol of the Higher Self

Surya-Vansa the sun race which, in Hindu thought, originated from Vivasvan, the Sun. His son was Manu, the father of the human being, whose two sons founded the two dynasties of the Sun in India. Ikshvaku founded the sun dynasty of Ayodhya, from which Lord Rama descends, and Nimi established the sun dynasty of Mithila.

swami title given by the guru to a sannyasi(n) who has achieved self-mastery

Tai Chi Ch'uan ancient Chinese martial art and method for spiritual development using slow, meditative movements for alignment with the natural flow of universal *ch'i* energy

tantra yoga yogic path of spiritual realization employing sexual energy to intensify and raise consciousness

tarot cards which portray occult wisdom in symbolic form and are used for divination

thangka religious scroll painting (Tibetan Buddhism)

Three Jewels, Triple Gem the Buddha, the Dharma (sacred doctrine of the liberating teachings) and the Sangha (practitioners on different levels of attainment)

tulku someone acknowledged as the present incarnation of a high being (Tibetan Buddhism)

Upanishads revealed scriptures which present the knowledge portion of the Vedas in essays on various aspects of divine wisdom; the source of Vedanta philosophy

vadi sukh spiritually transformed sexual pleasure

vasanas subtle desires derived from sanskaras, latent karmic tendencies of the personality left over from past lives

Vedanta system of mystical philosophy and rationale based on the final portions of the Vedas as expressed in the Upanishads

Vedas four ancient Hindu sacred books of hymns, verses, prayers and philosophizing which express the eternal truths revealed to rishis by spiritual illumination

Vishnu the Hindu god who, working continuously for the world's welfare, is said to incarnate as an avatar whenever righteousness needs to be re-established on earth and human soul evolution needs to be advanced

viveka spiritual discernment; the ability to distinguish reality from illusion, the true from the false

voluntary simplicity an attitude and lifestyle based on simplicity, high thinking, doing more with less

Vrindavan area in northern India where Sri Krishna spent his youth

wazifa (plural wazaïf) an invocation in Arabic which calls on one of the 99 qualities, or names, of Allah

YHVH 'I am who I am', four Hebrew letters representing the divine name of God in the Judaic tradition, a name considered so sacred and powerful it is never pronounced; a substitute is Jehovah, Yahweh or Adonai

yoga union; the spiritual disciplines one follows to yoke mind and body to the Whole; of the many forms of yoga, the path which emphasizes the physical body, hatha yoga, is most known in the West

yogi practitioner of a yoga discipline; one who has mastered a yoga system

yoni stylized female organ representing *shakti*, the divine energy which activates the consciousness of the universe

yuga 'age', a period of the world's existence; in Hindu thought, time is cyclic and unrolls itself in a succession of four ages – golden, silver, copper, iron – marked by a progressive deterioration of life on earth as humanity is increasingly distanced from the divine

zikr the invocation to remember God by repeating a sacred Arabic word or phrase, the foremost of which is *La ilaha illa 'lla Hu* ('There is no God but God')

Zoroaster (Zarathustra) Prophet of ancient Persia (6th century B.C.) who founded the religion of Zoroastrianism, whose adherents are followers of the light of the fire and the sun, and whose sacred scripture is the *Avesta*

Short List of Essential Concepts

awakening that stage in the embodied soul's evolution towards the divine when the inner being awakens and makes its existence known

divine couple refers to Sri Krishna and his consort Sri Radha, considered one soul in two bodies

enlightenment the eradication of ignorance and delusion along with the realization of one's innate Perfection; Self-realization

esoteric refers to hidden, mystical teachings about the fundamental principles or truths of life

global consciousness the view which considers the welfare of the whole planet before its individual parts

incarnation refers to a life spent on earth in a physical form

Perfection the state of being in total, continuous harmony with the divine consciousness and will; the luminous totality of our true and spiritual identity

Reality that invisible, eternal, unchangeable and indestructible source of life and existence behind all manifestation

realization when a belief, idea or aspiration become real through direct personal experience

reincarnation concept that the soul survives physical death and comes again into a physical body

revelation direct knowledge of the Truth, most usually by sight or hearing

right livelihood work that is consciously chosen, personally fulfilling, done with awareness, and helps serve the common good

Self the eternal, transcendental Supreme which is also a person's higher self and true identity

Self-realization to transcend the mind and recover one's true identity as the immortal Self; also termed realization of God, realization of one's Self, enlightenment, liberation, *moksha, mukti, nirvana,* Perfection

soul a person's true identity, the core of divine consciousness within the human body; identical with the Self, the Supreme

spiritual journey a person's spiritual development and progress on the road to Self-realization

spiritual sun symbol for the immortal soul, represents the Supreme Soul, the cause of all matter, the Sun behind our visible sun

List of Illustrations

1974, during Swamiji's first visit to me in Amsterdam.

11 The Sun, in a representation used on the front cover of *Als de zon spreekt* (published by Uitgeverij De Ster, The Netherlands, 1994), the Dutch translation of an earlier version of *The Call of the Sun*. The *Als de zon spreekt* (*When the Sun Speaks*) book cover was based on a sun to be found as a decorative detail in *Atlas Coelestis seu Harmonia Macrocosmica*, by Andreas Cellarius, published in Amsterdam in 1660/61. The *Als de zon spreekt* sun, which I created on a computer together with the Dutch publishing team, differs in several striking ways from the 17th-century sun which served as model. To begin with, it is colored green.

12 Swami Satchidananda, as I tried to capture his light on a photograph, just after I had interviewed him on matters of spiritual relevance. This lovely encounter took place at the home of yoga teacher Tulia van Twist in The Hague in 1975.

13 His Holiness the 16th Gyalwa Karmapa, giving photo *darshan* to me during a luncheon held in his honor by Ambassador and Mrs. K. S. Bajpai at the Embassy of India in The Hague in January 1975. This personal meeting occurred the day after the Karmapa, at the Kosmos Meditation Center in Amsterdam, initiated many people into his guru line of spiritual transmission.

The Kagyu tradition of Tibetan Buddhism traces its origins back to the great yogi-saint Milarepa, who is connected with the Immortal Babaji of the Himalayas. Milarepa, who had mastered the practice of producing inner heat, spent many years in the Himalayas, living in icy caves clad only in a thin cotton cloth. His most important student was Gampopa, to whom he transmitted the teachings which established the Kagyu tradition.

Om Mani Padme Hum, jewel (*mani*) in the lotus (*padma*), the mantra sacred to the bodhisattva Avalokitesvara, helps us attune with compassion, a fundamental aspect of buddhahood. Another fundamental aspect of buddhahood is wisdom.

14 Herakhan Baba, 'Babaji,' who lived among people in India between 1970–84, as I photographed him in September 1981. At that time I was staying in Babaji's ashram in Chiliyanaula, in the Himalayan region of Raniket, India. Along with many other Westerners and Indians we were

celebrating with Babaji the Hindu festival of *Navaratra* (Nine Nights), an annual observance honoring the Divine Mother.

One day Babaji selected some of us to accompany him on a pilgrimage to spiritual sites in the area which were connected with his ministry. The photo shows him at Siddashram, built by devotees of a great yogi, also called Herakhan Baba, who was experienced by people in Northern India between 1861 and 1922.

It is said that both Herakhan Babas were not born in the human way, but were Divine Materializations. They were each thought to have been forms of the Immortal Babaji of the Himalayas. To help people believe that Babaji is a real being, Paramahansa Yogananda (1893–1952) described in his *Autobiography of a Yogi* a visit he had with the deathless master in 1920.

Indian tradition says that the Immortal Babaji has appeared many times over the centuries in various ways. In *I am Harmony* (Spanish Creek Press, Colorado, 1990, p48), author Radhe Shyam writes that the second Herakhan Baba mentioned several of his earlier identities. Among them was the 11th-century Tibetan Buddhist yogi Milarepa. Herakhan Baba II also stated that he was a manifestation of Lord Shiva, who is known to have numerous forms.

15   Martinus, and I, outside his summer home in Klint, Denmark, in July 1975, after our journalistic interview. Under a bright sun I took some pictures of the loving sage and, at the end of the photo session, Denis photographed us together. Martinus departed this planet in 1981.

16   Swami Ranganathananda, and I, during a taped interview I made with him in 1975, at the home of Jo and Harma Orshoven, in Assendelft, The Netherlands. Photo by Denis.

17   Pir Vilayat Inayat Khan, and I, conversing on spiritual topics in The Hague in June 1975. Photo by Denis.

18   Pir Vilayat Inayat Khan, as I photographed him leading our afternoon session at the silent retreat in the Camp of the Eagles, above Chamonix in the French Alps, August 1975.

19   The Himalayan Master of the many names and titles, and I, as we were photographed together in May 1993 in the living room of my Amsterdam apartment, no longer on the Lauriergracht. Photo by Denish who, by then able to see

more clearly, had come to my home that day in order to offer his gratitude to Swami Purna.

Of H. H. Swamiji's many names and titles, only a few have been mentioned in *The Call of the Sun*. Other traditional titles of his (as noted in the glossary of *The Truth Will Set You Free* by Swami Purna: Element Books, Shaftesbury, England, 1987, pp148–51) include: *Ananda Peethadhisvara*, lord of the *pitha*, seat or conclave of *ananda*, bliss; *Avadhuta*, literally naked, the one who has relinquished all sects and creeds; *Brahmanista*, that one who belongs only to Brahma; *Satdarsanacarya*, the preceptor who has mastered the six great schools of Indian philosophy; *Vidya Vacaspati*, lord of learning; *Virukta Siromani*, he who has accomplished the supreme renunciation.

20   Irina Tweedie, and I, photographed together in December 1992, a few days after my 'reunion' meeting with Swami Purna.

21   Swami Purna, in London in December 1992, as I photographed him during our 'reunion' meeting. That encounter was in fact not really a 'reunion,' since during the 12-year 'separation' our spiritual link had continued. It was my ignorance which had caused me to think that he and I were apart.

22   Helena Petrovna Blavatsky (12 August 1831–8 May 1891), as she appeared in her best known photograph, called quite appropriately: 'The Sphinx.' The picture was taken by Enrico Resta at his studio in London, not quite two-and-a-half years before Madame Blavatsky's withdrawal from the physical world. Theosophists celebrate her date of departure, 8 May, as 'White Lotus Day.' H.P.B.'s masterwork, *The Secret Doctrine*, is considered to be a comprehensive sourcebook of the esoteric tradition.

23   The spiritual cremation rites of Pamela Knight, in Dharamsala, India, in December 1977.

Mrs. Knight, whose father had been largely responsible for the construction of the Indian railway system, had known Swami Purna from her childhood. Her wish, towards the end of her life, was to die in Swami Purna's presence. Having been trained by him to leave her body at will, she departed at the age of 75 at the exact time of her choice.

By Mrs. Knight's request, the cremation was performed in Dharamsala, close to the Tibetan people she had loved and generously supported through the years. Swami Purna conducted the ceremony with the assistance of lamas from the Gelugpa line of Tibetan Buddhism who are here seen chanting.

24 People lighting candles for Maitreya and the Masters, Surya the Sun, Mother Earth, and peace in the world. The candle-lighting initiates the public spiritual gathering held biweekly in Avenhorn, The Netherlands, by the *Stichting Spirituele Kring Emmanuel* (Spiritual Circle Emmanuel Non-profit Foundation). The association was founded in 1991 by Magnolia Huijboom (in the right-hand corner of picture) and Els Dijkstra. Several spiritual masters, including the Sun Master, transmit telepathic messages to the circle through Magnolia Huijboom.

This photograph was taken by me on 24 April 1996, when I was the evening's invited guest speaker. Most of these persons have read *Als de zon spreekt*. Having discovered the clues to the secret wisdom, and doctrine contained within its pages, the people in the circle recognize the higher identity of Swami Purna. They call him: Maitreya.

The attunement of my Dutch readers has greatly encouraged me.

Photo Copyrights and Credits

Index